Routledge Revivals

Walter Hawkesworth's Labyrinthus

T0347493

Walter Hawkesworth's Labyrinthus

An Edition with a Translation and Commentary

Volume II

Susan Brock

Routledge
Taylor & Francis Group

First published in 1988 by Garland Publishing, Inc

This edition first published in 2018 by Routledge
2 Park Square, Milton Park, Abingdon, Oxon, OX14 4RN
and by Routledge
52 Vanderbilt Avenue, New York, NY 10017

Routledge is an imprint of the Taylor & Francis Group, an informa business

© 1988 by Susan Brock

Publisher's Note
The publisher has gone to great lengths to ensure the quality of this reprint but points out that some imperfections in the original copies may be apparent.

Disclaimer
The publisher has made every effort to trace copyright holders and welcomes correspondence from those they have been unable to contact.
A Library of Congress record exists under ISBN:

ISBN 13: 978-0-367-19022-4 (hbk)
ISBN 13: 978-0-367-19031-6 (pbk)
ISBN 13: 978-0-429-19991-2 (ebk)

GARLAND

PUBLICATIONS IN

AMERICAN AND

ENGLISH

LITERATURE

Editor
Stephen Orgel
Stanford University

GARLAND PUBLISHING, INC.

Walter Hawkesworth's *Labyrinthus*

An Edition with a Translation
and Commentary

Volume II

Susan Brock

GARLAND PUBLISHING, INC.
NEW YORK & LONDON 1988

Library of Congress Cataloging-in-Publication Data

Hawkesworth, Walter, d. 1606.
[Labyrinthus. English]
Walter Hawkesworth's Labyrinthus: an edition with a
translation and commentary/ Susan Brock.
p. cm. — (Garland publications in American and
English literature)
Thesis (Ph.D.)— University of Birmingham, 1974.
Bibliography: p.
ISBN 0-8240-6381-3
1. College and school drama, Latin (Medieval and
modern)— England— Cambridge— Translations into
English. 2. College and school drama, Latin (Medieval
and modern— England— Cambridge. 3. English
drama— Translations from Latin (Medieval and mod-
ern) I. Brock, Susan. II. Title. III. Title: Labyrinthus
IV. Series.
PA8523.H85L313 1989   862'.4— dc19   88-38462

Printed on acid-free, 250-year-life paper
Manufactured in the United States of America

CONTENTS

Volume I

Volume II

ABBREVIATIONS OF STANDARD WORKS

Adagia   Desiderius Erasmus, Adagia quaecumque ad ?anc
                  diem exierunt, Paulli .anutii studio atque
                  industria (Florence, 1575).

Annals   C.H. Cooper, Annals of Cambridge, 3 vols
                  (Cambridge, 1842-5).

Athenae   Athenae Cantabrigienses, compiled by C.H.
                  Cooper and T. Cooper, 3 vols (Cambridge,
                  1858-1913).

College Plays   G.C. Moore Smith, College Plays Performed at
                  the University of Cambridge (Cambridge, 1923

Cooper, Thesaurus Thesaurus linguae Romanae et Brittanicae,
                  compiled by Thomas Cooper (London, 1578).

Elizabethan Stage E.K. Chambers, The Elizabethan Stage, 4 vols
                  (Oxford, 1923).

Progresses   J. Nichols, The Progresses, Processions, and
                  Magnificent Festivities of King James the
                  First, His Royal Consort, Family, and Court,
                  4 vols (London, 1828).

University Drama F.S. Boas, University Drama in the Tudor Age
                  (Oxford, 1914).

Jahrbuch   G.B. Churchill and W. Keller, "Die lateinischen
                  Universitäts-Dramen Englands in der Zeit der
                  Königin Elisabeth", Shakespeare Jahrbuch, 34
                  (1898), 221-323.

DNB   Dictionary of National Biography

MLR   Modern Language Review

PMLA   Publications of the Modern Language
                                 Association

STC   Short Title Catalogue

All references to the works of William Shakespeare are from the
Globe edition, edited by W.G. Clark and W.A. Wright (London, 1956).

All references to classical Latin texts are from the Teubner
edition, unless otherwise stated.

All references to classical Greek texts are from the Loeb edition,
unless otherwise stated.

ABBREVIATIONS FOR THE TEXTS
OF LABYRINTHUS

P   Printed edition of 1636

C   University Library, Cambridge, MS Ee.v.16

D   Bodleian Library, Oxford, Douce MS 315

Y   Yale University Library MS

N   Warwick County Record Office, Newdigate MS CR136/B761

L   Lambeth Palace Library, MS 838

J   St John's College, Cambridge, MS J.8

T   Trinity College, Cambridge, MS R.3.9

VARIANT READINGS

Prologue

line
number

3   hic L^c] his NLJ
    nihili ob] nihil ob Y ob nihili N
    facimus] fecimus N

4   merces] meres J
    nisi] nil nisi Y

5   Certissima C^c] Certissime CY

6   literato N^b] liberato NJ

7   praemii] praetii L

9   Labyrintho] Laborintho L Labyrinthus N
    nomen poeta] poeta nomen L

10   optumos DJT] optimos PCYN optimi L

13   nunc] iam Y
    prodit] prodest D

    om.] finis Prologi L

    Authore M^{ro} Hawkesworth Trinitatis Collegii quondam
        socio CYT] Authore T. Goffe ex ede Christi N^a om. PDNLJ
    Hawkesworth] Haukesworth CT Hauksworth Y
    quondam CY] olim T

Dramatis Personae

Tiberius 7 1. Tiberius J
senex 7 om. L
Domus Decani superioris D^b LJ 7 om. PCDYNT
Mr Hawkesworth D 7 Mr Haukesworth T Mr Hauksworth CYL om. PNJ

habitu foemineo, filius 7 habitu foeminio filius D filius habitu
    foemineo CYNT filius habitu foeminae LJ
Tiberii 7 om. CYNJT
Mr Verney CDLT 7 Mr Verneg Y om. PNJ

Goldingham CDYLT 7 om. PNJ

Cassander 7 2. Cassander J
*Domus Baccalaureorum in Medecina 7 Domus Bac. in med. LJ
    Domus Bac. in medio D^b om. PCDYNT
Ds Taverner D 7 Mr Taverner CYT Taverner L om. PNJ

Horatius .../ Lydia .../ Crispinus .../ Lysetta ...7
    Horatius .../ Crispinus .../ Lydia .../ Lysetta ... GYT
    Lidia .../ Horratius .../ Chrispinus .../ Lysetta ... L
    Lydia .../ Lysetta .../ Horatius .../ Crispinus ... NJ

Horatius 7 Horratius L Horatius, adolescens YT
Cassandri filius 7 filius Cassandri YNLJT
Ds Forrest CDYLT 7 om. PNJ

Lydia 7 Lidia L
Bing CYT 7 Binge D Cademan L om. PNJ

Crispinus J^c 7 Chrispinus LJ
Horatii servus 7 servus Horatii CYT
Thwaites 7 Thwaytes D Ds Thwaites Y Ds Twaites CT Ds Twayts L
    om. PNJ

Lysetta 7 Lisetta J om. L
Lydiae ancilla 7 om. L
Cademan CDYT 7 om. PNLJ

Synesius, senex 7 Sinesius senex C Valerius senex alias Synesius L
    3. Valerius senex alias Synesius J
Domus Decani inferioris D^b LJ 7 om. PCDYNT
Blaxton DY 7 Ds Blaxton CT Ds Blacston L om. PNJ

filia Synesii 7 Synesii filia Y filia Valerii LJ om. C
Ds North Y 7 Mr North CDL^c T Simson Mr North L om. PNJ

Faustulus .../ Caelia ... ⟧ Caelia .../ Faustulus ... NJ

servus Synesii ⟧ servus Sinesii C servus Valerii LJ
Ds Simpson CDYT ⟧ Simpson L om. PIJ

Caelia ⟧ Coelia C Celia N Caeliae L
nutrix Lucretiae ⟧ Lucretiae nutrix CYNLJT
Nidd DT ⟧ Nid CY Neede L om. PNJ

Piedro ⟧ Pedro L
Pacheco ⟧ Pachecno YN Paheo L
D'Alcantara DLJT ⟧ D'alcantara P Don Alcantara YN om. C
Semper e foro D ⟧ Semper a foro J om. CDYNT
Mr Kitchin CDLT ⟧ Mr Citchin Y om. PNJ

servus Piedri ⟧ servus Hispani CYT
Mr Freeman CDLT ⟧ Mr Freman Y om. PNJ

Cytharaedus ⟧ Cytharedus L Citharaedus CJT
Wilkinson CDLT ⟧ Wilkitson Y om. PNJ

Prologus Mr Hassall CT ⟧ Prologus Mr Hassell Y om. PDNLJ

Actus 1. Scena 1

Line
Number

Horatius_/ Horatio D
Horatius. Crispinus. CDYNLJT_/ Horatius et Crispinus P
Crispinus_/ Chrispinus L
Don Piedro T^c_/ Don Pidro T om. DNLJ

1   Don. O hermosa - D^b_/ om. DNLJ

4   coniecit_/ coniicit Y
      stringentem_/ stringente L
      aspexit_/ vidit Y

5   Quem ego, si_/ Quem si ego N
      rursus T^b_/ rursum Y om. T
      prodeambulantem CDNLJT_/ perdeambulantem P
          deambulantem Y^b deambulanem Y

6   inaniloquum C^c_/ ___ (illeg.) inaniloquum C
                                      inanilogum D

7   quantivis_/ quantumvis CY
      pretii_/ precii CY praetii DL

8   absterrere D^{b}J^b_/ absterere DJ

10   Meamne_/ Medeamne Y Meumne N

11   ob nihili_/ ob rem nihili CYT

12   Quem_/ Quam YN
      aequius_/ aequus Y
      illum_/ illud N

13   iracundiam L^c_/ il iracudiam L

14   Lucretius N^b_/ Lucretia N
      manere CYT^c_/ manerem PDLJT ut manerem N

15   praeteriit_/ praeterit Y

17   aedibus_/ edibus L

18   est ei_/ est et ei Y

19   in urbem CDYNLJT _7_ inurbem P

20   nunc _7_ om. NLJ
minas _7_ minis Y
qui _7_ quis CY dem qui N
commonstret _/_ commonstrat Y

22   Lepidae _7_ Laepidae DL

23   admittar _7_ admittor Y
noctem, sed _7_ sed noctem CY noctem L
unam _7_ unicam Y

24   queis _7_ quibus L
Iove N^c _7_ Iovem YN

25   sentio _/_ censeo T

26   exaruit _7_ erravit L
summus C^c _7_ ___ (illeg.) summus C

27   apud _/_ quid Y

28   laturum terris _7_ terris laturum Y
aeternam _7_ eternum N
Ha ha he _7_ Ha ha hae L

29   censeo CDYNLJT _7_ sentio P

30   Ridetis _7_ Rides L
Nae _7_ ne D
solem _7_ solum C solam L soli Y
solem Iovi _7_ Iovi soli Y
non _7_ om. N

31   ineundam _7_ ineundum CY
intelligo mihi L^c _7_ mihi intelligo mihi L

32   nolis D^c _7_ noles D id nolis CYNT

34   si forte C^b _7_ si fort _ (illeg.) C ad laevam L^c
offendes _/_ offendas CYT

35   Quocum _7_ Quo cum J Quoquam Y
communicat _7_ communicet L
formae _7_ formae suae Y
consilia _/_ concilia J

36   superimponantur ⟋ super imponantur DNJ   superimponuntur L
     reperiet ⟋ reperit L

38   hanc ⟋ nunc L
     age, age, age ⟋ age age CYT

40   Per aecastor ⟋ Perecastor CYLJT   Percastor N
     hoc quid ⟋ quid hoc CT   quid J
     sit ⟋ siet CY

41   dicam CYT ⟋ dico PDNLJ

44   Nempe D^c ⟋ Crisp. Nempe D
     sit ⟋ om. L
     vicinia ⟋ vicina N

45   Imo aliud J^c ⟋ Aliud ___ (illeg.) Imo aliud J

46   id ⟋ idem CYT
     Lucretius amicus C^c ⟋ amicus Lucretius amicus C

47   Lepidae ⟋ Laepidae DL

48   compareres C^c ⟋ comparares C   compareris N^{b}J
     uspiam C^c ⟋ etiam uspiam C

49   opportunius ⟋ oportunius DNJ
     quid ⟋ quod J

50   transigeres ⟋ transigere C^{c}YT^c transfigeres L
     Convenit ⟋ om. L

52   qui ⟋ quis C   om. N
     fuam ⟋ fiam CYT   suam L   om. N
     abstines ⟋ abstinens Y   abstinets L

53   oportet CYNLT ⟋ oportuit PDJ

54   adeo interdiu NLJT ⟋ interdiu PCDY

55   quicquam mi DNJ ⟋ quidquam mi P   quicquam mihi L
        mi quicquid CT^b mihi quicquid Y   quicquid T
     in vita D^c ⟋ invita D   invito N
     animo ⟋ omnino L   om. Y

56   perlegerit ⟋ pellegerit Y
     est ⟋ et L
     lepida DYLJ ⟋ Lepida PCNT

57   aliud _7_ illud Y
         Obsecro te _7_ om. Y
         numnam _7_ numne Y   nunquid L
         insanimus _7_ insanias Y

58   sumne _7_ summus Y
        *herus tibi _7_ tibi herus CYT

59   eloquutus _7_ elocutus CNLJT   allocutus Y

60   ergo CJYNLJT^b _7_ igitur P   om. T
         sic _7_ si L

61   Observent _7_ obssvent N
         sentiscat _7_ perscentiscat L
         prehendat _7_ praehendat CYT   perpendat L

63   expedit CYT _7_ expedi L   expetat PDNJ

65   Crisp. Sentio _7_ Sentio YL
         facis _7_ facio N
         videris _7_ om. N

66   Medius _7_ Crisp. Medius Y
         ut video _7_ ut ego video L   ut video ego J   ut ego
                                  videam N   ut videam Y

67   haec res _7_ res haec L
         aliquod magnum _7_ magnum aliquod Y   aliquod L
         evadat CDYNLT _7_ evadit PD^c   evadet J
         Agedum _7_ om. Y

68   Hor. Ego _7_ Ego L
         Affectas _7_ Affectus L

69   Hor. Abstine _7_ Abstine N   Hor. Astine J
         argumentis _7_ argumentis luam L

Actus 1.   Scena 2.

71   postquam _7_ postea NL
         Flaminia _7_ flamma L
         viderat _7_ viderit N
         Ardelia _7_ Ardelia L

72   stetisset _7_ petissit Y

73   famulatu me _7_ me famulatu L

74   multo est mihi aegrius NLJT] multo mihi est aegrius PD
      multo aegrius est mihi CY
    incoenatum] incanatum L

75   multo est CDYNLJT] multo mihi est P
    inaerem] om. (space left) L

76   frigens] fringens L

77   mihi nunc inanitate] mihi inanitate nunc NJ
      inanitate nunc L   inanitate mihi CYT

78   verum] vero Y

79   est] om. N
    unico] uno L

80   recipiat] recipiet CYNL^{b}T^{b} (illeg.) T
    beatus sum] om. L

82   hodie apud illum] apud illum hodie L

83   tum] tu C

85   <u>Gril</u>. Dii] Dii L
    quae velis C^{b}] (illeg.) C

86   Salve T^{b}] Vale T

87   Immo L^{b}] om. L
    Oh] ob Y
    haec] hec N   hic C   isthaec T

88   mali] male CYT
    tibi] om. N

89   es] is CLJT
    quid tibi vis CYT] quid vis tibi PDNLJ

90   nimium] omnium L

91   ] line om. Y
    te id CNJT] id te PDL

92   Quamvis] Quanvis D
    cum] dum Y
    interiore] interiori N
    expecter CNLJT] expector PY   expectar D

93 ad - C^c ⟧ ad latrem C

95 tuo T^c ⟧ tuos T

  nunc mihi exaudire C ⟧ nunc mihi exaudere T
    mihi nunc audire L audire nunc mihi Y
    exaudire mihi nunc PDNJ
  commodum CYJT ⟧ est commodum PDNL

97 istaec ⟧ isthaec N istac CT ista Y

98 paululum ⟧ paulum L
  hac ⟧ huc N om. CYT

99 si ⟧ om. L
  paululum sit CYNLJT ⟧ sit paululum PD
  paululum est T^b ⟧ paulum est N placet mihi T

100 supremi ⟧ suprema L
  regnum ⟧ reginam Y regna L

101 quapiam ⟧ quopiam N
  malum ⟧ mali Y
  istaec ⟧ isthaec CYN isthae T
  curatio ⟧ iuratio L

102 licere ⟧ lecere L
  rem meam CYLT ⟧ meam rem PDNJ
  sine ⟧ nisi L
  ted CT ⟧ te PDNLJ om. Y
  arbitro ⟧ arbitrio Y

103 id dii ⟧ dii id Y
  vero ⟧ om. CYNLT

104 si ⟧ om. N
  consilio ⟧ concilio D
  huc DNLJ ⟧ hic P om. CYT
  mittar ⟧ mittor N

105 ago ⟧ om. CYLT

106 fuit ⟧ fuerit N
  deluctari ⟧ delectari Y deluctare N

107 te L^b ⟧ ut Y om. L

108 quaeso, vale ⟧ vale quaeso N

109-10 O^b ⟧ lines om. C

111 nullus T^b ⟧ nulli T
priusquam N^c ⟧ priusquam huc venero N
quid T^c ⟧ quod NT
huc C^c ⟧ huic C

112 Quid ⟧ quod Y

115 abs te nunquam ⟧ nunquam abs te T nunquam a te CY
discedam ⟧ descedam L

116 Tiff, taff, toff. ⟧ tiff toff NNT tiff Taff L
tibi ⟧ tibi Grille beate N

117 argutari ⟧ argutarier N
mihi cum istoc D ⟧ mihi cum isto P mihi cum istocc NLJ
cum istoc mihi CT cum istoc argutari cum istoc mihi Y
licuerit CNJT ⟧ licuit Y licuerat $PDLJ^c$

118 ad ⟧ at DL
sumne ⟧ sumne YL

119 amore CDNLJT ⟧ amorae P

120 auspicatius CDNLJT ⟧ auspicatus P
cito cito cito ⟧ cito cito CT

Actus 1. Scena 3.

Lepidus. Crispinus. ⟧ Lepida Crispinus NNJ Lepida Chrispinus L
Crispinus Lepida CT

121 Stava la gentil dama ⟧ om. CTT^c
Stava ⟧ Estava T
la ⟧ lu T
gentil NJ ⟧ ggentil L gentill T gentle PD
*Buon di, buon di D (stage direction) ⟧ Buondi, buondi P
om. CNLJT
*Madonna Modina ⟧ Madonna modina PCD (stage direction) T^c
Madonna Madonna Y om. NLJT

122 Tib. C CDLJT ⟧ Tib. Ah PD^b C NN
lucentem ⟧ luculentem N
focum ⟧ domum Y
renidet ⟧ renitet Y

123   D^b] line om. D
quam] ac Y
incensa si foret] si incensa foret CYT   accensa si
                                       foret N
nempe] Tib. Nempe N nam C cum Y
oportet] oportuit L

124   Nae CYNLJT] Ne PD
horam ego] ego horam CYT
unicam ductam] unicam ductem N ductam unicam L
per lubentias] perlubentius N
aetati N^c] aetat Y aetatem N

125   Hah D^b] hah ha T ha ha ha C ha ha he Y om. DNLJ

126   uspiam si persederint] si persederint uspiam CT
       si procederint uspiam Y

127   Ilicet] Hae Y
Pish] mens pish L^c mens L mans J maugh CYT^c om. N

128-129 T^c] order of lines reversed in T

128   nequam T^b] om. YT
cantilenam T^c] cantilenam eccere T

129   at] et Y
haud refert] hanc refert L

130   sic] si L

131   preces anxie] preces anxiae CLJT anxias preces N
exquiruntur] acquiruntur L
poh D^c] proh D om. CYT^c

132   gemmis] geminis Y

133   ipsasque adeo Musas D^bN^c] ipsasque adeo musas musas N
      ipsas adeo musas D ipsasque Musas adeo C^bT
      ipsasque musas etiam C musasque ipsas adeo Y
meretriculas] meritriculas T meristriculas L

134   misericors D^b] misererres L om. D

135   Tib. Sat] Sat L
solae quae] solaeque CY
obveniunt CYNJT] adveniunt PD conveniunt L
ultro] om. C^cY

136 Ne _/ Tib. Ne L
mediam T̄ᵇ _/ om. T
obsitam _/ insitam CYNJT iustam L

138 nummum _/ nunum N

139 illud _/ id C
sospitent _/ hospitent L
et Lᵇ _/ om. L

140 amico _/ animo Y

141 fatigo _/ flagito N

142 id _/ idem Y

143 leviter _/ leniter D
crediderim _/ crederim L

146 Sim _/ Sin Y
et sum: an _/ resumat Y
de risu _/ et risu Y
quid _/ quicquid CYT

148 accurrunt _/ occurrunt Y
saepe _/ saepius N

149 item Nᵇ _/ idem NJ
nolle Lᶜ _/ nollem L
id inique CYT _/ inique id PDNLJ

150 amice _/ amici CYT
quod _/ quid L
consulant _/ consultant CYLT

151 cur _/ quod Y
autumare _/ autumant N

152 prae _/ plus Y
pudentem Lᶜ _/ impudentem L prudentem CYT

153 est esse CYT _/ esse PDNLJ
ha ha he _/ ha ha ha JT

154 mores Dᶜ _/ amores D
frequenter _/ comfrequenter L
huc _/ om. L
adolescentulos Dᵇ _/ adolescentes NJ adolescentos D

155   meas _/ om. N
       compluries DNLJ _/ complureis P   complures CYT

156   adolescentẽm _/ adolescentulum YL
       pol optimum _/ om. N

158   O Hispanus iste scurra _/ om. N
       iste CYJT _/ ille PDL
       Piedro _/ Pietro D^b
       Pacheco _/ Pachecho NJ Pacheo L
       D'Alcantara D _/ d'Alcantara PCYT Dalcantara NLJ
       tara tantara CDYNLT _/ tararantantara P farara tantara J
       farara _/ forará N ferara L om. CYT

159   Monere _/ Movere Y
      *denique ne quid hinc _/ me hinc denique ne quid YT
           mea hinc denique ne quid C
       ne quid CDLJT _/ nequid YN me quid P
       infamiae T^c _/ om. T
       admigret _/ admigrat D demigret Y

160   vero CYNLJT _/ quidem PD

161   de via _/ devia Y
       iis _/ eis N

162   olim _/ om. N
       consero _/ confero YLJ
       pol C^b _/ om. CYL
       illorum CDYNLJT _/ eorum P

163   aliquid L^c _/ aliquod L
       labis _/ labes LJ
      *permanesceret L _/ permanasseret PCDJT permanserit Y
                       permanare N

164   credam CYNJT _/ crediderim P crediderem D crederem L
       noctem _/ nocte CYN
       perpetim _/ perpetem DNL

165   corrumperet L^c _/ corrumpet CYLT
       cras discederet _/ cras descenderet Y descederet cras L
       virgo vitiosior _/ vitiosior virgo CYT om. N

166   Quamne _/ Quam CYT
       partui L^c _/ patrui partui L pressi Y

167   obtundit _/ obtundet Y

168   vel indies _7 indies vel CYT[b] indies T
       instarent _7 instaret L

169   Tiberi _7 Tiberio NLJ
       *crepuerunt fores _7 om. CDYNLJT

170   barbiton _7 barbyton Y barbaton N
       haec tempestas _7 tempestas haec Y

171   mi _7 om. CYT
       dominum _7 domum Y
       exhilara _7 exhillara L exhilera D
       tuum _7 tuam Y

172   canes CYNJT _7 canis PDL
       ut sint mihi _7 om. N
       mihi L[c] _7 tibi mihi L

173   Intus _7 om. N
       tecto _7 tectis CYT

174   focus T[b] _7 om. T
       lepos iocus _7 iocus lepos Y

175   sua _7 tua C
       vero D[b] _7 om. D
       harum me rerum _7 harum nec rerum L hay me xam Y

176   ceperit _7 coeperit C
       Stava _7 Estava CYT
       la gentil _7 lugentill CY lu gentill T
       dama CDYNLJT _7 dama. Buondi Buondi - Cantus P
          dama. Cantus Buon di, buon di, etc. D[c] (stage direction)

177   his _7 om. CY
       inspectoribus CDNLJT[b] _7 inspectatoribus PY speculatoribus T
       unum _7 unus L
       *praehenderem DL _7 prehenderem PJ prehendero N prehendam C
          praehendam YT

178   Primum T[b] _7 primi Y nimirum T
       ego illi pedes _7 ego pedes illi CJ illi pedes ego Y

179 Dein' LJ] Dein' vero PD Deinde CYNT
  manus et linguam illi CT] manus et linguam ei Y
   linguam illi NLJ linguam D manus huic et$_b$
            linguam PD^b

  praescinderem] praescinderim Y

180 quid] quod N quae CYT
  viderit L^c] videret L vidit Y
  tulerit] tulerat Y
  taceret] om. Y

181 innocens] imnocens N
  At] et Y erverem ut N

182] line om. CY
  istuc] isthoc N
  accurassem D^b] curassem D accurascem L
  ergo D^c] ego DNT
  machaeram hanc] hanc machaeram T
  quaeso] gestio T

183-187 Viveret? Lepidum hoc esset. Oh, quam acuta acies! J^c]
   Viveret? Lepidum hoc esset. Hor. sumne ego infelix./
   Viveret? Lepidum hoc esset. Oh, quam acuta acies J

183 Lepidum] lepidam N
  Oh] O NJ ob Y

184 ictu] istic C
  quis] quisquam Y

185 Cick ah D^b] Chick ah CT Cik ah J chick Y ah N om. D
  viveret] om. D^{b}Y
  Lepidum hoc esset CDNLJT] om. PD^{b}Y
  Deum Fidium, ut D^b] Deum fidem ut CT om. DYNLJ
  ego hoc nunc gestio CD^{b}T] ego nunc gestio P Hoc nunc
   gestio Y om. DNLJ

186 D^b] line om. DNLJ

187] line om. D
  Sumne] Summe YL

188 Ah. DNLJT] ha CY Crisp. Ah PD^b

189 Hum] Hunc CYNT
  eccere] ecce re N om. L

190   scelus $\overline{J}$ fretum Y
        istic malum tibi CT^b $\overline{J}$ istic tibi T istuc malum tici Y
          tibi istic PDLJ tibi isthuc N

192   <u>Crisp</u>. Quid ni $\overline{J}$ <u>Crisp</u>. Quid Y

193   Nae CDYNLJT $\overline{J}$ Ne P
        hic intus elegantes $\overline{J}$ intus hic elegantes CYT
           hic elegantes L elegantes intus N
        habes C^c $\overline{J}$ habes habes C

194   carnificem $\overline{J}$ carnifex NL

195   nusquam $\overline{J}$ nunquam Y
        vita $\overline{J}$ vitam Y
        memini $\overline{J}$ inveni L
        ex re ludicra $\overline{J}$ e re ludicra Y om. N

196   eram $\overline{J}$ om. CYT

197   D^b $\overline{J}$ line om. DNLJ
        illum $\overline{J}$ illud D^b
        perduint CT $\overline{J}$ perdant PD^{b}Y
        ita $\overline{J}$ ite C

198   Quam confidenter D^b $\overline{J}$ Quam confidenter Quam confidenter D
        autem sese intulit iam inde a principio D^b $\overline{J}$ sese intulit
          iam inde a principio CYT om. DNLJ

199   has T^b $\overline{J}$ hac L om. T

200   circum confulgebant $\overline{J}$ circumfulgebant CLT circum
          fulgitant Y confulgebant N

203   istoc $\overline{J}$ isthoc N istuc L hoc Y

204   sis L^b $\overline{J}$ sit L om. N

205   inspectu CDYLJT $\overline{J}$ aspectu P^m

206   ah ha $\overline{J}$ a ha CYT ah ah ah NJ ah L

207   hercle vero $\overline{J}$ vero hercle Y
        ah ha $\overline{J}$ a ha CYT ha ha L ha ha he N
        aliquid aliud CDYNLJT $\overline{J}$ aliquid P
        ha ha CY $\overline{J}$ ah ha T ha ha he N^c ha he he N ha PDLJ

208 Egon' D^c _7_ Egone CDNLJ Ego me Y
   interturbarem _7_ inturbarem TL

209 mediam usque ad _7_ ad mediam usque N mediam usque L

210 constiterim _7_ constiterem L constiteram CYT
   si _7_ om. L
   usque _7_ uspiam YN

211 Mira _7_ Mea Y
   suspicacem L^b _7_ suspicarem L
   sis _7_ om. L

212 <u>Hor</u>. Tactus _7_ <u>Hor</u>. Factus L Tactus CT Factus Y
   qui _7_ quid L
   de _7_ me N ne LJ
   fecit _7_ facit Y
   lusit _7_ facit Y

213 Ah _7_ O CYT
   mi, mi _7_ om. N
   impudens D^c _7_ impudens hem tibi D

213/14 quam ego te ob istam confidentiam/Non possum quin
    deosculer! Vah! delicias facis. Neutiquam nevis? D^b
   istam _7_ istanc CYT   om. DNLJ

214 deosculer _7_ osculer CYT
   Neutiquam _7_ nequicquam CYT
   nevis CD^bYT _7_ ne vis P
   Hem tibi D^b _7_ om. D

215 usu Y^c _7_ usus Y
   Heus tu _7_ Hem tibi Y

216 intelligo _7_ <u>Crisp</u>. intelligo N
   La la la _7_ La la la la la Y

      Actus 1. Scena 4.

Scena 4 _7_ Scena 3 N
Crispinus _7_ Chrispinus L
Lucretia ... Synesius. Horatius. Faustulus. _7_ Horatius Faustulus
              Lucretia CYT
Synesius _7_ Synaesius NL om. CYT

217 <u>Crisp</u>. Vide _7_ <u>Syn</u>. Crispine vide N
   hoc tibi _7_ tibi hoc L

218   Lydia Lydia] Lidia Lilia L

219   ] line om. Y
toties D^b] om. D
te] om. C
facies D^c] facies DNLJ

220   Lucretius CYNLJT] O Lucretius PD
Luc. Ohi me DN^{c}J] Luc. Ohime P   ohi me. Luc. Ohi me N
                                      Luc. Oh me CYLT

221   tibi sit CYNLT] sit tibi PDJ

222   gratiae] gratia N
est ego D^{b}L^c] est DY   et ut ego L
iussus] iussum Y   missus L
ut] ac Y
imperium D^b] imperio D
quem] quae N

224   illuxit] eluxit CDYNT
deos N^b] des N

225   defit DJ] desit PCNLT   deest Y

226   Lydiam] Lidiam L
virgo est, pulchra est] pulcra est, virgo est Y

227   quid est] quid T^c om. CY
quid] quod N   quem T   om. T^c
quaeris T^c] quaeris alium T   om. CY

228   Luc. At] At L
id L^b] om. L
dixi tibi L^b] tibi dixi Y   dixi L
penitus L^b] pentus L   potius Y
abs] ab N^c a CYLT

229   tanto D^c] sin tanto D
mihi] misi L
ipsi L^b] om. L

231   nunquam] nusquam CYT
negotii] negotium Y
sit] fit Y

232   an] om. Y
persequi] persequar YN
me N^c] Faust. me N   om. (space left) L
postules] postulas C^{c}YNT

233   nullas _7_ nullus NL
                 istuc _7_ isthuc N istic C
                 hercle _7_ certe L om. N
                 quod patrem _7_ patrem quod L
                 male T^b _7_ malum T

234   Lydia si ... at CT _7_ At Lydia si ... Y Si Lydia ... at
                                  PDNJ Si Lidia ... at L
                 Delia _7_ Belia L Ardelia J
                 Erminia _7_ Erimnia J Erimma L Erycinia Y
                 hic c^c _7_ haec CY
                 Lepida _7_ lepida L^c

235-6 Tibi nulla placet, aegre fert pater; et tu aetatem
                 corrumpis tuam./Quaeso, Lucreti. N^b _7_ om. N
                 nulla placet _7_ nullae placent YL
                 et tu aetatem corrumpis tuam. Quaeso _7_ et tuam
                 aetatem corrumpis quaeso tuam Y

237   rem _7_ nunc Y

238-9 Sane quidem huic rei subesse aliquid oportet,/Quod ille
                 sic solus se in consilium _7_ om. N

238   quidem _7_ om. L
                 huic L^c _7_ huinc L
                 subesse aliquid _7_ aliquid subesse L

239   se _7_ te C
                 consilium _7_ concilium D
                 sevocat T^b _7_ vocat LT

240   pertulerim _7_ pati L

241   hic D^b _7_ om. D
                 et est CYNLJT _7_ et PD

242   crediderim _7_ crederim L

244   Quid est ... sibi? Luc. _7_ Luc. Quid est ... sibi? Y
                 quid est? quid _7_ quid est quod Y
                 nepotes _7_ nepotem N
                 Iube _7_ Iubeo Y

245   ducturum _7_ ducturam Y
                 Qui CNJT _7_ Quid PDYL

246   Ah _7_ Oh CT O Y

248   quicquid sit *⸕* om. L
qui *⸕* quis CY
sim *⸕* sum N

249   Nullibi *⸕* Nullubi D
securius D[b] *⸕* reperies D
reperies depositum CYT *⸕* depositum reperies DNJ
    depositum invenies L invenies depositum P
mi Lucreti, Lucreti mi CYNLJT *⸕* mi Lucreti? mi PD

250   certe *⸕* forte D[b] om. D

251   Aut J[b] *⸕* om. J
perirem *⸕* perierim CYT
quam D[c] *⸕* quia D
sum, sum *⸕* su-- sum J

252   quid me *⸕* quid de me CT de me quid Y
<u>Faust</u>. Foemina? *⸕* om. L
<u>Luc</u>. Superi, si non forem. T[b] *⸕* om. LT
forem *⸕* taceam Y

253   T[b] *⸕* line om. LT
foemina CYT[b] *⸕* om. PDNLJ
nihil istuc *⸕* nihil isthuc N nihil istic C istoc nihil Y
prae ut *⸕* praeut NJT[b] verius ut Y

254   **Quod iam statim intelliges.** <u>**Faust**</u>. **Foemina?** T[b] *⸕* om. LT
intelliges *⸕* intelligas Y

255   **huius rei imprudens** *⸕* imprudens huius rei CY
te *⸕* om. L
et devestivi parvulum C[c] *⸕* parvulum et devestivi
    parvulum C et devestivi pervulum L

256   **totiesque** *⸕* toties L
quidni *⸕* quid ni CDNT quidem YL

257   **Ersiliae** *⸕* Ersillae J
celare *⸕* colare L

258   **istiusmodi** CYNLT *⸕* illiusmodi PDJ

259   **ipsi** C[c] *⸕* ipsum C
etiamdum non *⸕* etiam dum non D[b]NJ etiam non dum DL

260   <u>**Faust**</u>. *⸕* om. L
<u>**Papae**</u> *⸕* Pape LJ Papa D[b] om. D
Euge *⸕* om. CYT

261   **pernoscere** T[b] *⸕* penoscere T praenosceret L

262   rem ⌐ᵇ⌐⌐ om. DNLJ
    sic⌐⌐ om. CYT
    integram⌐⌐ integrum N

263   adiuta⌐⌐ adiuva CYT

264   matrem meam Ersiliam⌐⌐ written in larger letters in T
    Ersiliam⌐⌐ Ersilliam J
    vicinus Lᵃ⌐⌐ vicinius Y vi_inus (illeg.) L

265   haec⌐⌐ hic N
    at⌐⌐ ac C et N sed L
    ferunt⌐⌐ aiunt N

266   hic prudens⌐⌐ prudens hic N

267   uti CDYNJT⌐⌐ ut PL
    ingenium⌐⌐ ingenii Y
    cognati mox⌐ᵇ⌐ cognitum mox Y cognati N
    mox perviam Tᵇ⌐⌐ perviam NJT

268   et⌐⌐ est L

269   perstitit CDYᶜNLJT⌐⌐ praestitit PD
    integra⌐⌐ intigra L

270   At⌐⌐ at/At Y
    integra⌐⌐ intigra L

272   si compressu foeminam CYNLJT⌐⌐ foeminam si compressu PD

273   aureos Dᵇ⌐⌐ aures D
    in dotem dari⌐⌐ dare in dotem Y

274   maxime⌐⌐ maxima Nᶜ mascula maxima N

275   Oblata⌐⌐ Obleta L
    ultro fide⌐⌐ ultra fidem Y
    aetas Cᶜ⌐⌐ aedes C

277   Munerumque⌐⌐ mumerumque N munerum Y
    vitium⌐⌐ vestium L

279   At⌐⌐ et N
    comparet Tᵇ⌐⌐ comperit NJ competet T comptait L

280   cura factum⌐⌐ factum cura CYT
    ingenio meae CYT⌐⌐ ingenio PDNLJ

281   suae] om. L
    imprimis] imprimis CJT in primis Y
    istis ex] ex istis CYT

282   ope] opere L
    e] et L in Y
    vicinia] vicinae L

283   Quam CYNT] Quem PDLJ
    iam tum] iam tunc LJ iam N cum iam Y
    spectaret] spectarit D^c spectare D

284   prolem] probe L
    curavit] curavit et L
    commode] comode N percommode Y
    supponi] om. N
    masculam DYT] masculum PNLJ musculam C

285   gaudebat] audebat L

286   mihi] mihique Y

288   unam unice] unicam N

289   *De ferendo ... negotio] deferendo ... negotio NT
       deferendum ... negotium CY

290   provida] provida esset CYT

291   fidei] filii DT
    oppetiit] appetiit L

292   Rem admirandam] Admirandam rem N

293   Nutrix] om. N
    ut viderat C^b] ut videret L ut videam C om. N

294   fabricam] fabicram J

295   primo] primum Y
    participem] perticipem L

296   credo] om. N
    verita] merito Y
    incauta] incaute N

297   pater CDYNLJT] om. P

298   *commodam CYT] commodum PDNLJ

299   coepit CDYNLJT *]* cepit F
    magistros *]* magistrum CYNLJT

300   Quin *]* Qui L
    me cupit *]* cupit me Y

301   natae *]* nata Y

302   vibrare discunt *]* discunt vibrare N
    ineptae manus *]* manus ineptae CT   manus inepte Y
        imperitae manus L

303   una *]* unus CYT
    venerant *]* venerat CY^{b}T   venerit Y
    ahime *]* ahi me NJ   ah me CYLT

304   perderet CNLJT *]* proderet PDY

305   tum *]* tunc YN

306   oh *]* om. N
    conspicor *]* conspicer L

308   me *]* om. L
    concinnasti CNLJT *]* concenasti PD   coronasti Y

309   Ne *]* Nec CYT
    quod *]* quid Y
    reliquum L^c *]* reliquam N   requum L

310   commoda est occasio *]* comoda est occasio N
        occasio commoda est CT   occasio est commoda Y

311   te *]* om. NJ
    leva *]* atque leva Y   et leva N
    dolore *]* dolorum Y

315   fuerat *]* fuerit J   fuit L

316   Intelligo *]* om. N
    vestris amicitiis *]* nostris amicitiis N   vestras amicitias

317   fere *]* om. CYT
    eadem *]* ea LJ

318   namque *]* nanque C   neque Y

319   amorum *]* amorem C   om. L
    fuerat *]* fuit CYT

320   Laudare *]* Laudarunt CT   Laudarant Y

321-2 •D^b] lines om. CDYNLJT

323 viscret D^b] viserat D

325 Neque] Nec L
illuxit] eluxit YN

326 amplexu] complexu YN

330 Nempe istuc] Istuc nempe CYT Nempe id NL
hic] huic CNT hinc Y

331 •prohibessit] prohibescit PDYNJ prohibescet L
prohibescat CT
ausim L^c] ausam L

332 Diceret] Dixerat Y
proh] poh L
foeminae] feminae N foeminam Y
et] est L

333 bella N^c] bellas N

334 Ibi] ubi Y
uti] ubi L
ingenio N^b] ingeni N om. L

335 acclamantem me CNLJT] me acclamantem PD
acclamante me Y
deserere] disserere Y

336 Accurrere] Adcurrere CYLJT
ad patrem mox] mox ad patrem CYT
ibi] ubi Y
expostulare] exostulare L
iniuriam CYT^b] rem PDNLJT

338 amico quod] quod amico CYT
exciderem C^cL^c] excideram C exciderim YL

339 late] om. L

340-1 Quanto ... venis? Faust. Perge] Faust. Quanto ... venis?
Perge N
•amoris venis] amor invenis PDNLJ amor fuisti CYT

342 •Horatius CDYNLT] Horatius mediam per parietem PD^b
om. (space left) J

344   me diu rem CYT *]* diu me rem DNLJ diu rem me P
        sed L^c *]* om. L
        decipit *]* decepit Y

345   Cantabat *]* Cantavit Y
        sobolvit J^c *]* subsoluit suboluit J

347   prospiceret CDYNJT *]* perspiceret PL

348   rogaret D^b *]* rogasset D negaret L

349   Lepidae *]* Laepidae DL
        statim *]* saltem N affatim L
        intuli T^b *]* contuli T

351   fervere *]* fervet CT ferret Y
        crebra internuncia *]* crebra internuntia NL crebra in
          ternuncia J crebris internunciis CYT

352   mala *]* mali Y
        inconsultu *]* in consultu J inconsulto CNT inconsulta YL

353   mei D^c *]* meo CYNLJT
        plane *]* clam Y
        uti *]* ut J

355   rediit *]* redit L
        fidens *]* fidem CYT

356   tibi CYJT *]* ibi PDNL

357   venustum T^b *]* verum T
        unice *]* vince Y

358   ut *]* ubi CYT

359   praestarem CDYNLJT *]* praestiterim P praestiterem D^b

361   fuit *]* om. Y

362   cum illo sibi CYNLJT *]* sibi cum illo D^b sibi cum illa P
                             cum illo D

363   caute *]* autem Y
        ut rem CYNLJT *]* ut PD
        ageret *]* agerent CYT
        eius *]* om. L

364   •e NJ ⌐ a PLL ex CYT
fuerat ⌐ fugerat L
ei ⌐ om. Y

365   destinaret CYNLT ⌐ destinarat PDJ
fixu ⌐ filium CT filiam Y
rogari ⌐ rogare CYT

366   cuiquam ⌐ quod Y
ne vel CDYNLJT ⌐ ne P
permanasceret CT ⌐ permanasseret PD[b] permanserit Y
    permanaret DLJ faceret N

367   Interminari D[c] ⌐ Interminare D
aedes ... pertransiret ⌐ per aedes ... transiret CT
    per aedes transierit Y
tam ⌐ tum L

368   ubivis ⌐ verbis N

369   eum ⌐ cum C
ipsa ⌐ om. CYT
negligeret ⌐ negligerat L negligerit J
obvia ⌐ obviam Y obvium CT

370   Quin etiam ⌐ Quinetiam CT
aut literas ⌐ autem trans Y

371   Uni ⌐ Vin YNJ ut L
aut ⌐ et NJ
petere ⌐ peteret N om. CYT
ut ⌐ et N

372   caetero T[c] ⌐ caeterae T
penes CDY[b]NLJT ⌐ paenes P paene Y
nos una D[b] ⌐ una CDYNLJT
dispiceremus NJ ⌐ despiceremus PCDYLT
se ⌐ si CYT
sit ⌐ fit YT
promptum ⌐ promptam J prompum Y

373   evadas ⌐ evades Y
at ⌐ om. N
Oh D[b] ⌐ Ah D O J proh N et L

374   Audi T[c] ⌐ Audivi T om. Y
qua ⌐ quas Y

375   erat ⌐ fuit Y
censui ⌐ censeo L

376   at adeundam N^bT^b _7 ad adeundam NL   at adeu eandem T

377   annueret CDYNJT _7 annuerit PL

378   simulo C^b _7 simul Y om. C
       fingo _7 fingam Y

379   At T^c _7 Ac T
       geri _7 gero Y
       interiori CDYNJT _7 interiore PL
       se Horatius ut contineret _7 ut se Horatius contineret N
         Horatius ut contineret se CYT

380   ignis _7 om. N
       caetera _7 ceterae Y
       essent CDYNLJT _7 esset P

381   et _7 est Y om. L

382   At _7 et N
       potuit _7 poterit Y

383   rimator _7 miretur Y
       illud _7 illud illud N aliud illa L^a illa L

384   intelligo. Ne T^b _7 intelligone L intelligo T
       innotesceres T^c _7 innotescit T

385   nonne _7 non T

387   quin _7 cum N quum J

388   traduceret CYNLJT _7 introduceret PD

389   velle _7 vellet CYT
       in custodia _7 ad custodiam Y
       observatum inde adeo si _7 observatam inde adeo si N^b
         adeo ut observarem si CY
       accideret CYJT _7 acciderat PDNL

391   praesto CDYNLJ^cT _7 presto P percurrerem praesto J
       occurrerem NJT _7 occurrem CL accurrerem PD accurram Y
       index CNLJT _7 iudex PD inde Y

392   Istuc _7 istic CY
       idem N^b _7 om. N

394 Datur _⦎_ Datur CYT
in Y⁵ _⦎_ om. Y
praesenti CYLJᶜT _⦎_ presenti N praesente PDJ

395 ivimus _⦎_ inimus Y
viximusque mutuis CY _⦎_ viximurque mutuis T viximus
mutuisque PDLJ viximus mutuis N

396 dii CDYNLJT _⦎_ dii omnes PDᵇ
quam _⦎_ quin N
istaec _⦎_ isthaec DNT ista Y
est mira _⦎_ mira est Y

397 amabo ades _⦎_ amabo aede Y
inquit; ades _⦎_ ades inquit CT aedes inquit Y
abnegas Cᵇ _⦎_ ŏbnegas L attingas C

398 istuc _⦎_ isthuc N istic C istaeo Y
*pudentiae CDNJTᶜ _⦎_ prudentiae PYL impudentiae T

399 ah nequam CYNLJT _⦎_ at nequam PD

400 Ibi _⦎_ Ibo J
cum _⦎_ quin CYNLJT

401 Nae _⦎_ Ne P (catchword p. 17) D
te _⦎_ tibi CYNT
propter Lucretium multum _⦎_ propter Lucretiam multum N
multum propter Lucretium L

402 illi _⦎_ ei N

403 nunc illi _⦎_ tunc illi L
rursum _⦎_ rursus CYLT
nunc utrisque _⦎_ utrisque CYT
unicum _⦎_ unum CYT

404 uni _⦎_ vin' CYL
propter _⦎_ om. N
usque _⦎_ om. Y
advigilat _⦎_ advigilabat Lᶜ advigi ___ (illeg.) L

405 amando haud _⦎_ haud amando CYT
uspiam Cᶜ _⦎_ etiam uspiam C

406 ac _⦎_ ut N ego ut CYT
ut fiat Jᶜ _⦎_ fiat Y ut fuat J

407 hic _⦎_ hec N sic L
nunquam _⦎_ hic nunquam Y
hercle _⦎_ improbe DNJ improba L

408   ergo nunc $\rfloor$ ergo inquam CT inquam ergo Y
ab illo $\rfloor$ ad illum Y

408-9 hem inquam./Nunc a me illi alterum:$\rfloor$ om. Y

410   de $\rfloor$ ab de Y
illi $\rfloor$ om. CYT

411   Ausim $\rfloor$ Ausin' Y
id $\rfloor$ hoc CYT om. N
is $\rfloor$ ille N

412   agimus $T^c \rfloor$ egimus NT
propinantes CDYNLJT $\rfloor$ mutua propinantes PD^b
ita $\rfloor$ sic L
quisque $T^c \rfloor$ quisquam YT

413    $L^c \rfloor$ line om. L
id $\rfloor$ id quod L^c
in arduo $T^b \rfloor$ ad arduo T om. N
dum $\rfloor$ non Y

415   divellimur CY $\rfloor$ dividimur PDNLJT
id $\rfloor$ in L om. N
aegritudine $\rfloor$ aegritudina C

416   Quippe $\rfloor$ om. Y

417   Ego $D^c \rfloor$ Luc. Ego D
conscia $L^c \rfloor$ consciam NL

418   summa $\rfloor$ sumna C
•perceperam $T^c \rfloor$ perciperam L perceperim T

419   abfuit $T^c \rfloor$ adfuit T
gaudebam $T^c \rfloor$ gaudebat T

420   quae $\rfloor$ quod N

421   Postero $\rfloor$ Postremo N
autem $\rfloor$ om. N
accurrit DYNLJT $\rfloor$ occurrit PC
ovans $\rfloor$ amans Y

422   Vita et salus $\rfloor$ salus et vita N
author $J^c \rfloor$ aucthor author J

423   delicatam mollem $\rfloor$ mollem delicatam Y

426   est D^b ⨼ esse D fuit L
aegritudinis ⨼ aegritudini L
rivali CD^{c}NLJT ⨼ rivalem PDY

427   Et quia ⨼ At quia CY atque L

430   repetimus ⨼ repetivimus CYT
resecro ⨼ refero Y
tuam N^b ⨼ om. N

431   Lucretia ⨼ Lucreti N mala CYT

432-3 D^b ⨼ lines om. D

432   ergo CD^{b}YNLJT ⨼ igitur P
quo J^c ⨼ quod J

433   Iupiter! quid video? CD^{b}YNLJT ⨼ Iupiter! P

434   Luc. Ita ⨼ Ita C Ha Y
calamitas J^b ⨼ clamitas J

435   Quin J^c ⨼ quid quin J

436   Et ⨼ at YN
heus ⨼ hem Y
Ah. Horatium T^b ⨼ ad Horatium CYT
prosequor CDYT ⨼ persequor PD^{c}NLJ

Actus 1. Scena 5.

Lucretia CDYLJT ⨼ Lucretius PN
Lysetta ⨼ Lycetta C Lisetta L
Lydiae ⨼ Lidiae L

437   At heus CYT^b ⨼ At heus insuper NLJ om. PDT
  *Signior Lucretio C ⨼ Segnior Lucretio L Sig^{or}
    Lucretio JT^b Sg^r Lucretio Y Seignior N
    Lucreti Lucreti PDT

438   Lucreti ⨼ Lucretio NLJ
hem ⨼ om. CYNT
inquam ⨼ inquam inquam L
tune ⨼ tun' T

439   Quaeso, uti sint res meae, in pauca quicquid est
    conferas. ⨼ Lys. Quaeso ... meae? Lu. In ...
    conferas. Y
uti sunt D ⨼ ubi sunt PT uti sint CYLJT^b ut sint N

441   heus heus _] heus N

444   haec _] hic N   hoc L
       subcingula _] subingula Y   subcingulum L
       est _] om. Y
       scio: vale. _] om. CYT

445   Eia _] om. CYT
       Pugh _] Puh N   Pish CYT

447   despicatui CDYNLJT _] dispicatui P
       ita nunc dierum _] nunc dierum ita CYT   nunc dierum N
       es _] om. YN

448   haec sis D^b _] hec sis N   sis haec J   sis DL
       Lydia _] Lydya CD

449   ut L^b _] om. L

450   Elaborata _] elaboratum N
       mehercule _] mehercle DYNJT

452   Et _] om. NL
       Quin dicas _] dic CYNLJT
       nec D^b _] om. D
       haec usu CYT _] usu haec PDJ   usu hec N   haec L

454   Pugh _] Puh NT   Poh C   Pol Y

455   haec _] hae T
       an ad CYT _] ad PDNLJ
       reponitur CYNLJT _] om. PD

456   Luc. Quid ni _] Luc. Quidni YNL
       illo non _] non illo Y
       *possit CYNT _] posset DJ   potest PL

457   Lys. Quem C^c _] Lys. Quin C
       te huic _] huic te L
       et illius D^b _] illius DN

459   vides T^c _] vidis T
       sanguinis CDYNLJT _] virginis PD^b

460   Age age CYNLJT _] Age PD
       Unica _] una L
       tua T^b _] om. T
       sexcentum T^c _] sexentum L   sexcenta T
       tricis _] tricas CYT^b om. T
       istiusmodi _] huiusmodi L

461   intelliges] intelligas Y   intelligis NLJ
         inquam] om. N
         munia] munera CYNT
         ei T^b] om. T
         referre CYT] reponere PDNLJ

462   es] om. Y
         et T^c] om. T
         par C^c] pars C
         gratia T^c] gratiae NT

463   aliud CDYNLJT] illud P
         defit] desit CYL   deest N

464-5   ] lines om. L

464   ut D^b] om. DNJ
         sit] est J

466   forsan] fortasse CYT
         age age sis modo $D^b T^b$] age age sis ^{D} age age sic L
            age age N   age T
         personam hanc] hanc personam L

467   illa] etiam CY

468   quid J^c] quod J
         sit] om. L
         cuiusmodi] eiusmodi Y
         vobis CDYNLJT] nobis P
         istae si] si istae L
         fierent D^b] fiet D

469   si non fierent] om. N
         periret] perirent NJ   perire J^c
         mox] om. L
         hominum genus] genus hominum CYT

471   aenigmata $C^c J^c$] aenigmate C   ___ (illeg.) aenigmata J

472   nunc] om. L
         subdole] subolet Y

474   ago CYNLJT] agam PD

476   resiste N] restiti PDLJ   resta CYT

477   imprimis _] inprimis CYJ   in primis T

478   venio _] veni N

479   me T^b _] om. T
        facias _] facies Y
        efflictim CT _] afflictim PDYNLJ
        haec T^b _] om. T

480   nosti satis _] satis nosti L

482   Lassus _] lassus lapsus L^a   lapsus L
        quasi _] equidem L

483   Abalienasti _] Et alienasti Y
        nobis _] a nobis Y
        aliquot _] aliquos N

484   Exin' _] Cum CY
        internunciis _] internuntiis NT   inter nuntiis J
        egit _] agit YL

485   ergo T^b _] autem Y   ego T
        postremo _] postremum CYT
        te hoc rogat _] hoc te rogat YN   te rogat hoc L
        unice _] unicum CLT
        atque CYT _] et PDLJ   om. N

486   _] line om. CYNJT
        est _] om. L

487   Per lachrymas eius, et mortes, intimumque _]
        intimumque per lachrimas eius et mortes L   om. CYNJT

488   diu _] om. Y

489   vero _] volo Y   om. L

490   colloquii _] alloquii L

491   cum sola solo cum DN^bLJ _] sola solo cum PCYT^b
        sola solo ___ (illeg.) T   cum solus solo N
        fueris DNLJ _] fueri P   fuerit CYT

492   dimittas _] demittas NJ

494   et _] om. CYT
        Horatii _] Horratii C
        hoc causa _] haec causa L   causa hoc CYT
        superaddas _] superaddes Y
        insuper D^c _] etiam insuper D

495 nisi cui ⟋ cui nisi L
unus ⟋ om. CY
Cassander sit ⟋ sit Cassander N

496 •Quin etiamdum C ⟋ Quin etiam-dum D Quinetiam-dum PY
Quin etiam dum NJT^b Quin etiam dem L Quin porro T
clarius T^b ⟋ om. T

497 me C^c ⟋ ne C
dum ⟋ cum N
nunc iam T^b ⟋ nuncia CY inquam T

498 ego T^b ⟋ om. LT

499 Ibi T^b ⟋ ut T

500 Ubi primum ego illum D^bNJ ⟋ Ubi primum ego illam P
Ubi ego illum primum L Ubi primum illum D
Primulum ubi illum ego CT Primulum ubi ego illum Y

501 primulum ⟋ parvulum N om. CYT
hic ut ⟋ ut hic L
amet ⟋ amat L

502 pol ei ⟋ ei pol L

503 Lys. Quin ⟋ Quin J
haec res ⟋ haec L^a om. L

Actus 1. Scena 6.

Lepidus ⟋ Lepida DL

504 St ⟋ St st NL
Lep. Quo CDYNLJT ⟋ Luc. Quo P
itura T^b ⟋ ___ (illeg.) T

505 Ad ⟋ om. L
me moratur ⟋ moratur Y memorat L

506 quodam C^b ⟋ quovis C
rationem T^b ⟋ mentionem T

507 Mox ⟋ Non CY
retro reversura ⟋ retroversura Y retro reversuram N

508 illuc ⟋ illic Y illud N
intenderam T^c ⟋ contenderam T
descendero ⟋ descendam Y

509   ego *]* om. L
confectam *]* confectum DNLJ
nobis N^b *]* esse N

509-10   Lydiam/Nisi haec fuisset amica eius, et consodalis
Lepida *]* om. L

510   consodalis J^b *]* sodalis J
Lepida *]* Lepidae D

511   invenit *]* inveniat CYT
fugat *]* om. L

512   lepido *]* Lepido C Lepida YL
hilari laeto CNLJT *]* laeto hilari Y hilari PD
ingenio *]* animo N

513   Lydiam CDYNLJT *]* Lepidam P
plane uti *]* uti plane L

514   ei *]* om. L
in amore *]* in amorem YNJ amorum L

515/16 Lep. Ecce me, cick. Ah, quam elegans es?/Non sum ego virg
minutula, et perpusilla? CYLJT *]*
Lep. Non ... perpusilla? / Ecce ... es? PD^b
Non ... perpusilla? / Lep. Ecce ... es? D
Ecce ... elegans non ... perpusilla. N

515   me *]* om. L
cick *]* chick CYT om. N
Ah *]* ha L$_b$ om. CYT
elegans L^b *]* elegantem L
es D^b *]* om. DNLJ

516   sum ego *]* ego sum CYT
minutula CDNLJT *]* minutila PY
perpusilla T^c *]* perpusillata T

517   Lys. Quaeso *]* Lep. Quaeso N
manus *]* manum N

518   *]* line om. CYNLJT
Lep. Ha *]* Ha D^c

519   Lep. Est *]* Lys. Est N
lubido *]* libido CYT
collare *]* collocare N om. L

520   Istud] illud L
diffingere] defingere D   diffundere Y   diffstingere T
Lys. Immo] Lep. Imo, N
quaeso hercle] hercle quaeso YN   vero quaeso L
ut D[b]] om. DNJ

521   Lep. Hem] Lys. hem N
·istic] isthic N   istuc CYLT

522   Lys. Nihil N[b1]] Lep. Nihil N[b2]   Nihil N
Ha ha he D[b]] Ha ha ha DJ

523   nam, quid] nunquid L
istuc] isthuc N   istoc CYT   istic L
sic] sit YL

524   hac] om. Y
sic] om. J

525   ego] eo NJ
natam] te natam Y
esse T[b]] om. T
unice] vince Y   om. L

527   eone] adeone CYT

528   Quia T[c]] qui LT
amatorem D[b]] amatorum--D

529   nunc] om. CYT
abscessit] abcessit D   obsessit Y
refingam D[c]T[c]] refringam DYNLJT
denuo T[c]] modo denuo T

530   Lys. Pulchre N[c]] Lys. Pulchra N   Pulchre L

531   Lep. Ha] Ha C
Ha ha he D[b]] Ha ha ha DJ

533   erit L[b]] exit L
quid L[b]] om. L

534   concinnius] concinnus D   concimnius N   cominus L
iam multo est] multo iam est C[c]YT   est multo iam est C
    est multo iam L
credo] om. L
quam D[b]] quin D
antea] ante N

535   istic] isthuc N

536   id *]* om. Y
saeviter CNJT *]* severiter PD suaviter Y saviter L

537   lubet *]* lubes CNJ
haec mea *]* has meas CYNT
itidem C^b *]* etiam C

538   Age *]* Atque Y
ecce *]* etiam N
nimio iam *]* iam nimio N

540   Lys. Licet *]* Lys. Licet? non NLJ om. CY

541   Lep. A *]* Lys. A C Ah Y Lep. ah L
quid ad CYT *]* ad PDNLJ

542   praestigiatrix CYNLJT *]* praestigatrix PD

543   respuit *]* respicit L

546   Lep. Ita *]* Ita L
istoc *]* isthoc DN istioc T
ego munere *]* munere ego CYT
mihi *]* om. L

547   calamistra J^c *]* callamistra J
quot *]* quod C om. Y
Hispanica CDYNLJT *]* hyspanica P

548   forfices CDYNLJT *]* fornices P
crispatoria *]* Crispatoria CT Horispatoriae Y
monilia *]* monillia J

549   D^b *]* line om. D
Medius fidius *]* Mediusfidius CD^{b}T
mille mille mille *]* mille mille N
annulos CD^{b}YNLJT *]* amulos P

550   denique et CYT *]* denique PDNLJ
sexcenta *]* sexcentum CNLJT

551   O *]* Oh CY om. N
infacetum *]* inficetum J
respuere *]* respuerem NJ

552   per Venerem, inquam, vapulabit *]* inquam per Venerem
        vapulabit Y per Venerem vapulabit inquam L

552   heus *]* heu L

554   I *]* om. NLJ

555   Ducam _⌐7_ duco L
aliam _⌐7_ alium Ɔ

556   auferet _7_ aufferet Ɔ auferret NJ

558   nunc mihi _7_ mihi nunc Y

562   verius T^b _7_ virilis T

563   *vivit _⌐7_ vivet CYT
Lydiam qui _7_ qui Lydiam N

564   praeripiat D^{c}T^c _7_ praeripiet CYNLJT praeriperet Ɔ

565   te T^b _7_ om. T

566   Lydia _⌐7_ Lidia L
magis amat CYNLJT _7_ **amat magis PD**

567   ac _7_ om. **Y**

568   <u>Lep.</u> At _7_ At L
ego CDYNLJT _7_ om. P

570   <u>Lys.</u> Nae _7_ Ne L
hac _7_ **haec** C

571   <u>Lep.</u> Deliberatum T^b _7_ Deliberatum L <u>Lep.</u> Decretum T
tu D^b _7_ om. DNLJ

572   abstineres _7_ abstinueris J abstineris **T**

573   meam _7_ non L

574   **Nemon' CYT** _7_ Nemo PDNLJ
Non _7_ **Nos** D

575   primum _7_ primo Y
cape sis tibi CYJT _7_ **cape sis PD** **cape** tibi sis NL

578   iterum CDYNLJT _7_ **item** P

579   <u>**Lep.**</u> **Diu** _7_ Diu L

580   commoditatem hanc _7_ **comoditatem** hanc N hanc
commoditatem CYT

581   mihi _7_ om. N
operam L^c _7_ et operam **CYLT**

582   ] line om. L
       alluxit] illuxit Y
       tibi C^b] mihi C

584   Nil] nihil L
       tibi] mihi Y
       Omnes deos] Per omnes deos CT Per deos omnes Y

585   istuc] isthuc N istoc CYT

586   spes mea] mea spes L
       foemineis] foeminiis YL
       induar] induor NLJ
       licet] om. N

588   Cave] tace CYT
       merx mala] mea mala N om. L

589   Lys. Ita] Ita L
       animadvertens CT] animadvortens Y advertens PNLJ
                                  advortens D
      *iudicaram] iudicarem YNL indicarem J

590   contuens] contueris CYT

591   iocos] locos N ioco L
       suspirare] suspicare L

592   et] om. N
       porro] tibi CYT
       assolent T^c] assoleant assolent T

593   improbitas manus, osculi, incubitus, raucior vox NJT]
         raucior vox, improbitas manus, osculi, incubitus PDL
         improbitas manus, osculi incubitus, raucedo vocis CYT^c
       osculi] oculi N

594   nimio] nimium L

595   istuc] isthuc N istoc CY
       Mirabar] mirabor L

596   At] aut N Ab J
       cur habitu] habitu cur CYT
       sic dissimulas CDYNLJT^b] cur dissimulas PT
         sic dissimules L

598   caverem] caveam L

599   Nemon' CYT] Nemo PDNLJ
       Audi] Audi audi L

600 Malvezzi CYT[a] ⟧ Melvezzi J Melverzi N Mavezae L
Maluzzi D Malurri PT
factiosa ⟋ fastuosa Y

601 Mafoltiam ⟧ Mafolciam L Matoltiam CYT[a] malfoltiam N
Mafoliam T
cum ⟋ civum L
huc ⟧ om. CY

602 diu ⟧ iam diu Y

603 ut ⟧ est C
molimine ⟧ moltmine C
adeo et ⟧ adeoque CYT

604 utraque ⟧ om. N
Advorte ⟧ adverte CDLJT advertere N

605 ego ibi ⟧ ibi ego CYLT

606 innocuam ⟧ innoxiam Y

607 pro foemina ut ⟧ ut pro foemina CYT
dueerem ⟋ dicerem L

608 ut ⟧ et L
*creveram T[b] ⟧ creverem T metuerem CY

610 viciniam ⟧ vicinam L

611 simulas ⟧ simules N
nec ⟧ ne N
postulas ⟧ postules N

612 est nunc ⟧ nunc est N
uti ⟧ ut NLJ

613 sunt ⟧ sint C

615 hoc L[b] ⟧ om. L
istoc D[b] ⟧ isthoc N om. D
fruiscor CDYLJT ⟧ fruiscar P fruor N

616 sic ⟧ om. L
collibitum ⟧ collubitum L

617 contuear L[a] ⟧ contuar DLJ
alloquar ⟧ alloquer CT
*amplectar N[c] ⟧ amplecter CYNLJT

618 At _7_ _t Y
  hic _7_ om. L

619 praestas _7_ praestas L prestes N

621 deiuves L^a _7_ om. L
  tantum _7_ tantam N^c
  Falsa _7_ At falsa CYT
  fueris C^c _7_ fueras C

622 toxico _7_ toxica-L

623 •curassis CLT _7_ curasses PDYNJ

624 Cypri _7_ Cipri L Cypris CT

625 St CYNJT _7_ 'S't D Sancti P at L

    Actus 1. Scena 7.

Scena 7 CDYNLJT _7_ Scena 9 P
Tiberius _7_ Tiberio DNLJ
Puer CDYNLJT _7_ et Puer P
Puer.Cassander _7_ Cassander Puer N

626 hoc vesperi T^c _7_ hoc vespere Y hodie hoc vesperi T

627 Non non non _7_ non non L
  est coelum CYNLJT _7_ coelum est PD
  vide _7_ vidi T
  ut _7_ et CYT
  crocitant _7_ vocitant N vocitent J convocitant L

628 Cohibe _7_ Cohibe puer L
  •Canace _7_ Cannase NJ Canice PD Cuanae L Canae T^c
   canes CY choraster T
  Dorilas _7_ Dorilus L Dorylas CNT Aorylos Y
  Pu. Intrate N^b T^b _7_ Cass. Intrate M puer: intrate L
   Intrate T

629-30 D^b _7_ lines om. D

629 e regiam _7_ et regiam Y
  mansuefacta _7_ mansueta Y

630 Quam integre _7_ Oh quam integre YT O quam integre C^b
   O quam integra C

632   placide placide placide ⨼ placide placide Y

633   expedivit CDYNLJT ⨼ ex expedivit P
vesperi_CT ⨼ vespere PDYNLJ
ah mea ⨼ .om. N

634   <u>Pu</u>. Nae N^b ⨼ <u>Cass</u>. Nae N
fui infoelix ⨼ infoelix fueram Y
illic ⨼ illuc N
intereram ⨼ interreram L

635   <u>Pu</u>. Neutiquam N^b⨼ <u>Cass</u>. Neutiquam N

636   interereas ⨼ interereras C
<u>Pu</u>. O N^b ⨼ <u>Cass</u>. O N

637   **Ah** ⨼ **om. N**
convenerunt ⨼ **convenerint Y**
nostin' ⨼ **nosti N**
ad pedem est ⨼ **est ad pedem CYT**
montis C^c ⨼ **montes C**
Lernii ⨼ **Lerini** C **Lemnii Y**

638   tu ⨼ te L
•um J ⨼ hum CYT vin' PDL una N

639   <u>Pu</u>. Lemnium dicis N^b ⨼ <u>Cass</u>. Lemnium dicis N
     <u>Pu</u>. Leminam dicis Y
<u>Tib</u>. Lemnium ⨼ Lemnium L
Lemnium Lemnium ⨼ Lemnium Lemniam Y
lacum Lemnium T^c ⨼ lacum Lemniam Y lacum N lacum ipsum
ipsissimum ⨼ ipsissimam YN

640   ibi ⨼ ubi N
inquam ⨼ nunquam L

641   Signior ⨼ Seignior N Sygnior L S^{gr} CYT Sig^{or} DJ
Bentevoglio LJT ⨼ Bentvoglio PD Beute Voglio C
    Bente ^{V}oglio Y Bontevoglio N
Hernando NJT ⨼ Hermando PD Hemando L Herriando CT
    Ferriando Y
Del Humore C ⨼ Del'humore PD^c del Humore T Bel Humore Y
    Bel'humore D Belhumore LJ Bethumoro N

642 Il _]_ Ill NJ et L Item CYT
Cavaliero CNJT _]_ cavaliero PD Cavalliero Y caveliero L
Marte Bellonio CY _]_ Marte bellonio PL Marte-Bellonio T
     Martebellonio DJ Martebollonio N
di _]_ Di N de CYT

643 alii credo CYNLJT _]_ credo alii PD
nobiles et summi _]_ summi et nobiles CT

645 Hispania L^b _]_ Hispaniae L
aliquid _]_ aliquod C

646 Bene habet iuxta CDYNLJT _]_ Pu. Bene habet. Tib. Iuxta PD^b
conspicimus _]_ conspeximus N

647 exerto T^b _]_ porrecto T
manu T^c _]_ manus T

648 Pu. Ah N^{b}D^b _]_ Pu. At D Cass. Ah N
fui ego _]_ ego fui L
incommode _]_ commode N
tunc _]_ tum CNLJ

649 e _]_ a Y

650 Ambitiosis _]_ Ambitiosi Y Ambitio sis L
segregent L^a _]_ segragent D emergent L
emergant _]_ emergent Y

651 enim T^b _]_ om. T
mox illa laeta _]_ illa mox laeta Y illa laeta mox N
     illa mox lata L
cick _]_ cicke D chick CYT om. N
Hisp _]_ om. YN
Ah CYNLJT _]_ Ah. himpe etc. PD

652 ambientem _]_ abientem Y
tum _]_ tunc CT hanc Y
suspicere _]_ aspicere CYT

653 summa ... assequi _]_ in larger letters CT

654-5 _]_ lines om. L

654 Pu. Ah N^b _]_ Cass. Ah N
voluptatem regiam _]_ regiam voluptatem CYT

656   <u>Pu</u>. ʌh N^b ⟋ <u>Cass</u>. ʌh N
       iam CYT ⟋ om. PDNLJ
       Etiam CYT ⟋ Et iam PDNLJ

657   tum ⟋ tunc Y
       hanc ⟋ om. Y
       forte ⟋ forsan Y

658   Eccam ⟋ Ellam CYNT   illam LJ
       sub ⟋ ut sub C   et sub YT
       monstravit L^c ⟋ monstravet L
       neminem CYT ⟋ nemo PDNLJ

659   fere CYT ⟋ om. PDNLJ
       apparatur CYLT ⟋ apparetur NJ   apponatur PD
       ubi ⟋ ubi etiam Y
       hanc CYNLJT ⟋ hunc PD
       dicam tam diu D^b ⟋ tam diu D   tamdiu dicam Y
       gravidam CDYNLT ⟋ Gravida PD^cJ

660   <u>Tib</u>. Alitem ⟋ alitem L
       ibi ne T^b ⟋ ibine T   ibi me CN
       inclamo ⟋ clamo Y   milano N

661   paret NJ ⟋ parit PDL   parat CYT
       citus ⟋ cibus T   cibum CY   cito L
       celeusmate L^b ⟋ celesmate L
       videre ⟋ videro Y
       fas erat ⟋ falco ruit Y

662   cum ⟋ tum L
       semet ⟋ semel YL
       Cick ⟋ cicke D   Chic C   chick YT

663   rediit CDYNLJT ⟋ redit P
       *adibo CYT ⟋ ad i P   adii DNJ   om. L

664   confecit D^c ⟋ conficit CDLT

664-5   <u>Pu</u>. Tria?/<u>Tib</u>. Tria. <u>Pu</u>. Tria? <u>Tib</u>. Tria ⟋ <u>Pu</u>. Tria?
                                          <u>Tib</u>. Tria N

666-7   ⟋ lines om. L

666   occeperat ⟋ occeperit N

667   eccum ⟋ eccam N

668   Falco ⟋ Falio L

669   Illa CƆYNLJT _⫽_ ílle P
        ceu sagitta CLT _⫽_ seu sagitta PƊNJ   sagitta velut Y
        celer _⫽_ celeris N   om. Y

670   pernix T^{b}-_⫽_ perdix T
        Pirr T _⫽_ pir CJ   pit Y   om. PƊNL

672   Madre ella amour _⫽_ Madrella amour CYT^{b} Stava madre
            ellamore L   Stava Madre ellamour J   Stava hodre
            ellamour N   estava madie elamo T
        Pu. Cancro D^{b}_⫽_ Pu. Canero Y   Puer: L   om. D

Actus 1.   Scena 8.

Tiberius _⫽_ Tiberio NLJ
Lepidus _⫽_ Lepida CDYNLJT

673   Tiberi! Tiberi! Heus Tiberi _⫽_ Tiberio, **Tiberio. heus**
        Tiberio CYLT   Tiberi heus Tiberi **N**

675   Hem _⫽_ Tib. Hem N
        i intro _⫽_ om. L
        ocyus puer, bene D^{h} _⫽_ ocyus bene ƐNLJ   ocyus CYT

677   respicie _⫽_ respicies Y   respicit L

678   subita D^{c}_⫽_ subitae D
        mi res fuit _⫽_ mihi res fuit T   res mihi fuit NJ
           res fuit mihi L   res fuit CY

679   Tiberi _⫽_ Tiberio CYT
        filiam _⫽_ Lepidam CYT

681   Nunc _⫽_ Mane L
        hodie huc **venio** _⫽_ hodie huc veniam N   **venio huc hodie CYT**

682   Hum _⫽_ om. N
        adolescentem L^{c}_⫽_ adolescentulum L
        adolescentem pol optimum, filium tuum _⫽_ **filium tuum**
           adolescentem pol optimum N

684   optimum _⫽_ optimam N   om. CYT

685   **ego** _⫽_ **om. L**
        e D^{b} _⫽_ om. D

686   animus mihi CYNLJT _⫽_ mihi animus PD

687   Viro _/ Viri J
         filiam _/ om. N

688   Incommodum _/ In incommodum NJ
         mi _/ mihi CYNLJT
         inverteret D^b _/ inveteret D

689   in ingressu _/ ingressu CYL

690   Incommodum C^c _/ Incommodum mihi cederet C
         amicus _/ animus N
         commodum D^c _/ commoda DL

691   ille ad quid T^b _/ ad quid ille L   ille quid T
         valet _/ valeat N
         incommodat _/ incomodat N   non incommodat CY
             non incomodat T

692   ut _/ forsan CYT
         tuum C^b _/ suum C
         ha ha he CYNLT _/ ha ha ha PDJ

693-4   _/ lines om. Y

693   nolit _/ nolit ha ha he N
         haud D^b _/ om. D
         decet _/ decet Tiberi N

694   ha ha he CNT _/ ha ha ha PDLJ

694-5   ha ha he / Risus seni _/ risus seni ha ha he N

695   est umbra _/ et umbra Y
         et potus CYT _/ est potus PD^b om. DNLJ
         in febri CYT _/ in Febre PD^b om. DNLJ

696   focus _/ potus Y
         cibus _/ fidus Y
         potus _/ iocus CYT

697   Fa la la la la _/ Fa la la la N   Fa la la CYT

698   usque _/ imo usque Y

699   id _/ om. Y
         contumeliam _/ contumelia CY
         mei J^c _/ meam (?illeg.) mei J
         hoc T^b _/ om. T
         feram T^c _/ adferam T

700   mi DNJ 7 mihi PCYLT
        a risu ut 7 ut a risu CYT[b]   ut risu T

701   istuc 7 Isthuc N istoc CYT
        rideat 7 rideam N
        Tiberius 7 Tib: L

702   tristis 7 tristis tristis N
        Fa la la 7 Fa la la la NL

703   Cass. quin Jb 7 Quin J
        ilia om. L (space left)
        ridendo 7 ridendus L

704   per CYNLJT 7 et per PD

705   Nam quid 7 Numquid CT Nunquid Y

706   lepos 7 lepor L
        o hilaritas 7 et hilaritas L
        ego vos 7 vos ego CYT
        amo et colo 7 colo et amo L

707   Non 7 Neque CYT
        est invenustus 7 invenustus est CY
        filia 7 filius L

708   adeo 7 om. Y
        instructus 7 est instructus CYT instructas N
        filia quem D[b] 7 quem filia DNLJ
        depereat 7 deperiat L

710   defit illi 7 desit illi NT defit ei C ei desit Y
        basta 7 postea Y basta.i.sufficit N

711   hunc 7 hanc CYN

712   hercle 7 om. L

713   impetrabilior 7 imprecabilior J
        credo, esset mea filia D[b] 7 esset mea filia credo N
           esset credo mea filia J esset mea filia DL
        cum 7 iam N
        illa NLJ 7 illo CYT ea PD
        cubet 7 cubat L

714   aedipol CDYJT 7 edipol P aedopol N ædepol L

715   deridiculo] diridiculo L ridiculo YJ
pol hoc esset] pol esset hoc Y hoc pol esset NLJ

716   me nunc T^b] mini hoc T
mihi hem ergo] ergo mihi CYT
manum Y^c] ___ (illeg.) manum Y manum tuam NJ
    manus tuas L

718   gentium CDYNLJT] gentum P
fidem si] si fidem CYJT
hic T^b] om. LT

719   ridebo] rideo L

720-1   ] lines om. L

720   **vim feres**] **vini faeces Y**

721   Nec] Non Y

722   Tiberi] Tiberio CT Tiberius Y

723   iste C^b] est C ille Y
agrarius $C^b T^b$] agrag CT

724   a] e J
purgamentis] gurgamentis L
Aedipol] Aedepol YN

725   Valetudinarius] Valetudinaria NJ
Dispennat CDYNJT] Di pennat P dispenat L^b dispend L
et] ut CY
pandiculatur] pendiculatur L

726   accipitre D^c] accipitri DL

727   de filia D^b] filia D
filia CDYNLJT] filia. Tiberi? PD^b

728   Tib. Ibi] Ibi L

729   Cass. Eccere DLJ] Cass. Ecce re N^b Cass. Ecce P
    Tib. Ecce re N Eccere. Cass. CYT^b Cass. T

731   istiusque] istius N

732   Admisceatur] Admisceant N
*chelidonia J] Calidonia CYNLT Caledonia PD

733   <u>Cass</u>. Tangam _7_ tangam N

734   conditionis C^c _7_ conditiones ^{C}

735   Immo nihil _7_ Imo intus Y om. L
Vide _7_ vidi T inde L
modo _7_ om. L
ne quid _7_ nequid T

736   Ha ha he D^c _7_ Hah ha he T Ha ha ha DJ
puer _7_ puerum Y om. L
tuam NLJ _7_ tua PD tuum CYT
curassis _7_ curasses N cura sis CYT^c

737   viri a vitio _7_ a viri vitio CYT^c a vitio L $_\wedge$$^{om. T}$(space left)

738   oportet esse meum filium _7_ esse oportet meum filium CT
      esse oportet filium meum Y meum oportet esse filium
                                   NLJ

739   Tanto CYT _7_ Tanto est PDNLJ

740   <u>Cass</u>. Octodecim _7_ <u>Cass</u>. Octodecem J^c <u>Cass</u>. Cas.
                                           Octodecem J

741   quidem est _7_ est quidem CYT
illa CYNJT _7_ ista PDL

742   ea aetas CMJT _7_ aetas ea PD ea aetate Y ei aetas L

743   immergatur _7_ immergeatur L mergatur CYT
frigebit _7_ et frigebit Y

744   Ha ha _7_ Ha ha ha CT Ha ha he IN
vero _7_ om. CYLT
foemina est _7_ est foemina L

745   istuc _7_ isthuc N istud L istoc Y

746   Ah _7_ En CYT
es J^c _7_ est CYJT

747   simul _7_ simul etiam CYT

748   Bene bene _7_ Bene habet N

749   Optime _7_ om. Y
•condormierint DJ _7_ condormierunt PCYT condormirent NL

750 Ne _7 Me NL
hercle vero _7 vero hercle L
nihil CDYNLJT _7 nullus P

751 si T^b _7 om. T
iam _7 om. L
deveniret _7 deviniret L
gravidus _7 gradibus N

752 tu, tu _7 tu CYT
derisor tu _7 derisor te T
deridicule _7 ridicule CYNLJT

753 inquire _7 inquiras L

754 hae _7 haec N
possit _7 potest N

755-7 * _7 In CYT these lines occur after l. 775. The
readings however have been collated here.

755 Tib. Ita DNLJ _7 Ita CYT   Tib. It P
ha ha he, ut CDYNLT _7 ha ha ha, ut PD^b J
natum te _7 te natum CYNT
ha ha he CYNLT _7 ha ha ha PDJ

756 facias _7 facis ⌐
ha ha he CDYNLT _7 ha ha ha PD^b J

757 Cass. _7 Cassander CYT
Ha ha he CDYLT _7 Ha ha ha PD^b J   Ha ha N

758 Ha ha he CDYNLT _7 Ha ha ha PD^b J

759 Ha ha he stupide CYT _7 Ha ha he ND   ha ha ha PD^b J   om. L

760 Satin' _7 Statim NLJ
Iupiter _7 om. CYT
materies in mundo _7 in mundo materies Y

761 deridiculi J^c _7 deridiculo L   derid___li d_____
(illeg.) deridiculi J
credit C^c _7 credet C
sui CYT _7 ejus PDNLJ
compressu D^b _7 __ pressu (illeg.) D

762   gravidam Y^c] gradidam Y
si] om. Y
sciret J^c] s___je (illeg.) sciret J

763   hasce CYT] has PDNLJ
rerum gereret] rerum gerreret L rerum gererent N
    gererent virum Y gereret rerum CT

764   magis filiae ut L^b] ut filiae magis Y magis filiae L

765   eccas eccas eccas] eccas eccas CYT
una nunc] nunc una CNT nunc uni Y
Ah ha] ha ha N ah ah LT

766   Ah ha] ha ha N
tara ran tan tan tan] tara rantantan N tarra tan
    tan tan D ta ra ran ta ra tan CT tarara tara tan Y

767-8 In Y lines 767-8 are written twice, once before l. 766
    i.e. Y$_1$ and once after it in the correct position
    i.e. Y$_2$.

767   Ah ... ah ... ah Y^1] Ha ... ha ... ha Y^2

768   istoc ex Y^1] isthoc ex DN ex isto Y^2
esse te plane CNJT] esse plane te PDL te esse plane Y

769   Lyd. Ah] Ah L

771   commoda] commode Y
gignendis J^c] gi gignendis J

773   faxis CY] facis PDNLJT
modi] modo CYT

774   vide] vid L

775   Lepide C^b] Lepida CY
CYT see lines 755-7.

776   est] sit CYT
eiusmodi] huiusmodi NLJ

777   opprime] occupa opprime N

778 tange mihi hanc _/ tange hem hem Y
   tange tara _/ tara N
   tara ran tan tan tan tan _/ ta ra ran tan tan CY
    Tara ran tan tan NT

Actus 1. Scena 9.

Lepidus _/ Lepida PCDYNLJT

779 labella _/ lubella L bella CY
   auferes _/ auferres DL auferri Y

780 Venerem Y^c _/ venerem PYL

783 Ah mori CYNLJT _/ Mori PD
   non deamem D^c _/ non amem CYT dedam non deamem D

784 aliqua _/ aliquas NL
   suas _/ om. L (space left)
   mortes D^b _/ mores N motus LJ^b m_t_s (illeg.) D

785 Illamque o nimiam _/ o miram CYT
   morum CDYNJT _/ moris L oris P

786 ad conspectum CDYNLJT^b _/ conspectum PT

787 Patrisque _/ Lyd. Patrisque N

788 Lyd. Lepida L^b _/ lepida N Lep. Lepida L

789 At _/ Ah J

790 Lep. Qualis _/ Lyd. Qualis CYT Lep. Quale LJ qualis N
   haec _/ hoc LJ^b om. J
   est CYNLJT^b _/ o est PD om. T
   hoc D^{b}T^b _/ om. DT

791 Lys. Superbias _/ Lys. Superbiam CYT superbi N

792 _/ line om. L
   Lep. Et _/ Et CYNT

793 inexperta _/ experta L

794 exinde est _/ exind'est LJ^c exind'est est J

795 me nunc CYT⏋ nunc PDNLJ

796 ut⏋ om.-L
tum⏋ tun N tu L
stulta tum⏋ stulta dum L
intelliges⏋ intelligas Y

797 iam CYNLJT⏋ nunc PD

798 qui te temnit⏋ qui te contemnit C^{b}YNJT qui sic
  contemnit C om. L
qui te⏋ atque te NJ

799 Lep. Quem⏋ quem L

800 hercle⏋ om. N

801 quam te⏋ te Y
amem CYT⏋ amo PDNLJ
et quam CDYNLJT⏋ quam P
chara⏋ charae C

802 mea rosa⏋ rosa mea Y
ah⏋ om. CYT

803 tuas⏋ tuasque N

804 unquam⏋ om. CYT
uspiam crudelitas CDYN JT⏋ crudelitas uspiam PD^b
  uspiam credulitas L

805 Quin⏋ qui L

806 ⏋ line om. J
per vices rideo, et⏋ videret L (space left)

807 Lys. Nae⏋ Nae J
multum huic⏋ huic multum CT
debes y^b⏋ deb__ (illeg.) Y
quae c^c⏋ qui CN

808 Lep. O ⏋ Lyd. O Y O J^c
coelestium D^b⏋ om. D
scelestissime L^c⏋ scelessime scelestissime L

810 aspernantur $\bar{J}$ aspernuntur L

811 istuc DLJ J isthuc N istud P istoc CT istaec Y
     enim J om. CYLT
     efflictim adeo te CYLJT J afflictim adeo te PD
         te afflictim N

813 emortuus J mortuus D

814 esse J om. L
     alium J aliam Y

818 at J et N

821 quis J qui L

823 **ille me** J **me ille CYT**
     Admodum J **Ad modum J**

825 **Sane insane CYT** J **Sane PDNLJ**
     Lys. Certe J Lyd. Certe N

826 Lyd. **Certum** J certum N

827 ac **est** $\bar{J}$ et Y est L
     ipsi qui amat J ipse qui amat N tibi ipsi L

828 amicus J animus CY

829 scit J sit Y

830 sum particeps J sum perticeps J particeps sum L
     ergo J om. CYT

832 Multo J Lep. Multo N
     is te CDYNLJT J iste P

837 est J om. CY
     Lep. Mea J me Lep. Mea C

838 ingenio J ingenii N

839 tu J tum N
     quae T^b J quum L cum T
     es et vicina CYT^b J es et vicinia N et vicina es PDLJ
         et vicina T
     aut $\bar{J}$ om. N

840   mercatum nunc feci NLJ _/ nunc mercatum feci CYT
        mercatum feci PD
       hoc L^b _/ om. L
       fiet igitur _/ igitur fiet CYT   fiet N   siet igitur L
       subservi _/ subserva L

841   iubet _/ iuvet J
       unum tantum ut C^b _/ ut unum tantum C
       obsurdeam CYJT _/ absurdeam L   obsurdiam PD   observiam N

842   fecit _/ om. N

843   mihi fueris _/ fueris mihi Y

844   qui _/ quae CYT

845   meo pro Lucretio _/ pro Lucretio meo CYT

846   amicus _/ amans Y
       meus L^b _/ tuus YL

848   mortem et vitam _/ vitam et mortem CT   vitam per mortem Y

849   si quid _/ siquid YNL

850   Lucretium ut convenias _/ ut Lucretium convenias L
       ut convenias Lucretium J

851   hunc _/ nunc L
       doceas _/ edoceas CYT
       meos CDYNLJT _/ meas P
       at sic T^b _/ at sit T   et sit CY   et fac sis L
       istuc _/ istoc CYT^c istic T   om. N

852   ut hac proxima _/ hac proxima ut CT   hac proxima Y
       ut haec proximo L
       ipso T^b _/ om. YT
       possim _/ possem CNLJ^{b}T`

853   tuo J^c _/ tibi tuo J

854   in me CYNLJT _/ me PD
       dubium _/ dubium certe Y

855   demeream CYNJT _/ demerem L   demerear PD

856   prosperare 7 pro parte Y
             intelligam 7 intelligo CYT

857   quicquid 7 quicquam NLJ
             id T^b 7 om. NJT

858   Sponden' ergo 7 Spondeo CT   Sponde Y
             facturam 7 facturum YN

859   <u>Lyd</u>. Da 7 Lydia da CYT

860   Ah 7 <u>Lyd</u>. Ah CYT
             utinam 7 uti J

861   Lepida 7 Lepidus L

862   Ancillare huic 7 Comitare hanc Y
             ne C^c 7 ne te C   me N
             incedat T^b 7 discedat T

863   Fiet 7 Fiat CT

864   osculum CYT 7 om. PDNLJ

Actus 1.   Scena 10.

Lepidus 7 Lepida CDYNJT

865-70   All Lysetta's speeches are assigned to Lydia in N.
            These errors will not be included in the list
            of variants.

865   Hem 7 Lepida CYT

868   tu 7 om. Y

869   ubi 7 ubi tu L
             Non CDYNLJT 7 Nonne PD^b
             me dem 7 dem me L   me CYT

870   <u>Lys</u>. Quale 7 Quale L
             est hoc 7 enim hoc Y
             frangam T^b 7 om. T
             quod demoliar C^{b}D^b 7 quos demoliar C   quo demoliar D

872   O 7 oh CT   om. L
             Lepide 7 Lepida CYLT

873   Lep. Lysetta _7 lep. Lyset L^c Lyset lep. Lyset L

874   Numnam _7 numnam L

875   Lys. Quid C^b _7 quid C
         Lep. Ita N^c _7 Lyd. Lep. Ita N
         Regina _7 Lucina CYT

876   supremus T^b _7 om. T
         patruus eius _7 eius patruus L
         Saturnus _7 Saturnius L

877-8   avique et proavi, omnisque divum domus - /Lys. Quid hi autem? _7
         Lys. Quid hic autem? Avique et proavi ... domus. Lys.
         Quid hic autem? C Lys. Quid hic autem? Y

877   Et Castor _7 et ecastor L
         omnisque _7 omnesque N
         divum _7 Deorum CYT

878   hi _7 hic CYT
         Lep. Iuno _7 Iuno C
         filia C^c _7 filius C
         et Saturnus _7 Saturnus L
         patruus C^b _7 pater C
         maritus Iupiter _7 Iupiter maritus L

879   Lys. Dic _7 Dic L
         ita me, ita me _7 ita me, ita mei CY   ita mei, ita mei T

881   perduint CYNJT _7 perdunt L   perdant PD
         Lydiam _7 Coeliam Y

882   Vale CDYNLJT _7 Val P
         Lepide! Lepide! Lepide! Hem Lepide, _7 Lepide Lepide hem
            Lepide L

883   habe animum _7 animum habe Y

884   te T^b _7 om. T
         illius T^b _7 om. T

885   Ain' vero _7 Amo vere Y

886   Ain _7 Anne CYT
         Lys. Faciam _7 Lep. Faciam CN

887   Lys. Videbis C^b ⟧ Lyd. Videbis C   Lys. Videris NLJ
      tu ⟋ tum L
      iam nunc hanc DNLJ ⟧ nunc hanc P   nunc iam ᴗ
         iam nunc C^cYT
      vobis ⟋ om. N

888   modo aliquid mox ⟧ mox aliquid CYT
      fiet ⟧ fiat YJ
      metuas CYNLJT ⟧ dubites PD

889   Hem istuc ⟧ Item istuc CT

889-91   Lys. Immo nimium est, nolo./Lep. Hem inquam./Oportet
        inquam. ⟧ om. CYT

891   gratiam T^c ⟧ gratiam nunc T

892   Lep. Per ... paenitebit. ⟧ Per ... paenitebit. L
        Per ... faxo ego. Lep. Istiis ... paenitebit. Y
      te D^b ⟧ om. DN
      paenitebit T^b ⟧ paenitet T

893   Lys. Vale ⟧ Vale L

894   hominum ⟋ atque hominum Y
      animus ⟧ animius N
      rediit ⟧ redit Y   reliit L

895   Lysetta quod ⟧ quod Lysetta iam CYT   Lyset. quod L
      promisit D^bNLJ ⟧ promiserit PDCYT
      sum deus, sum deus, sum deus. ⟧ sum deus, sum deus. CYLT

Finis Actus Primi ⟧ Actus Primi Finis CJT   om. DL

Actus 2. Scena 1.

Lucretia / Lucretius PCDYNLJT

2 Horati $\underline{J}$ Horatio NLJ Horatium Y
   Lucreti $\underline{J}$ Lucretio NLJ

3 visi D^bJ^c $\underline{J}$ om. D vs visi J
   inde te $CYNLJT^a$ $\underline{J}$ te PD^cT ... te (erased) D
   vidi C^c $\underline{J}$ video C

4 ted erga CDYT $\underline{J}$ te'd'erga NJ te erga P sed erga L

6 te mihi C^c $\underline{J}$ te non viderim mihi C

7 totam $\underline{J}$ totam, totam Y
   credo $\underline{J}$ addo L
   quaestione $CYNLJT^c$ / quaestionem PDT

8 a te D^b $\underline{J}$ te D

10 *hercle $\underline{J}$ vero CYT

11 fere DCYNJT $\underline{J}$ om. PL
   culminis $\underline{J}$ cumulus L

12 istuc $\underline{J}$ isthuc NL istud CYT
   suspirii CNLJT $\underline{J}$ suspiri PD supplicii Y
   nunquid $\underline{J}$ numquid DNLJ
   mali CNJT $\underline{J}$ male PDYL

13 aedipol $\underline{J}$ aedepol YLJT
   vide sis CDYNLJT $\underline{J}$ videsis P
   o Dio $\underline{J}$ O dii o L O Dii CYJ^cT
   es mihi T^a $\underline{J}$ mihi es NJ mihi sis L mihi T

14 L^a $\underline{J}$ line om. L
   medius fidius $\underline{J}$ mediusfidius CN
   oppilationes DJ $\underline{J}$ opilationes PNL^a oppilationem CYT
   aut aquam CYNJT $\underline{J}$ aut aqua PD om. L^a
   intercutem DNJ $\underline{J}$ inter cutem $PCYL^aT$

15 tempore $\underline{J}$ tempori J
   huic CDYNLJT $\underline{J}$ hic P
   intelligo tibi NLJT $\underline{J}$ tibi intelligo PD^b est tibi CDY

16   est⟩CDYNLJT⟨7 om. PD^c
        istuc 7 isthuc L isthoc N om. Y
        prospectum CDYLJT 7 profectum N perspectum P

17   quam 7 qua N
        suspirat‾CDYNLJT 7 suspira P

18   qui 7 cur CYNLJT
        hosce CYT 7 hcs PDNLJ
        multos T^a 7 om. T

19-20   iam denuo. Quid avertis autem? Aedipol profecto coniicio
          hercle. / En iterum   7 om. CYT

19   iam denuo 7 iamdiu N
        autem DNLJ 7 me P
        hercle J^c 7 autem hercle J
        aedipol 7 aedepol NLJ
        profecto L^b 7 om. L

20   En 7 tu L
        sic CYNLT 7 sis PDJ

21   Quaeso 7 om. CYT

22   At ~~PDNLJ~~ 7 Ah CYT
        quae mihi 7 mihi quae N

23   nunc pol 7 pol nunc CYT
        loqueris 7 liqueris N

24   quicquid enim in vitạ mihi CYNLJ^bT 7 quidquid enim in
          vita mihi J quicquid mihi in vita PD

25   omne C^c 7 omnem C
        acceptum 7 acceptam Y

26   ~~istuc~~ 7 isthuc N istud CYT

27   forsan haud CYNL^aJT 7 haud PD forsan L
        in vita 7 in vita ob ⋅/ vita L^a in / vita L om. N

29   Line 29 is copied twice in L, once before l. 28 and
          once in its correct position; the first version
          has been deleted.
        ut compos CYNJT 7 compos ut PDL

30   istuc] isthoc N
     vere] veri T
     atque] et CYLT
     diceres.C^c] disceres C

32   dispice] despice CYNLJT
     impera] respice N

33   recuso] recusem C
     habear] haberer N
     ego] om. L

34   meum] mecum Y

35   secretum] saeculum L
     advorte T^c] adorte T

36   ] line om. L
   *illum quem CYNJT] illam quam PD

37   me in amicitiam] in amicitiam me CYT

38   spectat] spectet N
     adeo tam similis, Horati tibi] Horati tam similis tibi CYT
     similis] similes L
     Horati] Hor / Horati L^a

39   eo solum] eum solo Y

41   L^a] line om. L
   *me] mihi L^a
     quam cum] quam Y qua cum N
     contingat CYT] contingit $PDNL^a$ contigit J

42   Adeo C^c] Adeoque CY
     et tuo] ut tuo YL at tuo N

43   rerum] verus CYT

44   abiret CNLJT] abieret PDY

45   quam ego] ego quam L

46   adolescentem T^c] adolescentat T
     ibi ipsa] ipsa ibi CYT   ibi ipsu N
     ibi Y^c] ibi lu Y
     alium] aliam Y

47   agerem _7 ageretur L

48   ergo _7 ego CYT
         agi _7 age Y egi J
         praetuli _7 protuli Y

50   facio _7 fiam J
         'inter _7 ego CYT^a (illeg.) T

51   esset _7 erit Y

52   animo . _7 anim = / animo L^a

53   Tantane _7 Tantaque L^b Tantque L
         cuipiam _7 accipiam Y quaepiam L
         siet _7 sit CYT
         amplexu CYJT _7 amplexa PDL amplexus N
         quem _7 quam YJT^c

54   alio _7 alia CYT
         internosceret _7 inter nosceret D innotesceret N
         Facile ... animus _7 written in larger letters in J
            and underlined in T
         sperat _7 spirat CY
         amantis animus L^a _7 om. L

55   line 55 _7 underlined in T
         priusquam D^c _7 priusquam quam D prius quam YNJ

56   hic _7 his CYT

57   hac re _7 hoc Y
         possim _7 possem D possit YL om. N
         amantem ... decipit _7 written in larger letters in J
            and underlined in T

58   Ahi _7 Abi Y
         illam, illa _7 illam sed illa CY
         decepit _7 decipit N decoepit L

59   hunc _7 hanc NLJ
         amplexa, amplexus _7 amplexa, amplexa L amplexus,
            amplexus L^a

60   in timore spem quaerens, in dolo fidem, in flammis
            refrigerium. D^b _7 om. DNJ

quaerens _/_ querens L
flammis _/_ flamma C^bYT luctu C

61 charissime CDYNLJT _/_ clarissime P
amicos inter _/_ inter amicos N
quales _/_ qualis L

63 quod _/_ quid YNJ

64 inde _/_ om. CYT
sum _/_ sim C
hoc _/_ haec L

66 tam N^b _/_ qam N
quam / quid L

67 quoquam _/_ quopiam CY

68 hercle _/_ mehercle N
non solum liberali, nobilique honesto et tuo CDYLJT _/_
    non solum liberali, nobilique et tuo P
    nobili non solum liberali et honesto et tuo N

69 adeoque _/_ adeo Y

70 ego _/_ om. Y
ni _/_ in L
devinctus _/_ divinctus l devinc=/ divinctus L^a
    districtus NJ astrictus CYT

71 continerem _/_ continere N
iniuriam L^a _/_ m ... iam (illeg.) L

72 •ipse ut CDYNLJT _/_ ipse P
ulciscerer _/_ ulsciscer J

73 fisam J^c _/_ fisum N fid fisam J
tibi _/_ tui N
duram - _/_ durram L^a
crudelem o _/_ o crudelem N

75 atque _/_ et Y

77 culpa _/_ is culpa CY

79 pacto _/_ pacta CYT
ubi _/_ cum NLJ

80   mihi _7_ me CT
        praeripere alterius gaudium _7_ gaudium alterius praeripi L

81   amicam _7_ amicum Y

82   haud _7_ non N
        amicam _7_ amicum N

83   Ohi me DNLJ _7_ O hime P   Perii CYT

85   non _7_ num L

86   Ha, ohi me! ha L^cJ _7_ Ha, oh ime! ha P   Ha ohime ha D
        Ha ohime me ha L   aha ohi me ah N   Ah, ohime, ah CY
        Ah, ohi me, ah T

87   *resiste N _7_ restite N^c restiti PDLJ   om. CYT

88   mehercle _7_ mehercule CT

89   ut saluti aliquid _7_ saluti aliquid ut N
        advorsi _7_ adversi CYLT   ut advorsi J

90   est hic _7_ hic est Y
        atque _7_ et CY

91   solus C^b _7_ sol_ s (illeg.) C

92   habuisse aliquid de rebus meis CYLJT _7_ habuissem
           aliquid de rebus meis N   aliquid de rebus meis
           habuisse PD

93   verum L^c _7_ utrum L
        rerum _7_ verum C

95   Perillae _7_ Perrillae D   perillae L
        suae amicae _7_ amicae suae CYT   om. L
        iamdudum CDYNLJT _7_ iam dudum P

Actus 2. Scena 2.

Crispinus _J_ Chrispinus L

96   Crisp. Amicus ut hic siet? _J_ Hor. Amicus ut hic siet? J^c
        Crisp. Amicus ut hic siet? / Hor. Amicus ut
                               hic siet? J
    Hor. Atque _J_ Atque J
    Crispine _J_ Chrispine L

97   vivusne _J_ vivus ne CDYLJT vivus N
    sum _J_ sim CYT

99   here D^b _J_ om. D
    est _J_ om. CYT

100   Enimvero _J_ Quin vero L
    eloquere YNLJT _J_ loquere PCD

100-1   Crisp. Nae, tu Lucretium hunc amicum elegantem
        habes? / Hor. Qui istuc? _J_ om. N
    habes CDYLJT _J_ habet P

101   tuas _J_ has L
    Perillae _J_ perillae L

102   Lepidae _J_ etiam Lepidae L
    perquam _J_ per quam CT
    eam CYNLJT _J_ illam PD

103   amoris _J_ amores T
    tui _J_ hic L
    pacto _J_ pact - (illeg.) Y

104   est tibi _J_ tibi est Y
    eam CDYNLJT _J_ illam P
    gravidam T^c _J_ gravdam T

105   Etiam et CYT _J_ Et iam PDNLJ
    eam _J_ eam / eam L

106   primo congressu _J_ congressu primo CYT
    est _J_ om. L

107   brevi posse eum _J_ brevi posse eam N eum brevi posse Y

108   metuo quo haec res evadat _J_ quo haec res evadat
                                     metuo CYT
    evadat CYT _J_ evadet PDL evadit NJ

110   Te ultimo die Veneris _/_ Ultimo Veneris die te L

111   hoc _/_ haec CYT
obstupuit J^c _/_ obstupiit C   obstuc obstupuit J
    distupuit L

112   Lepidae _/_ lepidae T Laepidae L
cognitissima CYNLJ^{c}T _/_ cognotissima PD notissima
    cognitissima J

114   fuisse tuis die Veneris ultimo eam arbitreris CYT _/_
    eam fuisse tuis ultimo die Veneris arbitreris PDNLJ
fuisse _/_ tum fuisse L
ultimo die Veneris D^b _/_ die Veneris ultimo CYT ultimo
    veneris D ultima die Veneris N

115   mecum una _/_ una mecum Y
coenae _/_ coena NJ

116   reverteremus _/_ reverteremur L reverterimus CYT

117   perrexit _/_ perexit CDT

118   dormivit _/_ dormiit CYNLJT
magis _/_ maius L

119   (inquit) ego Lepidae _/_ ego Lepidae (inquit) CT
    ego inquit Lepidae Y ego Lepidae N
atqui _/_ atque CYNT
abest J^b _/_ est J

120   saepicule _/_ saepiuscule CYLT
oboriretur CD^{b}Y^{b}L _/_ obiretur D _ boriretur (illeg.) Y
    aboriretur PNJT

121   habet _/_ habelt D

122   Interime _/_ Interrime J

123   tandem _/_ tantum N

124   tradidi etiam et armillas _/_ tradidique etiam armillas Y
quam primum _/_ quamprimum CYNLJ

125   has _/_ eas Y
detulit _/_ detuli L

126   ubi _/_ ut N
agitur _/_ igitur Y

128   quicquam _7_ quidquam N
          commercii _7_ commersii D   comercii N

129   eiusmodi _7_ istius modi Y

130   cogitasse N^b _7_ eogitasse N
          nedum CYL _7_ ne dum PDNJT
          desponsatam CDYNLJT _7_ desponsata P
          esse _7_ fuisse CYT

132   tuum _7_ om. CYT
          ne verbum _7_ neqverbum L
          unum L^b _7_ unquam L

134   Nimio _7_ Nimium L
          velim _7_ vellem N

135   Quid ni _7_ Quidni CDYLT
          credas T^b _7_ om. T_b
          morerer _7_ morear D^b

136   haec _7_ om. CYT

137   non _7_ num L

138   Ultimo eam die Veneris NLJ _7_ Ultimo die Veneris eam PCDYT
          totam noctem _7_ tota nocte Y
          amplexibus _7_ complexibus CT

140   Here _7_ om. L
          Lucretius ille _7_ Lucretio illi Y

144   Eloquere _7_ Hoc eloquere Y
          inquam _7_ in quam N

145   quod _7_ quid Y
          huc _7_ hic Y
          usque sutelis suis _7_ usque sutellis suis T   sutelis suis usque

146   deluserit CYNLJT _7_ deluderet PD
          ego ut perfidum _7_ ut ego perfidum N   ego perfidum ut LJ
          creduam CNJT _7_ credam PDYL

147   meum _7_ mecum NLJT

148   simulavit] simulabit L

149   dissimulavit] dissimulabit L
           suis N^b] tuis NJ

150   tu D^b] om CDNLJT
           arbitraris] arbitreris N

151   Mancipium] Mancipium es Y
           perfidiae] perfidiis N

152   periurii] periuriis CYNT
           huiusmodi] eiusmodi Y
           consimilem] consimiliter L

154   amare aiunt CYT] amare ais PDLJ   ais amare N

156   eam] eum L

157   Respondisse] respondere N
           se] om. CYT
           cogitare] cogitasse L

158   eam] om. CYT
           eam uxorem CYT] se uxorem PD^b eam DNLJ

159   est] erat L
           ut D^b] om. D
           ducat] duceret L
           qua] quae NT qui L

159-60   pro arbitratu frui] frui pro arbitratu N

160   innupta] inupta L

162   inconciliare] inconsiliare DT
           connititur D^{c}N^b] connitetur D comittetur N
           efficerem] effecerim CYT
           advorte] adverte L

164   consentiant] consentiunt T

165   se] se quidem Y
           pridem CDYNLJT] pridie P
           conciliasse] consiliasse DT

166   Tu] Tum Y
           ex te gravidam esse] ex te esse gravidam Y
              gravidam ex te esse L

169 millies CDYNLJT ⟋ milies P
accubui ⟋ occubui Y

170 Neque ⟋ Nec CYNT

171 Et ⟋ Atque CY
cuiquam ⟋ cuipiam N
credo ⟋ credam CYT

172 fuisse D^b ⟋ ___ (erased) D

173 Lepidam D^c ⟋ Lydiam Lepidam D
id ⟋ hoc CYT

174 huiusmodi ⟋ has Y
*suspicarier technas ⟋ suspicari technas PDNLJ
         technas suspicarier CYT

175 audies ⟋ audias Y
est ad te iterum ⟋ est iterum CT   iterum est Y

176 appellas CDYNJT ⟋ apellas PDL
Lepidam ⟋ Lepida L Lydiam N
qua astutiis DYLJ ⟋ quibus astutiis PCNT
adducas ⟋ inducas N

177 eam ⟋ etiam Y
impediant ⟋ impediunt L

178 nisi ⟋ mihi Y
eam CYNLJT ⟋ illam PD
abripias CDYNLJT ⟋ arripias P

179 obstas ⟋ obstes CYT

180 illum ⟋ tuum CYT
pateris J^c ⟋ tibi pateris J patieris Y
tibi glaucomam JT^c ⟋ tibi glaucamam L   tibi glauconiam C
         tibi glaucenam Y tibi nebulam T   glaucomam tibi PD
         glaucomam N
ob ⟋ ab Y
oculos ⟋ oculis YN
obiicere ⟋ abiicere Y

181 Ut D^b ⟋ Et DYNJ
credas ⟋ credis N
non ⟋ cum L
recusat ⟋ recuset N

182 si quae ⟋ siquae L

183   fiant ⟧ fient YNLJ

184   Hercle N^c ⟧ Eheu Hercle N
cum ⟧ et NJ

185   somnum ⟧ somnium CT
video ⟧ videro Y

186   Eamus CYNLJT ⟧ Eamus ad coenam PD^b om. D

Actus 2. Scena 3.

187   quae ⟧ que Y qua N
aquell ⟧ a quell CT a quel Y aquel NJ aquet L
*villiaco CT ⟧ villaco PDNJ villico Y vellan L
m'a traydo ⟧ m'atrido CT in altrido Y in a traydo NJ
    m'a h_aydo (illeg.) L
traydo ⟧ traydo Jesus Jesus L

188   Bide oide bide ⟧ Vide Vide vide CT Vide Vide Y
virum ⟧ birum DNJ

189   Lepidam Lepidam meam C^{c}YJT ⟧ Lepidam meam PDL
    Lepidam meam Lepidam meam C meam Lepidam N
visere ⟧ bisere DNJ

190   Doh ⟧ Poh CYT Don L
reniego ⟧ remiego L reheego J rem ego CYT
del ⟧ dee L
*mondo ⟧ mundo CYT
villiaco CYT ⟧ villaco PNLJ villacco D^c villa___ (illeg.) D
holla ⟧ o la L
mochacho ⟧ mochaco C machacho YN mochacco J

191   Signior$_{or}$ ⟧ Segnior D Seignior N Sennor L Seg^r CT Sg^r Y
    Sig^{or} J
Signior. Don. ⟧ Sg^r Don ... Y Seignior Don ... N
Burrachio ⟧ di Barachicho Y

192   Gril. Don Piedro L^b ⟧ Don Piedre Y Don Piedro N
    Don. Piedro L

193   esclavo ⟧ esclamo L^b escdamo L
Pacheco ⟧ pacheco T Pachecho N

193-4   <u>Gril</u>. Don Piedro Pacheco. / <u>Don</u>. D'Alcantara ...]
       Don Piedro Pacheco d'Alcantara ... Y
       <u>Gril</u>. Don Piedro Pacheco <u>Don</u> Alcantara / <u>Don</u>. ... N

194   D'Alcantara] d'Alcantara CY Alcantara N
       D'Alth D'Alchantara J D'Alchantara J^c
    villiacoCD^{b}YT] villiac_ (illeg.)Y villaco PNLJ villacco D

195   D'Alcantara C^c] D'alcantara T Don Alcantara C
       Don Atlantara N D'Altantara J D'abantara D
       Alcantira L
    villiaco] villiacco D villiacho D^c villaco NLJ villico Y
    Pacheco] Pachecho N pacheco T pachaco L
    D'Alcantara] d'Alcantara CT de Alcantara Y
       D'Alatantara DJ Don Atlantara N

196   Beso] <u>Don</u>. Beso Y
    Beso las] Besolos LT biso has N Desolos C De solos Y
    manos] manus NL manes Y
    de v merced J] de v mercede DL dev'mercede P
       de vi mercedem CYT de vinererd N

197   <u>Don</u>. Las piernas CT] <u>Don</u>. Los piernos PDLJ de las piernas Y
       Don / Piernos N
    villiaco CYNJT] villiaceo P villiacco D villaco L

198   Age] <u>Don</u>. Age N
    Age age] Age CY
    istoc] isthoc DN istuc L
    viro] biro DNJ
    sat] satis Y

199   Te decet] dedecet L

200   At] om. Y
    detergere prius J^b] prius detergere CYT detergeri prius N
       detegere prius J

202   tu] om. Y
    bide] vide CYLT
    excute J^b] exute J

203   Oh] O C
    ad N^c] bide ad N
    bide bide L^b] vide vide CYLT

204 Bide ⌐ Vide CYT
hic ⌐ om. CYT
tibialia J⁰ ⌐ tibi alia CYLT tibiliia J
lindamente, lindamente D ⌐ l'indamente l'indamente P
    lindamentae lindamentae J lindamenta, lindamente CT
    lintamenta lindamente Y lintamente lindamente N
    leviter leviter L
Doh ⌐ Don L doch J pol CYT
mochacho ⌐ machacho NT macheco CYJ

205 pro equo aut mulo Cᶜ ⌐ pro mulo aut equo C
circumcontemplare CDLJT ⌐ circum contemplare PYL⁰
    circum contemplari N

206 Penula ⌐ Pennula N
decet D⁰ ⌐ ___ (erased) D
Perquam CDYNLJT ⌐ Per quam P
optime ⌐ optume J

207 Elegantemente ⌐ Elegante mente J Eleganter CYLT

208 omnes exemplum ⌐ exemplum omnes CY
habent L⁰ ⌐ habeat L
in ⌐ om. N
vestibus ⌐ bestibus Tᶜ

209 O ⌐ oh L
bide ⌐ vide YNL
has ⌐ sas Y
Mochacho ⌐ machacho LJ Mochaco CT Macheco Y

211 An nunc ⌐ sum nunc Lᵃ
varvam D⁰Jᵇ ⌐ varbam DJ barbam YNL

213 Mal ⌐ Mall Y Male N
fuego D⁰ ⌐ fu ego CT fa ego DY furgo L
os ⌐ om. N
abrase LNJ ⌐ ab rase P obrase L pabrase CT probaste Y
villiaco CYT ⌐ villaco PDNLJ

214 O ⌐ oh LT

215 varvam ⌐ barbam YNL
aspergi odorifera Dᶜ ⌐ asperge odorifera D odifera aspergi L
    odorifera aspergi L⁰

216 citharaede ⌐ citharaedo D⁰ cytharaede YN
aedes ⌐ aedeis J

217 concelebras ⟋ conceterras L
bolo C^c ⟋ volo CYJ
salutare hodie ⟋ hodie salutare CYT

218 Alla ⟋ Atta CT
Hispaniece ⟋ Hispaniesse J Hispanisse NL Hispanissa CYT
←alla gala, alla gala ⟋ ala gala, ala gala LJ

219 cum ⟋ cui L

220 hic ⟋ istic N
nunc incipe ⟋ om. NJ

221 ⟋ line om. P
ego interim illus fenestram suspirans contemplabor ⟋ om.
interim ⟋ om. D
Gril. Incipe ⟋ Incipe N

222 Don. O ⟋ Don O N Don. Oh LJT
galano ⟋ gallano J Gallana CYT
o gentil ⟋ oh gentil L o gentill J o gentis C om N.
Por dios ⟋ Per dios CYLT
olla maravilla ⟋ alla maravilla D ala maranilla J
  ara maravilla L ara mara milla N ata mara milla CT
  attamara mille Y
gratiosamente ⟋ gratiosa mente YJ gratida mente N
doh DL ⟋ poh NJ hoh P om. CYT

224 occentem ⟋ accentem YL
Grille ⟋ Grylle YT

225 quid si ego CYNJT ⟋ et ego PDL
adiutabo L^a ⟋ advitabo L adiuvabo CYT

226 Buenos dias ⟋ Buenos dios NJ Burnos dios L om. CYT

227 Ala ⟋ Alla CYT
senniora D^cJ ⟋ fenniora P sennora DL semnor N
  sora CT sera Y
galana ⟋ gallana CYT
gentil ⟋ gentill LJ

228 Gril. Quem ⟋ Quem N
Don ⟋ om. N

229   <u>Don.</u> O ⫽ Don. Oh Y O N
      <u>Burrachio</u> ⫽ Borachio T Borachico Y
      non ⫽ num L
      bidisti ⫽ vidisti YLJ audivisti N

231   Neque ⫽ nec N

232   Doh ⫽ Poh CYT
      reniego ⫽ remiego L renego N cein ego Y
      los cielos D^b ⫽ lo los cibos D los cietos Y del mondo NL

233   per estas ⫽ por istas NJ per istas CYT
      varvas ⫽ varbas D verbas N vulnus L larvas Y
      eloquuta PD ⫽ elocuta CNLJT om. Y

234   Pacheco ⫽ pacheco C Pachecho DYN pachecho L
      D'Alcantara ⫽ d'Alcantara YT d'alcantara C Don
          Alcantara N D'Atlantara L
      *buon giorno ⫽ bon on giorno NJ vium giorno L
          me recommenda PD om. CYT
      ala senniora vestra ⫽ ala signa vestra NLJ om. CYT

236   <u>Don.</u> Malos ⫽ malos CYT
      annos ⫽ avos L

237   Neque ⫽ <u>Don.</u> Neque CYT
      ego D^b ⫽ om. D
      picaro ⫽ picare Y picato L
      vagamundo ⫽ vagamondo NL va gumbo CT vaguuve Y
      ministril ⫽ ministrill CT ministret NJ

238   etiam ⫽ et iam Y om. NJ
      *respexis ⫽ respicis CYT
      berbero ⫽ berbere N verbero CYL^cT

240   Mercedem ⫽ om. N
      Al NJ ⫽ at L il PDT i C^cY i ___ (illeg.) C
      diablo ⫽ diabolo CT

241   Non ⫽ Et non Y
      Grille ⫽ Grylle T
      viginti C^c ⫽ viginta CT^c 20 L

242   viginti ⫽ 20 L
      <u>Don.</u> Abi C^b ⫽ Abi C
      nunc iam ⫽ iam nunc CYT

243   <u>Cith</u>. Dii Y^b _/_ <u>Gri</u>. Dii Y

244   Esclavo _/_ Esclama L
    mio _/_ meo CY imo L
    hic nos CYNJT _/_ nos hic PDL
    mihi L^a _/_ --- (illeg.) L

245   servolus CYNT _/_ servulus PDLJ
    bolo _/_ volo CYJT
    uti _/_ ut N
    ediscas meos CYT _/_ addiscas meos N   meos addiscas PDLJ

246   et tu CYNLJT _/_ tu PD
    esto _/_ isto N
    irascor _/_ irascar Y

247   de cavaliero _/_ de Cavalliero CY de Cavalearo J
        delavagliero L
    deiera tu CYT _/_ tu deiera PDNLJ

248   Por dios _/_ Per dios CYLT
    por todos _/_ por tedos N per totos CLT per toto Y
    los santos L _/_ lossantos DJ lassontos P lassantes CYNT
    poh _/_ per CYT
    reniego _/_ reni ego D remiego L rein ego Y
    Emperador _/_ emperador T imperador N imperator Y

249   bonae rei _/_ boni N
    alicunde _/_ aliunde CYNLT
    corraseris _/_ convaseris Y
    communices D _/_ communi --- (erased) D^c

250   aeris _/_ aeros T
    opsonii _/_ obsonii CYLT

251   Bolo _/_ Volo CYT
    enim _/_ etiam CYT
    id _/_ ego N ego id N^b
    e _/_ a N

252   ego _/_ om. N
    harum _/_ earum Y
    sim D^c _/_ sum DYNLJ
    indigus _/_ indigens CYT

253   por tua DLJ _/_ portua P pro tua N per tua CYT
    vida _/_ vide Y bide N
    itane _/_ ita ne YN

254   es D^b] om. DNLJ
villiaco CY] villaco PNLJ villacco D

255   suffuratus] suffucatus L

256   vero] om. Y
tuae manus] manus tuae Y

257   por] per L pol CYT
vida] vide Y
del CYNLJT] d'el PD
Emperador] imperador N imperator Y

258   vel] bel J
biris] viris CYLT

259   Serva, serva CYNLT] Serba, serba PDJ
vorax CYNLT] borax PDJ

260   ventriones CYNLT] bentriones PDJ
carnivoros CYNLT] carniveros J carniboros PD

261   insalata] in salata CNT
colta] coltu T collu C colla Y
di mano] dimano J di manno N di manu CYT
fanciulla DL] fanci ulla P sanciulla CT saucivilla Y
    faciulla J facilla N

262   vini] bini NJ una CYT
sorbitiuncula $CDYNJT^b$] sorbitiunula T sortiuncula P om. L

263   modica modica] modica CYT
aedipol] aedepol YL

264   sum nactus] nactus sum C

265   tres dies nos alet] nos alet tres dies Y

267   Vamos, nunc Grille vamos C] Vamos nunc Grylle vamos T
    Vamos nunc Grille PD Vamos Grille vamos J
    Vamos. Gril. I prae here N Vamos vamos N^b
    Eamus nunc Grille eamus Y Eamus nunc Grille L
atque audin' N^b] om. N

270-274 D^b] om. D

271   Vamos _7_ Vamus N Eamus Y

273   confeceris _7_ conficeris Y
        hinc _7_ tunc CYLT

274   rursum incipe _7_ rursus incipe NLJ incipe iterum CYT

275   Don. Vamos, vamos. <u>Gril.</u> Vamos, vamos D^b _7_ Don. Vamos,
        vamos. L Vamos Grille vamos. Gr. Vamos vamos D
        <u>Don.</u> Eamus, eamus. <u>Gril.</u> Eamus. Eamus. Y

        Actus 2. Scena 4

Scena 4J^b _7_ Scena 3^a J
Piedro _7_ piedro L Pedro J
Tiberius _7_ Tiberio N

276   Signior _7_ Seignior N Senior J Sennor L Sg^r CYT
        Oh _7_ Ohi N

277   Bene facis _7_ Benefacis NT

278   virum noveris esse illustrem NJ _7_ noveris virum esse
        illustrem CYT virum esse illustrem noveris PD
        virum noveris illustrem L
        filiae _7_ filliae L

279   At ~~PYN~~ _7_ Ad CDLJT

280   Don Pacheco _7_ don Pacheco DYT Don pacheco L
        don pacheco C Don Pachecho N
        Piedro Pacheco _7_ pietro pacheco L Pedro Pachecho N
        D'Alcantara _7_ d'Alcantara CDT dalcantara J
        de Alcantara Y D'Ascantara L Don Alcantara N

281   meam _7_ ego meam Y

282   dignam _7_ dignum L
        propterea nec _7_ tam ob causam agitur L

283   inducere D^c _7_ ... (erased) inducere D
        possum _7_ non possum L

285   tu _7_ om. NJ

286   istuc 〕 isthuc N istoc YL
exurge 〕 exsurge L surge N
sis 〕 om. Y

287   Grille 〕 Grillo L Grylle T
villiaco 〕 villaco NJ villacho L om. Y
est hic CYNJT 〕 hic est PDL
e 〕 ex L

289   Verum J^c 〕 Don. Verum J
Tiberi 〕 Tiberio CYNLJT
por vida 〕 porvida N per vida L per vita CT per vitam Y
Emperador 〕 Imperador T imperador N imperator Y
tecum 〕 om. CY

290   *E iuro CT 〕 eiuro PDY et iuro L Ei vero J ego ei N
a los cielos T 〕 alos cielos PCD alios cielos Y
    ad cielos J ad ciolos L vero ero N
iuro 〕 vir N

291   tibi 〕 om. L
hercle 〕 hercule CT
Gril. Et 〕 Don. At Y
por dios ╱ per dios CYN por coilos L

292   por todos los santos 〕 per todos lassantos CT
    per totos lassantes Y per tedas lassantes N
    per totlos los santos L

294   nihili CYT 〕 nisi PDNLJ
sumus 〕 summus C
tu - Don. 〕 ha. Don. Y Don. tu N

295   Rex eris 〕 rexeris J

296   lubet 〕 libet N
mihi hanc in uxorem 〕 mihi in uxorem hanc Y
    hanc mihi in uxorem N

297-8   〕 lines om. CYT

299   lubet hanc Y^b 〕 lubes hanc Y
accipere 〕 om. L

300   in mundo plurimae D^bJ^c 〕 ___ (illeg.) D in plu mundo
    plurimae J

301   Revera CYNLT _/_ Rebera PD Benera J
expetissunt CYNL _/_ expetissent J expetiscunt PDT

302   ac _/_ et CYNJT
extra L^c _/_ extram L
hanc unam _/_ unam hanc CYT hanc tuam N
Reginas _/_ Reginae CYT
ha ha he _/_ ha ha hae D ha ha ha LJ

303   _/_ line om. YN

304   _/_ line om. PYN
deligas _/_ diligas D

305-7   _/_ lines om. YN

305   coenam _/_ prandium L
mavolim _/_ mavolem J mavelim CLT

307   aut _/_ et J
ha ha he _/_ ha ha hae D ha ha ha LJ

308   Ita CYNJT _/_ Ha PD Ah L
villiaco CYT _/_ villaco PDNLJ
pocas pallabras _/_ hocas palla bras Y

309   _/_ line om. L
te D^b _/_ om. D
id _/_ om. N

310   Remittas quaeso _/_ Remittas obsecro NJ <u>Tib</u>. Quaeso ergo ut
remittas L Remittas CYT
munus aliquod _/_ aliquod munus CYT pignus aliquod L
marito _/_ merito D

311   hodie composui CYNLJT _/_ composui D composui hodie PD^b

312   e mui J _/_ emui P emay L emni D omni N e mal CT et mal Y

313   eius pater _/_ pater eius CYT

314   Operi, operi _/_ operire operire L o heri, heri Y

315   gratias _/_ tibi gratias CYT

316   Quorsum vero _/_ verum quorsum CYT
circumfert _/_ circumfers L

317   ab aliquo e principibus Y] ex principibus ab aliquo N
        ab aliquo ex principibus PDL^C no—

ab aliquo e principibus Y] ex principibus ab aliquo N
ab aliquo ex principibus PDL^{C}J ex ab aliquo
ex principibus L ab aliquo e Principibus C
ab aliquo e princibus T

318   Non C^c] Don C

319   Archidux] Archideux C Archi Deux T
    Mediolanensis] Medialanensis J Mediolavensis T
    novit me, novit me] novit me CYT
    haec] hec N om. Y
    varia J^b] varria J

320   epitaphium est] est epitaphium CYT
    Imperatoris C^b] imperatoris YLJT om. C
    Caroli] Charoli T

322   humillimus] humilimus C
    Oh] ah Y
    Vicerege J] vicerege DLT Vice Rege P vice Rege C
        vice rege YN
    Neapolitano] Neopolitano CL

323   Hoc CYLT] Hah PD ha J hu N
    Oh] O CY ah L
    Madonna] madonaa L
    Iomora CD] Iomoro T Iamora P Jimoro L Samorra Y
        o mora N io morae J
    ah] oh. N

324   Bide, bide, bide] Bides bide bide L Vide, vide, vide CYT
    reperi] repperi T
    ad] a N

325   e] a Y
    calamo T^c] clamo T
    emanarunt] emanaverunt L

326   versiculi] versiculos L
    quisquam] quispiam C
    meliores dabit versus CYT] versus meliores dabit PDNJ
        tibi meliores dabit L
    age] om. Y
    me amet] meamet CT memet Y

327   Verum] om. N

329   hic importune] importune hic L hic oportune D
            hic opportune YJ
        solicitat] sollicitat CDYLJT

330   ] line om. L
        Necesse CDYNJT] Nec esse P
        incoepto CYJ] in coepto T incepto PDN
        dimoveam] dimoveas Y

331   pas qua] pasquae L pas quae CT pas que Y
        del dios] Des Dios C des dios Y des Dios T
        a quell CT] a quel Y a el PDL a ell J ell N
        villiaco CYT] villaco PDNJ^c vilaco L vellaco J

332   evulgavit] emulgavit CYT divulgavit N

333   ] line om. L

334   ] line om. N
        Utinam] <u>Tib.</u> Utinam L
        illo] eo CYT

335   ante coenam] multo mane L
        hinc aufugisset] fugisset CYT

336   Por il cuerpo santo D] por ill cuerposanto J
            per il cuerpo santo L Pol il cuerpo santo P
            por ill merpo santo N Per il santo CT Periit, sentio Y
        de la] te la Y
        Letania CYNT] letamia J latinia L ketania PD
        illum rursus offendero] rursus offendero, illum N

337   iste] ille CYNT

339   non] annon CYT
      *Don? Sane.L] <u>Don.</u> Sane CDYT Sane PNJ
        egregius] <u>Tib.</u> Egregius CYT
        es L] est L
        per deos] por dios D per dios N

684

340   Obsecro] Tib. Obsecro D
fili mi] mi fili CYT
libido] lubido L

341   Fa la la la] fa fa la la la L
elegantes T[b]] eleganter L egantes T

342   risus argumentum] argumentum risus N
O] a N
ridicule C[b]] dulcissime C
ha ha he] ha la la L

343   aestimant] existimant J

344   ego CNLJ[T]] om. PDY
in uxorem huius me] in uxorem me huius C
    me in uxorem huius Y

345   insanivit] insanibit L
protinam] protinus N
Grille. Gril. L] Gril. PDCYNJT

346   mi CYT] mihi PDNLJ
hodie] om. N
precibus PD] prece CYNLJT

347   herum me] me herum CYT

348   te] om. L
vamos, vamos] vamos L eamus, eamus Y
oh si] poh si CNT doh si L si Y
Horatius nunc obviam] nunc Horatius obviam Y Horatius N

Actus 2. Scena 5

Horatius] Horatio D
Lucretia CT] Lucretius PDYNJ Lucr: L

350   abscessitne] abscessit ne CD

351   lenior] levior CYLT

354   semper tecum] tecum semper CYT
adest J[c]] abest adest J

355   iam nunc] nunc iam N

357   ] line om. N

358   est meum] meum est CYLT

359   et CDYNLJT] om. P

361   ut] et L
contempler] contemplor CL   contemplar J
intus] dictus L

362   transenna] transcenna Y
et] at L

363   evenit mihi] mihi evenit N

364   cluet CYT] probet PDNJ pudet L

365   et] ex N
suis D^b] om. D
veniret CDYNLJT] transiret P

366   non] cum L

367   aliquanto] aliquando L^b

368   meam] meum D

370   partui] patrui C

371   deliciae] delitiae DNT diliciae Y

374   vestros sermones] sermones vestros NL

375   istud] illud CYT isthuc N istuc LJ

376   istud CDYT] istuc PLJ isthuc N
Lucreti] om. N
Verum in amore est hoc vitium:] underlined in T

377   Credit tantum quod videt] underlined in T; in
        larger letters in J
credit] credet Y
videt CYNT] vidit PDLJ
mi si me LJ] mi si PD si me CYNT
istud] istuc LJ
effexis] efficis J efficias CYT

378 Luc. Nempe _/_ nempe N
   istoc _/_ isthoc DN
   ego nomine _/_ nomine ego N
   quicquam _/_ quidquam L

379 Impetrasti _/_ Luc. Impetrasti N
   geramus _/_ agamus CYT

380 te Lepida CYNLJT _/_ Lepida te PD
   conspiciat _/_ aspiciat L

381 istoc _/_ isthoc L isthuc N istuc J
   Luc. J^c _/_ Lep. Luc. J

382 hac CLJT _/_ hic PD hoc Y huc N
   luscinia DYNT _/_ Luscinia PCJ Lusania L
   et _/_ est et Y

383 solatur _/_ salatur Y
   Lucreti CYNLJT _/_ om. PD
   occasio CDYNLJT _/_ ocasio P

385 Iupiter Iupiter _/_ Iupiter Iuppiter J

386 me mala Y^b _/_ mala Y me in mala L

Actus 2. Scena 6.

Lepidus _/_ Lepida PCDYNJ Lep. LT
Lucretia _/_ Lucretius PDYN Luc. CLJT
Horatius _/_ Horatio D

387 tamen Y^b _/_ tamem Y
   mea _/_ om. N

388 Quid _/_ Quod CYNT
   suasu iam meo _/_ iam suasu nunc meo Y

389 praeriperet _/_ praeciperet C
   istuc L^b _/_ istoc L isthuc N
   alloquar _/_ alloquor C
   hunc CDYNLJT _/_ hanc P
   ergo CDYT _/_ ego PD^{c}NLJ

390   re alia CDYNLJT *]* alia re P
        sic D^b *]* hic CDYT
        ut *]* et C   et ut Y

391   perplexabili *]* et perplexabili N
        alte et clare *]* clare, et alte CYT

392   Lydia *]* ut Lydia Y

394   promoveam *]* praemoveam D

395   Quid *]* Qui CT   Quia Y
        si *]* sic Y
        mea istaec C^e *]* istaec mea C   me isthaec D
             mea isthac N   mea istac L
        opera *]* operera L

396   Et *]* om. N
        nollem *]* nolle L

397   supprimam N^c *]* supprimam supprimam N   supremam   L
        vero *]* ut L
        dictum *]* dictum esse CYLT

398   exaudiat T^b *]* audiat T

399   Lep. O si CDYLJT *]* O si PN
        Lydia *]* Lepida N
        proviseret *]* praeviserat N
        Lysetta, Lysetta *]* Lysette, Lysetta L

400   Lys. Quid J^b *]* Lyd. Quid J

401   Lep. Curre C^{b}DYNLJT *]* curre C   Lyd. Curre P

402   esse dicito *]* dicito esse J   esse N

405   *illum *]* illam PCDYNLJT
        Lucreti CYNJT *]* Signior Lucreti PD   Sigor lucretio L
        vales *]* valeas Y

406   Madonna Lepida *]* Madoma Lepida L   Lepida J   om. N
        istuc *]* istoc Y   isthuc N
        quam *]* quae D
        et L^b *]* ut CYLT

407 Bellissimam _/_ Bellissima D
   optime _/_ optume T
   sim _/_ sum N

409-10 Lucretia's speech is distinguished by italics in P and by
   larger letters in NJT _/_ In C only Qui te omni
   observantia/ Amat et colit intime is distinguished. No
   distinction is made in DYL.

409 Luc. _/_ om. J
   te _/_ om. N

410-12 Hor. De me nunc sermo est, / Dixit servus quidam tuus, qui
   te omni observantia/Amat et colit intime. _/_ om. Y

411 quidam _/_ quidem T

412 At _/_ om. CYNJT
   est _/_ fuit N

413 Oratio is distinguished by italics in P and by larger letters
   in CDNJT _/_ There is no distinction in YL.

414 Ibi nomen _/_ nomen ibi Y
   memoravit _/_ commemoravit N

415 Non CYNJT _/_ nonne PDL
   sum CYNLJT _/_ om. PD
   servus tuus is distinguished by italics in P and by larger
   letters in CDNJT _/_ There is no distinction in YL.

417 Servus? Imo dominus, Lucreti is distinguished by larger
   letters in CDNJT _/_ There is no distinction in PYL.
   Servus C^c _/_ Servus Servus C

418 Potius, et patronus meus is distinguished by larger letters
   in CDNLJT _/_ There is no distinction in PY.
   patronus D^c _/_ p___ (erased) patronus D

419   illud _/_ illa N
tulit _/_ tulit! dominum me et patronum / Illa
      appellavit suum: L
lepidum NT _/_ Lepidum PCYLJ Lepidam D
Lucretïum! _/_ Lucretium amicum summum! / Optimum,
      elegantem! vin'ad! L

420   es Y^c _/_ est Y
modesta nimis _/_ modesta CYT

421   existimes _/_ existumes L aestimas Y

422   mea _/_ me J
solitam ut facias gratiam is distinguished by
      italics in P and by larger letters in CDN^bLJ.
      The phrase is underlined in N. _/_ There is no
      distinction in YT.
facias gratiam CYT _/_ gratiam facias PDNLJ

423   audi _/_ aidi L age N

424   illud _/_ illa Y
gratiae _/_ gratia Y
sit gratiae _/_ The phrase is distinguished by larger
      letters in L.

425   exhibendam _/_ exhibendum J
fac _/_ om. CYNLJT
Hac nocte is distinguished by italics in P and by
      larger letters in CD^bNJT _/_ There is no
      distinction in DYL

426   Mihi ut accomodes tua _/_ The phrase is distinguished by
      larger letters in N.
mihi _/_ om. CYT

428   The line is distinguished by italics in P and by
      larger letters in CDNJT _/_ There is no distinction
      in YL

429   The line is distinguished by italics in P and by
      larger letters in DNJT _/_ libentissime only is
      distinguished in L. There is no distinction in CY.
quousque _/_ quoque L^c quoque nocte L
lubentissime   _/_ libentissime CDLJT

430   mihi noctem _/_ noctem mihi L

432-3   nam lubentius / Hoc faciam, quam tu expetis ut
           fiat is distinguished by italics in P and by
           larger letters in NLJT _/_ nam and quam only
           distinguished in D. There is no distinction in CY.

432   nam _/_ nunc Y

433   hoc _/_ istoc Y
           quam D^b _/_ quod D
           expetis CYLJT _/_ expectes PD expectas N
           certe _/_ recte J

434   et   _/_ ex CYT
           puellis D^b _/_ om. D

435   choragium _/_ coragium (underlined) D

437   tam _/_ tum YN
           ibi _/_ sibi J

438   quam NLJ _/_ qua PD om. CYT
           lepide CNLJT _/_ Lepidae PDY

439   esse CDYNLJT _/_ om. P
           O _/_ oh C

440   ut D^b _/_ iam ᴗ
           quo _/_ ut Y
           Lep. Petas L^a _/_ Luc. Petas L

441   Iocaris nunc quidem _/_ om. CY
           Verum L^c _/_ Luc. Verum CL
           Verum aliam si concederes is distinguished by larger
              letters in CNJT _/_ There is no distinction in PDYL.
           concederes / concesseris Y

443   Impetrasti is distinguished by italics in P and by
           larger letters in Y. It is underlined in D^c _/_
           There is no distinction in CDNLJT.

444   fuerit _/_ fuit Y

446   per fenestram is distinguished by italics in P and by
           larger letters in DNL _/_ fenestram only is
           distinguished by CJT. There is no distinction in

447   pertica CNLJT _/_ portica PD   per tricas Y
            porrectas CYLJT _/_ porrectus N   porrecta PD

448   appensas _/_ appensus N
            est _/_ om. DN

448-9   e fenestra hac quae absque transenna est/Supra
                 portam conspicere potest plane is distinguished
                 by italics in P and by larger letters in CDLJT _/_
                 In N plane only, is not distinguished. There is
                 no distinction in Y.

450   Audi _/_ Audii L
            compareret D^b _/_ comparet D.

451   possit _/_ potest Y

452   Fiet, fiet; libenter fiet is distinguished by italics
            in P and by larger letters in DJ _/_ There is no
            distinction in CYNLT
            libenter _/_ lubenter L

453   unica _/_ amica Y
            om. _/_ Cum me propter quid petitur, quam statim,
                                     quam alacriter,
               Quam libere et libenter spondet! et tu Lucreti,
               Quanta cum venustate, quam decenter te
                                 intulisti? L

454   Ubinam _/_ Ubi CYNLJT
            nunc _/_ tu nunc N

454-5   eius habes tam sinceram CLJT _/_ eius habes tam
                 synceram Y   habes tam sinceram eius PD   habes
                 huius tam sinceram N

456   <u>Lys</u>. Ecce T^c _/_ <u>Lys</u>. et <u>Lyd</u>. ecce T

457   Lepida C^c _/_ Lysetta Lepida C
            convoca D^b _/_ con ___ (illeg.) D

458   est situm _/_ situm est CYT   est situs N

459   Lucreti in te _/_ in te Lucreti L
            situm est _/_ est situm L
            et tibi _/_ tibi CY

459-60   Et tibi/Et amicae tuae facere gratissimum is not
distinguished in CDYNJT $\int$ The words are
distinguished by italics in P. tibi, only,
is distinguished by larger letters in L.

462   te percepi J^oT^b $\int$ te percoepi L percepi JT
<u>Lep</u>. In $\int$ in N

463   Et tibi et amicae tuae facere gratissimum is
distinguished by italics in P and by larger
letters in CDNLJT $\int$ There is no distinction in Y.

465   quaenam CDNLJT $\int$ quae nam PY

466   *quaecunque $\int$ quicunque CYNJT
*amet $\int$ amat CYNLJT
Verum nomen is distinguished by larger letters in
CNLJT $\int$ There is no distinction in PDY.

469   Quae hercle non aliter quam caste et honeste amat is
distinguished by italics in P and by larger
letters in CDNJT $\int$ Quae hercle, only, is not
distinguished in L. There is no distinction in Y.

470   improbulae $\int$ improbatae Y
illae $\int$ istae NJ
Lesbia $\int$ Lesbii N

471   Aut $\int$ et Y^b om. Y. Distinguished by larger letters
in LJ
Horatii Lydia is distinguished by italics in P and by
larger letters in CLJT. The words are underlined
in D^c $\int$ There is no distinction in DYN.
Horatii CYNJT $\int$ Horatii tui PDL
Lydia $\int$ Lydra L
O $\int$ Oh C
fide et caste et sancte CYT $\int$ fide et sancte PDNLJ

472   Te lydia, ibi $\int$ Te Lydiam CYNJT Se tibi L
nominavit $\int$ nominabit L nominabat N
insuper $\int$ et insuper L

473   nisi caste $\int$ incaste N

474   Promeruisti tu hercle is not distinguished in CYNLJT $\int$
The phrase is distinguished by italics in P and
by larger letters in D.
tu $\int$ om. N

475   Nihil huic ut abnegem, quam pari affectu intime ac
        vere amo is distinguished by italics in P and
        by larger letters in CDNLJT.⦌ There is no
        distinction in Y.
    ut ⦌ om. CYT
    quam ⦌ quem Y
    ac ⦌ et N

476   om. ⦌ num posse illum/Si velit, tibi quicquam ut
        abneget, quam pari affectu/Intime ac vere amat. L

478   non Y^b ⦌ om. Y

480   efficacius ⦌ efficatius DL

481   Lepida ⦌ Lepidae C

482   hac nocte is not distinguished in CYNLJT ⦌ The
        phrase is distinguished by italics in P and
        by larger letters in D

483   quo CDNLJT ⦌ quod Y quae P
    indutae ⦌indutus N

484   tam ⦌ tamen N
    submisse ⦌ summisse J

485   Proin' ⦌ Proine Y
    sic ⦌ om. Y
    mihi tu tuas ⦌ tu mihi tuas Y mihi tuas CT

486   Hunc ⦌Iam Y
    ut ⦌ om. Y
    accomodes ⦌ accommodes CDLJT

487   'St ⦌ S't DJ St CNLT om. Y
    <u>Lys</u>. Promisit ⦌ <u>Lyd</u>. Promisit Y

488   rogandus ⦌orandus N

489   ut ⦌ om. N
    huic ⦌ huius Y

490   tute ipse ⦌ The words are distinguished by larger
        letters in CLT.
    has ⦌ The word is distinguished by larger letters in CT

clanculum per tenebras is distinguished by
italics in P and by larger letters in CDNLJT/ There is
no distinction in Y.
adferres mihi / The words are distinguished by larger letters
in CT.
* adferres T^b / afferres Y aferres T adferes L adferas J

492   Per posticum? Fiet, fiet is distinguished by italics in P /
There is no distinction in CDYNLJT.

494-5   Fac igitur ad decimam ut venias--/ Et te videam is
distinguished by italics in P and by larger letters in CT /
videam, only, is distinguished in D. fac and et te are
not distinguished in L. te is not distinguished in J. There
is no distinction in YN.

494   ad decimam ut / ut ad decimam CYT

495   Et te videam / Et te rideam L om. N
          Lys. Fac inquit ad decimam ut venias / om. N

496   Veniam CDYNLJT / The word is distinguished by italics in P.

497   Lyd. Iam CYNT/ Lys. Iam PDLJ

498   O me CYNJT / Lyd. O me PDL
          Lepidam / lepidam T Lepidum D

500   Nec munera, nec pater / om. N
          nec tu CYNLJT / ne tu PD
          tu ipsa / tuipsa YL

501   mea / om. CYT
          fere / om. CYT
          prospere CNLJT / Propere PD per se Y
          confecit mihi / fecit CYT

Actus 2. Scena 7.

Horatius ⟧ Horatio D
Lucretia ⟧ Lucretius YNJ

502   Hor. Nequeo ⟧ Luc. Signior Horatio. Hor. Nequeo N
             Luc. Sig^{or} Horatio. hor. Nequeo J
         mox ⟧ om. N

503   vitae CYNLJT ⟧ vita PD
         meae CDYNJT ⟧ mea P
         fidei CYNLJT ⟧ fidii D fidae F

504   ut ⟧ om. CYT

505   Oh mi ⟧ O mi J om. N

506   Hor. Quid Y^b ⟧ Quid Y

507   quadamtenus ⟧ quadantenus DYNLJ quadam tenue CT
         saltem CYNLJT ⟧ om. PD

508   O ⟧ Oh T om. N

509   has N^b ⟧ manus N
         sustentatrices ⟧ sustentrices LJ

510   ni D^c ⟧ nisi CDYNLJT
         et ⟧ ut Y^b om. Y

511   aedipol ⟧ aedepol L
         quod ⟧ quam quod CYT

512   Quam ⟧ Quod CYT
         meo tu ⟧ tu in meo CT tu meo Y

513   *Anne ⟧ An YL

514   clusam D^c ⟧ clausam CDYNT
         latere ⟧ laturum N

515   nihili L^c ⟧ nihilo L
         si C^b T^b ⟧ cum C om. T

516   Quali ⟧ Qualis CYT
         illum ⟧ ipsum N
         seipsum ⟧ se ipsum DT seipum Y

517   istuc] isthuc N istud Y
mei] meum Y
cuipiam] cuiquam L

518   evenit] eveniat N
mali]-male L

520   non]· cum L

521   Male te C^c] Mali te C

522   mei] mihi NJ

524   Horati] om. NJ
tua] hac CY
percipio] percepi N percaepero L

525   tu ipse] tuipse N
vel illa N^b] vell illa N
accumbit] accumbet CYLJT occumbit N

526   Hor. O C^c] Hor. Hor. O C

527   Fasne CNLT] Fas ne PDYJ
sugere] sapere Y

528   *suaviolentem T^c] suaviolentam NT suaveolentem LJ
       suave olentem Y
nocte te] te nocte N

529-34   C^c] confusion in order of lines:line 532 is found
       before line 529 and in its proper position in
       CN. lines 532-3 are found before line 529
       only, in Y.

529   Illasque D^b] Illasne Y Illas ne D Illas N

530   O] om. CYT
mea animula] animula mea Y

531   turturilla D^c] turturulla D turtucilla Y
te] om. N
amplectar CYNLJT] amplecter PD

532   Iterumne ego lacertis immoriar tuis; ah] omitted in N
       from the version of the line found in the
       correct position.
Iterumne] Iterum L
ego lacertis] lacertis ego N
immoriar] emoriar Y
ah] o Y oh N

534   quod _7 quid N
sic D^b _7 om. CDYNT

535   aliquandiu _7 aliquamdiu T aliquando NL

536   rimatores _7 rivatores L ianitores Y

537   _7 line om. CYT
praepedimenta LJ _7 perpedimenta PD impedimenta N

538   secum igitur CYNLJT _7 igitur secum PD
saltem _7 om. Y

539   mea prece _7 prece mea N

540   certe _7 certo NLJ
iri CY^{b}NL _7 ire PDJT ___ (illeg.) Y
se _7 om. N

541   deterreri J^c _7 deterrere J

542   noctem _7 nocte L

543   offenderet _7 offenderit N
se dato _7 sedato NJ

544-5 transire / Inde tibi e fenestra se libere spectandam dare_7
       om. N

545   tibi _7 ibi L
se _7 si L
spectandam _7 spectandum L

546   O _7 Oh YT
hic _7 his L^{b}T

547   dedit D^b _7 dabit D

548   Quaeso _7 O quaeso Y
*abrepat _7 obrepat YL
opportunitas _7 haec opportunitas J haec oportunitas N

549   ipse _7 om. Y
ego _7 om. Y
faciam _7 fiam CYT

550 successerint _/_ successerunt Y succurrerint L

551 quaenam D^b _/_ quanta D
  mora _/_ om. CY blank space left in T

553 enim CDYNLJT _/_ en P

554 ego CYNLJT _/_ om. PD
  angustum _/_ an gustum Y
  hoc _/_ om. L

555 Namque _/_ Nam Y

558 Aut N^c _/_ at aut N

560 sibi _/_ tutibi L

Actus 2. Scena 8.

Lucretiae _/_ om. N
Lucretia Horatius CLJT _/_ Lucretia Horatio D Lucretius
  Horatius PY Horatius Lepida Lucretius N

562 hic _/_ om. Y
  fuat _/_ fiat C siet Y

563 Hor. C^c _/_ Hor. Hor. C
  Introivit _/_ Introibit L

564 adest CYNLJT _/_ est PD

565 vita mea J^c _/_ vita meam J

566 morigeram _/_ morigerum Y

568 tuae _/_ an tuae NJ
  faciam C^b _/_ fugam C

569 Immo _/_ Imo CDYLJT In N
  exuperant _/_ exsuperant DL

570 perpetuo ut _/_ ut perpetuo L

573 primum Y _/_ primus PCDNJT perimus L
  video _/_ hic video N
  atque _/_ et Y

574 hanc N^b _/_ om. N

575 hercle C^b _/_ om. C
ego _/_ om. CYT
cordi· D^b _/_ vidi D
esse charum _/_ charum esse NJ

576 non charum _/_ charum non Y
ergo D^c _/_ ego D

577 tu te C^c _/_ tute CT tete Y

578 quod _/_ quid N
prius _/_ verius Y

579 ut _/_ om. .Y

581 Fac _/_ Hoc Y
te _/_ om. L

583 huc C^c _/_ hic CYN
transeas _/_ transeam Y
pericli   _/_ periculi CYNLJT

587 ipsissima _/_ ipsissimo N

589 utriusque CYNJT _/_ utrisque PDL
atque CYT _/_ et PDNLJ
vota eadem _/_ eadem vota CT vita eadem N vota Y

590 gaudia T^c _/_ gaudio N gaudias T
mea _/_ meo N

591 meos CDYNLJT _/_ meas P

592 anima T^b _/_ (illeg.) T

593 ut _/_ om. N

594 ne quis _/_ nequis YNL

598 Luc. Dii _/_ dii N

599 venio venio Y^b _/_ pereo venio Y

600 ipso _/_ ipso ipso L

Actus 2. Scena 9.

602 obvenisset *J* evenisset Y

603 Hem *J* Eih N Ohe L Tib J
ubi *J* tibi Y
istuc *J* isthuc quaeso N
quomodo *J* quo modo DT

604 posticum *J* posticam J porticum N

605 viri *J* veri Y vir J
istoc *J* isthoc DN istuc YL

606 nonne *J* non Y
hac *J* haec L

607 **colloquuta** *J* **collocuta** CYNLJT

608 et iam modo **etiam** *J* etiam modo etiam N etiam
modo CYT
his ipsis *J* hos ipsos Y ipsis N
oculis *J* oculos Y

610 sim *J* sum CYN
mortalium *J* om. CYT

611 alius T[b] *J* aliud T
vidit CYNLT *J* videt PDJ

612 tuus *J* om. L
iam *J* om. Y

613 enarravit *J* enarrabit L
sua *J* tua Y
famelicus *J* familiaris L
eccos J[c] *J* eccas NJ
opportune *J* oportune DN apporte L

Actus 2. Scena 10.

Actus 2 L^c _7 Actus 3 L
Piedro _7 piedro L
Horatius _7 Horatio N

614   illi _7 illius NJ
lachrymae D^c _7 lacrymae LT lachrimae NJ lachymae D
obortae sunt YJT _7 sunt obortae PD abortae sunt CLJ
paene _7 pene CNT om. YL
valedixeram CDYNLJT _7 vale dixeram P

615   mi _7 mea Y moi NJ
hermosa CYNT _7 hersnosa J formosa PD om. (space left) L

616   Por _7 Per CYNT
dios _7 deos Y
gallantamente CNLT _7 gallanta mente J galata mente Y
     gallantemente PD

618   iam pugnare _7 pugnare iam N
Vis? Si me L _7 ubi nunc es Lucreti? L

619   fortassis L^b _7 fortasse YNL
hanc _7 om. N
gratiam _7 gratia L

620   interimi _7 interime L
Grille _7 Grylle T
vamos _7 ramos L eamus Y

621   Crisp. Heus _7 Gri. Heus Y
screator _7 senator CY
famelice CYNLJT _7 familice PD

622   Quam _7 Quem L

623   hunc tu CYNLJT _7 tu hunc PD
Grille _7 Gril. J
Vamos, vamos CNJT _7 vamos, vamos L vamos PD
     eamus, eamus Y

624   tecum _7 om. Y
experiri _7 experire D

625   <u>Gril</u>. Mitte N^b _7 mitte N

626   Quid _7 Quin N
Vamos, inquam, vamos _7 eamus, inquam, eamus Y

628   abiures _7 abvires L

629   Lepidam _7 Lepudam L^b

630   intimi _7 integri Y
notas _7 notasque N
deditque _7 dedit YN

631   Ego vidi por mia vita DNLJ _7 Ego vidi por mea vita PCT
      Pol mea vita ego vidi Y
*apertissimamente _7 apertissima mente PDNJT
    apertissime mentem CY apertissime mente C^c
    opertissima mente L

632   <u>Hor</u>. At _7 <u>Hor</u>. Atque CT At J
ego _7 ego inquam N
moneo te _7 te moneo N
ac _7 et YN
siquidem _7 si quidem C siquid N
curae CYNLJT _7 cura PD
sit tibi _7 tibi sit L
vita _7 vitae NJ
salus _7 salutis N

633   aedibus abstineas _7 abstineas aedibus N aedibus ut abstineas J
devites _7 ut devites N

634   mavelis _7 ma velis L mavoles J
<u>Don</u>. Lepida _7 Lepida L
signior _7 Sg^{or} CT Sg^{or} Y Sig^{or} DJ <u>Don</u>. Sigor L
por vida LJ _7 por vido N porvida T provida P pro vida D
    poriuda C perinde Y

635   Del _7 Vel CYT
sois CYJT _7 ceis L dis PD vis N
*coragio D _7 coragis P choragio CYT corragiosa NJ
    corragiasa L
y'honrado _7 y'hon rado C y honorado J y honrada L
    honorado N quam hou cado Y

635-6   ego pariter/Ac fortunas tuas post_7 pariter/Ac fortunas
    tuas ego post N

636   fortunas et virtutes _7 virtutes et fortunas Y

637   fruere T^b _7 serva T
  est _7 es L
  viro _7 vero J

638   sibi _7 tibi Y
  verum _7 om. Y
  istud _7 illud Y isthuc N istuc LJT

639   videas CYNLJT _7 vides PD

640   hac nocte _7 om. N

643   Hor. Age _7 Age J
  Tu ad _7 om. N
  praestolare statim NJ _7 statim praestolare PD
    prestolare modo L praestolare CYT

644   horam decimam _7 decimam horam J

646   Pocas _7 Hocas Y
  pallabras _7 palabras J
  ego hic _7 hic ego N
  Adios _7 a dios Y

647   Gril. Adios _7 Gril. A dios Y Grille Adios N

Finis Actus Secundi Y^b _7 Actus Secundi Finis CJT Finis Actus
  Tertii Y om. PDL

Actus 3. Scena 1.

Horatius _/ Horatio J

1   Atque _/ At L
    undequaque est _/ undiquaque est C est undiquaque T
        undique est N
    conticinium L^c _/ contacinium L conticinnium T
        silentium N

2   omnia sunt plena _/ sunt plena omnia L

3   _/ line om. NJ
    Praeterea _/ Praeteriit L om. CYT
    dudum _/ om. L

4   _/ line om. NJ
    animo _/ animae Y
    here _/ horae CYT om. L
    ipsa _/ ipsae C ipsius Y

5-6   Fingis ex tuo desiderio horas, scio ego nondum adesse
        decimam. / Hor. Mittamus ista, ego _/ om. CYNJT

6   ad _/ Hor. Ad CYJT
    propius _/ proprius L
    meo more _/ meum amorem CYT

7   vide, ubi primum ad eam accesseris, attentis utare
        oculis. _/ om. Y
    accesseris _/ accedis L

8   Adduce _/ Adhuc Y
    ad _/ om. L
    si quis _/ siquis DNL
    subsit _/ subest Y

9   aut _/ autem N om. Y

10   indicium _/ iudicium NJ inditium L
    ducier Y _/ duci PCDNLJT
    eamque CYNLJT _/ eam PD
    brachiis _/ in brachiis NLJ

11   diutius me ludos fieri _/ me diutius ludos fieri L
        me ludos fieri diutius CYT

12   illecebra Y^c _/ Hor. Illecebra Y
    ista CYT _/ illa PDNLJ
    consilium _/ concilium D consiliud Y
    istuc _/ isthoc N illud CYT
    e _/ ex CYT

13   hoc est, stabile est hoc mihi CYLJT⟧ hoc est, stabile
        hoc est mihi N hoc, et stabile est mihi PD
      dubites⟧ debites Y^b pebites Y

14   etiam⟧ om. L
      iram D^c⟧ ___ iram (erased) D
      depaciscar⟧ depasciscar N^c depascitur N
      hoc⟧ hic Y
      mene⟧ mihi N

15   vir es C^{c}DYNLJT⟧ vires PC
      ego⟧ om. N
      interim hic⟧ hic interim L
      adeas CYNT⟧ ades PDLJ adis J^c

16   ille CYNLJT⟧ ex illis aedibus PD
      subducat⟧ subducet L
      hoc supicaris⟧ est hoc suspicionis CYT

17   Accedamus⟧ accedam Y
      ad⟧ ut ad Y
      propius⟧ proprius L

18   concede⟧ consede Y
      sis⟧ sit L
      ac⟧ et CYT

Actus 3. Scena 2.

Don Piedro⟧ Don CT
Grillus⟧ Grillo J Gryllus T
Horatius⟧ Horatio J
Crispinus⟧ Crispino J

19   serius⟧ servis CYT
      quam⟧ quod CYT

20   occiso Y^b⟧ occioo Y
      cuius⟧ ac eius L
      mihi praetereunti⟧ mihi praetereunti mihi Y
      complacuit⟧ om. N
      hoc erat CYLJT⟧ hic erat N om. PD

21   mansuesceres⟧ mansuesceris DNJ
      verum⟧ interimeris verum N

22   fere nunc CYT⟧ nunc fere PDNLJ
        Poh⟧ oh T O CY
        illiberal'mente JT⟧ illiberall'mente C illiberalment N
            illiberalimente PD illiberalle mente Y illiberalamete L

23   baxo⟧ bacso J bucso N om. CYT
        pensamento⟧ pensamente CT pensa-mente Y
        Pensamento⟧ Pensamente CYT
        tam diu⟧ tamdiu YL
        fuisses⟧ fuisti L

24   opinarer te habuisse CT⟧ opinarem te habuisse Y
            habuisses PDNLJ
        luculentum⟧ luculentam Y

25   Poh, poh⟧ Doh, poh DL
        o vil o ingentil L⟧ ovil o ingentil N ovil o engentil J
            vil o ingentil D vilo ingentil P o vil o gentil CT
            oh ville oh gentile Y

26   Poh⟧ om. Y
    *hercle est⟧ est hercle CYT
      atque⟧ aut L

27   Poh⟧ Proh Y
        servidumbre⟧ servi dumbre NJ servi domtre L servi drunke Y
        mihi famulari si cupias, meo frui comilitio⟧ mihi famulari si
            cupias, meoque frui comilitio LJ mihi si famulari cupias
              meoque frui comilitio N meo si cupias frui commilitio CYT
        comilitio⟧ commilitio CYLT

28   ferre⟧ sufferre CYT

29   non⟧ haud L
        famem ego⟧ ego famem Y
        iam⟧ om. L
        fero⟧ fere C ferrem Y
        nemine⟧ nemini J

30   benignus T^{b}⟧ begnus T
        villane⟧ villani J villain NL villiaco CYT
        esclavo⟧ esclano N esclamo L

31   *Hisios del⟧ Hisiosdel PD huio del J hunc del N huic det L
        hiscas a del CT his cas a del Y
        abaxati⟧ ah excute CYT
        ego⟧ ergo Y
        maiori⟧ maiore D^{b}
        fame te CYT⟧ te fame PDNJ fame L

32   se *⟧* te Y
         pascant *⟧* pascunt NL
         age D^c *⟧* atque age D

33   cibus, cibus, cibus. Y^b *⟧* cibus, c_bus, cibus (illeg.) Y
            cibos, cibos, cibos. L
         herus *⟧* servus N

34   servus. *⟧* herus N
         est CD^{c}YNLJT *⟧* om. PD

35   Assiste *⟧* Asiste L
         nunc contra CYT *⟧* contra PDNLJ

36   praxin *⟧* praxmi T
         opportunitas *⟧* oportunitas DN

37   Oh, oh, oh. CYLJT *⟧* Oh, oh. PDN

38   **coenula** *⟧* **coenacula CYT**
         hercle *⟧* **om. CYT**
         perinde NLJ *⟧* **proinde PD om. CYT**
         ac *⟧* ac si N   tanquam C^{c}Y   tranquam T   quasi tanquam C
     ⋆**fuero** *⟧* furo D fuerim C fuissem C^{b}T etiam Y

40   Dein' *⟧* Die Y
         istius dimidii dimidio CYT *⟧* dimidii istius dimidio PDLJ
            dimidio istius dimidii N
         sic CYT *⟧* om. PDNLJ
         hic *⟧* om. N

41   deminuatur *⟧* diminuatur CYNJT
         quotidie aliquid *⟧* aliquid quotidie CYT
         ah *⟧* oh L
         me nunc NJT *⟧* de me nunc C ex me nunc Y **me PDL**

42   oliva *⟧* obiba L
         te *⟧* om. PDNLJ
         saturabis *⟧* saturaberis NLJ^b **saturabaris J**

43   <u>Gril.</u> Uva *⟧* <u>Gril.</u> Una CT

43/4   Don. Unica uva passa inquam. /<u>Gril.</u> **Unica** uva passa? *⟧* om.
       Unica *⟧* om. **N**

45   D^b *⟧* line om. DL

45   credis etiam? /<u>Gril.</u> *⟧* credis. <u>Gril.</u> etiam N

46   D^b _/ line om. D
         <u>Gril</u>. Credere malo quam experiri _/ om. L
         experiri D^{b2} _/ experire D^{b1}

47   ista una _/ ista uva LJ uva ista unica T uva istac
         unica C una istac unica Y
      ut abscedat aliquid etiam CYT _/ ut abscedat etiam
         aliquid NLJ aliquid etiam ut abscedat PD

48   aetheria _/ aetherea CYNLJT

49   aura! aura! _/ aura CYT
      ha ha he _/ ha ha ha LJ

50   camelionte _/ camelione T cameleonte NL chameleonte YJ
      me _/ om. YL

51   hoc ego _/ ego hoc CT ego haec Y
      longo _/ om. L
      et assidua experientia CYNLJT _/ om. PD

52   iudicans _/ indicans DJ
      una _/ re CYT
      potissimum _/ praecipue CYT

53   feculentis _/ faeculentis CYNLJT
      hisce _/ hisse L

54   crede _/ credo C
      serve Y^c _/ serv (illeg.) Y
      sunt _/ om. L

55   Tum _/ Tu L
      sum _/ sim CT
      quicquam _/ quidem CYT^b qudem T

56   audi porro _/ porro audi CYT
      haec _/ mea Y

57   Sic edimus _/ Sice edimus N edimus sic L
      consilia CYNLJT _/ concilia PD
      bibimus praecepta _/ praecepta bibimus Y

58·   hic _/ om. CYT
      interpello _/ interpellem Y

59   O _7_ Oh YT om. N
minime minime D^b _7_ minime CDYLJT om. N
nondum _7_ non dum D nedum L
signum e fenestra est _7_ est signum e fenestra CYT

60   <u>Crisp</u>. Quid CYNT _7_ Quid PDLJ

61   condimentorum D^c _7_ condimentu D

62   admovent _7_ adiuvent N
appetitus CYNLJT _7_ appetitum PD
irritant _7_ irritunt N

63   proin _7_ prout Y
sinapi _7_ et sinapi CYT

64   esset C^c _7_ esset esset C
ego _7_ om. CYT

65   assolent CYLJT _7_ solent PDN

66   peccatum _7_ om. Y
quodvis _7_ quotidie CYT
admitterem _7_ admittem L admittere vellem C^cT
    vellem admittere CY
quo expiarem ieiunium _7_ om. CYT

67   peccata D^c _7_ ___ (erased) peccata D pecata L

68   <u>Don</u>. Praeterea L^b _7_ <u>Don</u>. Denique odores L
tibi compares CYNLJT _7_ compares D compara P

69   eam _7_ quam L
cogitas D^b _7_ cogites CDYN
excidet CDNLJT _7_ excidit PY

71   coenam _7_ coena CYT

72   odores Grille _7_ odores Grylle T odores. <u>Gri</u>. Y
valde _7_ Wailes Y om. L

73   Grille habeo C _7_ Grylle habeo T <u>Don</u>. Grille habeo Y
    habeo PDNLJ
ego CDNLJT _7_ om. PY
Indicum _7_ Iudicum N
vel _7_ om. NLJ
ita _7_ ite N

74   Ne _/_ Me Y
        istoc _/_ isthoc DN istuc C
        vicini _/_ propinqui CYT

75   continere _/_ contineri J
        comedam _/_ comederem N

76   Taedet _/_ Tedet L

77   Hem _/_ <u>Don.</u> Hem Y
        pecus _/_ pectus Y

78   <u>Don.</u> Esclavo _/_ o esclavo Y
        <u>vis</u> _/_ esse Y
        Horati _/_ Horatium Y

Actus 3. Scene 3.

*No scene division here in N.
Don Piedro _/_ Don. CYT pietro L
Grillus _/_ Gryllus T

81   Mediolanensem _/_ Mediolavensem T

82   minus _/_ minos D
        <u>Hor.</u> Tune NJT _/_ <u>Hor.</u> Tunc L <u>Hor.</u> Tun' C <u>Hor.</u> Tu PD
          <u>Cris.</u> Tune Y

83   edocueras _/_ edocuerat L
        hic _/_ sic L
        qui CYNLJT _/_ quia PD
        viveret _/_ iuveret C

84   Mitte istaec, mitte istaec _/_ Mitte isthaec, mitte isthaec DN
          Mitte istaec, mitte CYT

85   mi _/_ om. N
        aliquid _/_ om. CYNT
        quod _/_ quid N

86   Nostin' _/_ Nosti L

88   ades _/_ accedas CYT
        huc _/_ suc L
        propius D^c _/_ proprius DL
        dato CYT _/_ aliquo PDNLJ
        whew _/_ whuh CT Whu whu NJ whish Y fis fis L^b om. L

89   habitat D^c _/_ habet DLJ

90   at _/_ om. N
integerrimum DNJ _/_ integerimum L integerrimam PD^c integrum CYT

91   *Whew whew _/_ Whew PD Whu whuh C whu whu NJT whish whish Y
         fis fis L
nutricem _/_ nutricum L
secedite _/_ secede CYT The word is underlined in C.

Actus 3. Scena 4.

Scena 4 _/_ Scena 3 N
Nutrix _/_ Nutrix Luc. L
Lucretia _/_ Lucretius YNT
Don Piedro _/_ Don. CYLT
Grillus _/_ Gryllus T
Crispinus. Lucretia. Don Piedro. Grillus. _/_ Lucretia. Don. Grillus.
   Crispinus. L Lucretia. Crispinus. Don. Grillus. CYT

93   me tibi _/_ tibi me L

94   apud _/_ ad Y
diutule CYNJ _/_ diutile PDLT

95   Exores CDYNLJT _/_ Ex ores P
me hoc cupere CYLT _/_ hoc cupere me PD hoc me cupere NJ

98   etiam _/_ et iam Y

100   dii tibi CYNT _/_ tibi dii PD^{b}LJ tibi D

100/1   duint/ Foelicissimam. Hor. Immo Lepida, mea vita, ut nox
        haec mihi _/_ om. Y
duint D^c _/_ dent CT dant dii duint D

101   mihi D^b _/_ tibi D

102   penes te _/_ paenes te C
est _/_ om. CYT

103   animi J^c _/_ anima J

104   *pertinget _/_ pertingat LT
tui L^b _/_ om. L

105   commemoras _/_ mea moras N
splendens _/_ splendidus CYT

106   radiis _/_ -om. Y
hasce _/_ has L

107   dixisses _/_ dixisti L
flammeam _/_ flammeum N
facem _/_ faciem Y

108   indies _/_ et indies N
Quod si CDYNLJT _/_ Quodsi P

109   istius ignes pectoris CYJT _/_ ignes istius pectoris PDL
          istius pectoris ignes N

110   noctu _/_ nocte CYT
ille _/_ om. NJ
ut _/_ et L
luceret _/_ lucet N
Verum _/_ Luc. Verum L Vero N
anime mi _/_ animo meo Y

112   Luc. Ingredere _/_ Hor. Ingredere N

112-13 Hor. Don?/Don. _/_ Hor. Don. Don./Don. CY Hor. Don Don DL
        Don. N

113   Con il diablo NLJ _/_ Coll ill diablo PD Con. ill.
          diabolo T Ill Diobolo C Indiabola Y
doh _/_ poh CT proh Y

114   digna _/_ dignum C dignun Y[b] dignus Y
adierit _/_ adiecerit Y
est indigna _/_ indigna est N

115   illud _/_ om. N

Actus 3. Scena 5.

Scena 5 ⟧ Scena 6 L   Scena 4 N
Crispinus. Don Piedro. Grillus. ⟧ Don. Grillus. Crispinus. Y
    Lepidus. Don pietro. Grillus. Crispinus. L
Don Piedro ⟧ Don pietro L   Don. CYNT
Grillus ⟧ Gryllus T

116   tuis et auribus CYT ⟧ atque auribus tuis PD^bNJ tuis DL

117   me mei D^b ⟧ mei D mei mei N
        Mavortis ⟧ mavortis D

118   hoc ⟧ hic Y
        oneraverim CYNLJT ⟧ oneraveram PD

119   hercle si mihi ⟧ mihi hercle si Y hodie si mihi NJ
        offerret ⟧ offert Y offerat N

120   Quarum D^b ⟧ Quorum D
        vidi nullas ⟧ nullas vidi Y
        in N^c ⟧ vidin N

121   conscivit ⟧ concivit L
        illi ⟧ ille Y
        Is ⟧ si NJ te L
        intercessit ⟧ interesse L

122   Quod ⟧ Quid N
        illum ⟧ om. CYT
        adversari CYNLJT ⟧ aversari PD

Actus 3. Scena 6.

Scena 6 ⟧ Scena 5 N
Lepidus ⟧ Lepida CYNT
sub habitu Lucretiae part of a stage direction in DJ ⟧ om. CYNLT
Piedro ⟧ pietro L om. CYNT
Grillus Crispinus ⟧ Crispinus Grillus CY Crispinus Gryllus T

123   adest CYNLJT ⟧ est PD

124   O ⟧ Oh T

125   facinus audax ⟧ audax facinus Y
        solatio ⟧ solatium CYNLJT

126   Line is written in larger letters in J and underlined in T
pericula _] periculis Y
ex CYNLJT _] omnia, ex PD
iisdem Y^b _] eisdem YN

127   inferas _] inseras Y
Lepide _] Lepida YN
audacia nunc opus est et confidentia J^b _] Don. Quis est?
   quis est inquam J
plurima _] plura D^b

128   auspicato CYNLJT _] auspicabor P auspicabo D
nunc CYNLJT _] om. PD

129   est? quis _] est hic? quis CYT
est inquam _] inquam Y

131   sit iste CD^cLJT _] ille sit iste D sit ille PN sit ipse Y
maritus _] amator CYT

132   annos _] avos L

133   Aha _] ah ha Y ah ah C^c Lucret ah ah C

135   Ve con dios _] Ve condios CT Vae condios Y
passate _] pascate CYT
con dios C^c _] condios CY

136   Petre _] Petro L
Petre CYNJT _] Petro L Piedre PD
Piedro _] pietro L
Pacheco _] pacheco C Pachecho NY
D'Alcantara _] d'Alcantara Y del'Cantara CT
   Don Alcantara N

137   Piedro _] Pedro J pietro L
Pacheco _] pacheco CL Pachecho N
D'Alcantara _] d'Alcantara Y dalcantara T del Cantara C
   Don Alcantara N
iam _] om. CYT
hinc te _] te hinc CYT

138   faxim _] faciam CYT
Petre CYNLJT _] Piedre PD
Lepida ut CYNJT _] ut Lepida PDL

139   Iterumne _] Hemne C Henne Y Hemmne T
Petre CYNLJT _] Pietre PD

141   propterea⌐ praeterea Y
alius illam iam⌐ alius iam illam J iam alius eam CYT
    alius iam N
exclusus⌐ exclusus exhilarus D^b exhilarus D

142   Etiamne CDYNJT⌐ Etiam-ne L Et iamne P
ubi⌐ ubi? ubi Y
es⌐ est CT

143   tu ubi ut CYJT⌐ ut tu ubi PD ubi ut tu YN tu ut L
sis⌐ sit C

144   Si quid⌐ Siquid NL
in te viri est⌐ est in te viri CT est inte viri Y
in me viri est⌐ est in me viri CT

145   Grille⌐ Grylle T

146   Don. Hem⌐ hem Y

147   Gril. Nunquam⌐ Nunquam CYNT
mihi commovit⌐ commovit mihi CYT

148/9   The order of lines is reversed in Y except for
        Abiitne which retains its cofrect position.
   tantum CYNLJT⌐ tamen PD
   careas gloria decertandi mecum⌐ gloria decertandi
     mecum careas CYT

148   Abiitne CDYNJT⌐ Abiit ne PL
abii⌐ abeo Y

149   in te⌐ inte L

150   *Ast CY⌐ At PDNLJT
Oh, oh, oh-⌐ oh. oh. CYT

151   Hem D^c⌐ Item Hem D
sequere⌐ se quere T
vos N^c⌐ vos vos N

153   Vamos Grille, vamos⌐ Vamos Grylle vamos T Eamus
        Grille eamus Y

153-4   supplicium de illo / Cras sumam in luce commodius: vamos,
        vamos.⌐ om. YL

155   Gril. Vamos⌐ om. L
Vamos ... vamos⌐ Eamus ... eamus Y

156   <u>Lep</u>. Nunc ⨼ L<u>u</u>c. Nunc Y
       auspicatius C^b⨼ auspicatuu C

158   •annon⨼ nonne CYT

159   huc ⨼ hic L
       Lydiam CDYNLJT ⨼ Lepidam P

160   mihi etiam ⨼ etiam mihi CT   etiam Y

161   et ⨼ om. Y
       quod ⨼ quin L
       intromittar ⨼ intro mittar T

Actus 3. Scena 7.

Scena 7 ⨼ Scena 6 N
Lepidus ⨼ Lepida NY
sub habitu Lucretiae L ⨼ sub habitu Lucretii PCDNJ sub habitu
    Lucret. T om. Y

162   Lysetta? Lysetta cito cito N ⨼ Lysetta Lysetta cito CYT
         Lysetta? cito cito PDL cito Lysetta cito T
       Lydia? Lydia ⨼ Lydia Y

163   moram ⨼ moras L
       quid ⨼ o quid CT
       properas ⨼ perperas T

164   ubi ⨼ <u>Lep</u>. Ubi N

165   <u>Lep</u>. Eccum ⨼ <u>Lyd</u>. Eccum N
       tu ⨼ om. N
       numquid ⨼ <u>Lep</u>. Numquid N nunquid CY nunquam L

166   tam Y^b ⨼ sum Y
       ego ⨼ om. CYNLJT

168   comitas ⨼ unitas Y
       morum ⨼ mirum L

169   uni ⨼ vin' NL

170   te geris ⨼ tegeris L

172   mihi *J* om. N
             Gratiae CDYNJT *J* gratiae PL
             Veneres *J* veneres DYN

173   Cupidines *J* cupidines L
             hum, hum, hum. *J* hum hum. N   hem, hem, hem. CYT

175   ego id *J* id ego N
             te *J* a te N
             velim *J* vellem CT
             suavissima mea *J* mi suavissima L suavissima NJ
             e *J* ex CYT
             forma *J* formae CYT

176   Eque DNLJ *J* Eoque CYT Atque PD[b]
             iamdudum *J* dudum CYT

177   *J* line om. L
             idque *J* Id N Atque Y
             te *J* a te N[b] om. Y
             rigore *J* om. N
             simulato *J* simulavi CYT

178   Recondidi *J* Et recondidi CYT
             ut quam non *J* ut quam cum L ut cum non CT cum Y
             tuus esset CDLJT *J* esset tuus PYN
             certus CDYNLJT *J* rectius P

179   raro *J* vero J
             solidus est et stabilis CYT *J* solidus et stabilis est PDNL

180   expertus nunc vero *J* nunc vero expertus N
             amas *J* me amas CYT

181   ignem hunc *J* ignem hunc/Ignem hunc CYT
             erumpere *J* erumpe L corrumpere CYT
             sinam *J* non sinam CYT

182   mihi *J* meum N

183   numquid *J* nunquid YL
             non *J* num L
             vera *J* vere CYT

184   Huc usque *J* Hucuque DJT
             non *J* cum L
             pessume N *J* pessime PCDYLJT
             quam *J* quem N
             ne *J* quam me L me L[c]

regerat *7* regeret J ageret N
aliud CYT *7* om. PDNLJ
a hum *7* ha hum CYT

185   At *7* Ut N
amaverim CNLJT *7* amaveram PDY
iam diu CNLT *7* iamdiu YJ iamdudum PD

186   amoris *7* amaris L
mori me CNLJT *7* me mori PDY

187   ut T^a *7* om. T
redamares *7* red (space left) C credo - Y

188   inexpertam *7* inexpertem Y
virgunculam *7* virgiunculam NJ virginculam L

191   fuerim *7* fueram N
impetrabilis T^a *7* impetrabile T inpenetrabilis L
precor *7* praecor DL
cui *7* tui Y

192   unice *7* vince Y
hak hum *7* hauk ham N hachum J hah hem L ha hum CYT

193   Lucreti mi *7* mi Lucreti L
quando *7* quanto N
promiseris *7* promisseris D
aeque T^c *7* et T om. Y
amare velle te C^c *7* velle amare te C amare te velle L

194   quantum *7* quaestum L
coniugi *7* coniuge L

195   *ne DNLJ *7* me CYT te P
sponsam *7* sponsam, sponsam Y

196   nisi T^a *7* illeg. T
pro T^a *7* om. T
Lepido T^c *7* Lepida N Lepidum T
Sed NLJT *7* om. PCDYT^c
hak hum *7* hauk hum N hachum J hah hum LT ha hum CY

197   tibi C^c *7* tuum tibi C

198   mea Lydia T^c _/ mea Lydea T om. N
        ut _/ et CT

199   tutelae _/ tutela YL
        pudicitia _/ pudicitiae Y
        sint _/ sunt CYNJT

200   se quis T^c _/ se CY se si quis T
        ergo _/ igitur CYT
        Lucreti _/ Lucreti mi Y
        descendero _/ defendero L

201   Nempe vereor _/ Vereor nempe CYT
        non _/ om. N

203   _/ line om. L
        Vera _/ Vere CY Vero T
        ariolare DNJ _/ arriolare P Hariolare T hariolaris CY
        hum CYNJT _/ om. PD
        maior esse nulla perfidia potest _/ maior esse perfidia
           nulla potest J nulla maior potest esse perfidia CYT
        data fallat C^bNJT _/ data fallit CY datae fallor PD

204   decipiat _/ deripiat J decipit CYT
        fidei CYNLJT _/ fidii PD

206   obsignaveris _/ assignaveris Y designaberis L

208   Lydia C^cT^c _/ Lepida Lydia C Lepida T

209   sis _/ scis L
        ergo Y^c _/ eggo Y
        si quid _/ siquid N

210-11 Non poteris dignoscere, quia ubi modestius me habeam,
        id me scilicet/existimes _/ om. L

210   poteris CYT _/ potes id PDNJ
        dignoscere _/ cognoscere CYT
        quia _/ quin Y

211   iuraverim T^c _/ iurat_erim (illeg.) T
        aut _/ et Y
        hum hum _/ ha hum CYT hah hum L hachum J hauk ham N

212   credas _/ credes N
        illi _/ ei N
        Lydia T^c _/ Lydea T
        descendam _/ defendam L

213   fefellero _/_ fellero N
       perfidissimus _/_ perditissimus L

214   ad te iam _/_ iam ad te CYT

215   ne T^c _/_ non T

216   fac nunc _/_ nunc fac CYT
       praesenti et constanti _/_ constanti et praesenti N
          praesenti et constante L
       Lepide _/_ Lepida CYNLT

217   e manibus T^c _/_ om. T
       elabetur DNLJ _/_ elabitur P elabatur CY elebatur T
       tibi moriendum esse _/_ moriendum esset tibi N
       sentio CYNLJT _/_ censeo PD
       protinam _/_ protenam D

218   fidem tibi _/_ tibi fidem CYNT

222   me sic _/_ sic me CYT

223   Annon _/_ An non CT
       si quid _/_ siquid YLJT
       placeat _/_ placet Y
       et _/_ om. CYT
       non allubescat tibi $CNLJT^b$ _/_ tibi non allubescat PD
          non adubescat tibi Y non allubescit tibi Y

224   quomodo _/_ quo modo L
       ego sum _/_ ego non sum N

225   faceres _/_ facere C
       sentio CYNLJT _/_ censeo PD
       ames CYT _/_ amas PDNLJ
       perperam CDYNLJT _/_ properam P

226   Lysetta _/_ Lyd. Lysetta N
       quaeso _/_ quaeso ubi es L

227   impedita T^c _/_ impeta T

228   haec _/_ hoc N

230   sic T^c _/_ (illeg.) T
       ab _/_ om. Y
       hoc _/_ isthoc N istoc J
       paterere _/_ patereris N
       fieri C^b _/_ facere C

231 virum T^c _/ verum T

232 spectate CDYNLJT _/ spectatum P
    probum C^c _/ dignum probum C
    adfuisses _/ adfuisset L

Actus 3. Scena 8.

Scena 8 _/ Scena 7 N

233 Nequaquam N^b _/ Neququam N

235 pomerio _/ pomaerio CNLT pomario Y

236 respondit CNJT _/ respondet PDL respondebat Y

238 inquam _/ unquam N om. Y
    inquisitum CYT _/ inquesitum D inquaesitum PNJ
     in quaesi tum L
    intro _/ om. N

239 et sobrie cubitum ut _/ et sobrie ut J ut sobrie N

240 dein _/ donum N

241 ornet T^c _/ ornat T
    et _/ ut NJ
    Lepide _/ lepide D Lepidae T Lepida CYN
    istuc _/ istoc CYT isthoc N
    solatio _/ solatium Y

242 abieris CYNLJT _/ aberis PD
    praegnantem _/ pregnantem D te praegnantem CT

243 sunt hic _/ hic sunt N sunt hae Y

Actus 3. Scena 9.

Scena 9 _/ Scena 8 N
Crispinus N^c _/ Crispinus Crispinus N
Horatius. Crispinus. Tiberius. _/ Crispinus. Tiberius. Horatius.
                      CYNJT

244 Quid est? quid fit? _/ Quidem quid sit? Y Quid est L
    Lepidamne _/ Lepidam ne L

245 audio _] audeo L

246 Nondum _] Non dum D

247 Crisp. Ubi nunc est igitur? Hor. Mox aderit ad fenestram. _]
                      om. Y

  Crisp. Quid T^b _] Grill. Quid T
  moratur T^c _] moretur T
  Hor. Credo Y^b _] Tib. Credo Y

249 alloquatur CDYNLJT _] alloquitur P
  here L^c _] here aedibus L

250 dubitando _] dubitanda CYT
  monebam _] monebat L
  Hor. Qui Y^b _] Tib. Quid Y Hor. Quid L
  istuc _] isthuc NT

251 tu postquam _] postquam tu CNLJT
  ingressus _] ingressa N
  ex _] et CYT^c
  Lepidae _] lepida CY
  egreditur $CDNLJT^c$ _] aegreditur P aggreditur YT

252 Quid _] Quod N
  tuas _] tum Y
  cum Lydia _] cum Lidia D^b fuit Lidiae D ad Lydiam Y

253 facit _] fecit N
  et _] om. L
  Quid et? _] Quid est ? L

254 putas T^a _] pactus NJT pactus es N^b
  te _] om. CYNT
  Lepida D^b _] Lydia D
  Lydia CD^bYNLJ _] Ludia T Lepida PD
  aliquid _] aliquo Y
  modo _] om. L

255 qui _] quin T quae J
  sic _] om. Y
  comminisceris _] comminesceris L cominisceris J^c
     comminisceres J commisceris D
  Quam _] Quid L
  iniquum _] inquam L

256 sint _] sunt N ·
  alii _] id alii CY
  suadeant _] suadent NJ
  iis _] eis N iisdem Y.
  non _] ut L
  habeas C^b _] habes CY

257 quin _7 quia N
etiamdum _7 etiam dum CDNL^cJT etiam hic dum L
illum _7 illam NJ

Actus 3. Scena 10.

Scena 10 CLYLJT _7 Scena 9 PN
Lucretia _7 Lucretius CYN
sub habitu Lepidi J^c_7 sub habitu Lepidae PDYNJ Lucretius sub habitu
   Lepidae is a stage direction in CT om. L
Horatius _7 Horatio D om. CNI

258 Lepida CYNJT _7 om. PDL
descende obsecro ad ostium D^b_7 om. DL
obsecro _7 quaeso CYT
ad ostium _7 ad hoc ostium CYT^c
secede tu NJT _7 secede tum PD^b secede Lepida DL om. CYT^c

259 Vita et lux _7 Vita et salus C Vita lux et salus Y
te _7 me Y om. N

260 amaverim _7 ama, veram Y

261 Quid ni T^c _7 Quidni DL Quid T
meminerim _7 memorem N

262 sic _7 sic semper CYT
pectore _7 in pectore CY

263 in _7 om. N

264 me _7 om. N

265 Ignoscas CDYNLJT _7 Ignosce P
mihi _7 mi N
mea CYT _7 mihi PDNLJ ·

269 haec _7 haec mea CY haec meae T hoc N
ex _7 ex ex T

270 hoc est _7 est hoc L
contumeliae T^b _7 contuliae T
haberi _7 habere CYT^c ·

271 istaec _7 isthaec DN haec CYT

272   vox T^{c} _/ uxor T

273   tuam CYNLT _/ tuum PDJ
si quid _/ siquid T
amari _/ amare CLT amore Y
Ohime _/ Θhi me NJ

274   est haec CYNJT _/ haec est PDL
inhumana vis _/ inhumanitatis L

274-5   quae vox foeminae. <u>Crisp.</u> Tiberius est./<u>Tib.</u> Horati?
    Lepida? Crispine? Quis est? _/ om. J
vox T^{c} _/ uxor T
foeminae _/ foeminea N foeminia L

275   Quis _/ Quid CYT^{a} om. L
est _/ om. L
nemo est T^{a} _/ om. T
aufugere T^{c} _/ aufugugere T

276   Lepida _/ lepida D
est haec aliqua J _/ et haec aliqua L est aliqua haec N
   haec est aliqua CYT est haec PD
supposititia _/ suppositia L
non _/ num L

277   An _/ A Y
ha ha he CYNT _/ ha ha ha PDLJ
tamen si T^{c} _/ tamensi T

278   velit _/ vult Y

        Actus 3. Scena 11.

Scena 11 _/ Scena 10 PN
Lepidus _/ Lepida N

279   te _/ om. Y
perimus DNLJT _/ perimis PC primus Y
*desaltus CYJT _/ desultus PDNL
quin cito _/ cito N

280   bene _/ bone Y
Hem pallium, hem petasum NLJ _/ Hem pallium, hem
   petacium PD Hem hem petasum pallium CYT

282   te _/ tute N

283 habet C^c ⟧ amat habet C

284 Lys. Abi ⟧ Abi J
   te T^c ⟧ om. T
   auferas ⟧ inferas N
   Vale. ⟧ Lys. Vale J^b

285 Lep. Vale T^c ⟧ Lys. Vale T

286 in vita T^c ⟧ invita T
   admiscetur ⟧ adiiciatur Y

287 Hem DNLT ⟧ Lys. Hem PD^bJ Tib. Hem CY
   Lepide Lepide T^c ⟧ Lepida Lepida CYNJT

288 Tib. Deos ⟧ Deos CY

289 hic est ⟧ est hic CYN
   carnifex ⟧ carnufex L

289-90 carnifex/Lep. Iam C^c ⟧ carnifex? mutuatis Lucretii
    vestibus insinuavit se apud Lydiam./Lep. Iam C

290 haec ⟧ hoc N
   Hei ⟧ heigh CYT

291 sedato ⟧ sodato N
   te ⟧ tibi LJ om. N

293 elusa ⟧ clusa CT clausa Y
   Hei. Tib. O DNLJ ⟧ Heigh. Tib. O CYT Tib. Hei. O P

294 est T^b ⟧ om. T

294-5 mutuatis Lucretii vestibus insinuavit se apud Lydiam./
   Nempe hoc illud erat ⟧ om. L
   insinuavit ⟧ insinuabat Y

295 illud erat ⟧ erat illud Y
   iam T^c ⟧ eam T

296 Quid T^c ⟧ Quod T
   huic ⟧ hic Y

298 ut ⟧ om. N

299 lepidus DNJ ⟧ Lepidus P Lepidi CYT om. L
   senex ⟧ om. L
   placide ⟧ placide placide NLJ

301   <u>Tib</u>. Lucreti J^c _] <u>Tib</u>. Lyd Lucreti J

302   Lucretium T^c _] Lucretum T
me _] meum N

303   Nomen _] om. Y
Tiberius _] Lucreti CYNT

304   Tiberi! obsecro C^{b}J^b _] Obsecro C Teberi obsecro J
te _] om. Y
Tiberi visus _] visus N
mihi D^b _] om. D
hercle D^b _] om. DN
hanc vocem _] vocem hanc N

305   dic amabo, dic sodes _] dic sodes, dic amabo N
num non _] numnon N
Lepidam C^c _] Lydiam Lepidam C

306   dicis T^c _] dices T
hoc YNJ _] hac PCDLT
*noctis CYNJT _] nocte PDL

307   Id _] Pol NLJ

310   profecto profecto _] profecto Y

311   _] line om. N
Tu, tu CYLJT _] tu, PD
tu Lucreti T^c _] tu Lucrti T tu Lucretius L Lucreti tu J

312   es _] om. N
moror T^c _] morer T

314   Lydiam T^c _] Lydeam T
ut _] at L
visas _] vises NLJ
eiah D^b _] ei ah J eia L eih T oh N etiam D om. Y
age age _] age Y
revortemur CT _] revertemur PDNLJ
statim CYNLJT _] om. PD

315   est T^b _] iste T om. NJ
esse id CDNLJT _] id esse Y esse P

316   delicias _] delitias DT
modo ex illius _] ex illius modo N
egressus _] aegressus D ingressus L
sis _] es Y
aedibus _] aedibus eia NLJ aedificio CYT

318   vidit T^c _] videt T

319 non T^c ⟧ num T

320 Immo T^c ⟧ Ego T
sum ⟧ tum NJ
domi D^b ⟧ om. D

322 Censeo ⟧ Ego vero L

323 Age ⟧ Aeque Y
ergo ⟧ vero L

324 tecum ⟧ te cum C

325 Bono, bono ⟧ Bono YN

326 ego ⟧ ergo J
hunc ⟧ om. L

327 et ⟧ O Y
etiam iam DNLJ ⟧ itiam iam T etiam CY iam P

328 mihi nihil ⟧ nihil mihi N

329 eamus, eamus ⟧ eamus N

332 fortasse ⟧ forsan Y

333 ero tibi ⟧ tibi ero N
senex es ⟧ annos habes L
est CYNLJT ⟧ om. PD

334 placet CDYNLJT ⟧ placeat P
comitarer ⟧ commitarer T

336 istuc ⟧ isthuc NT
ita tu vis NJ ⟧ tu ita vis PCDYT tu vis L

337 Eamus, eamus, eamus ⟧ eamus eamus N

338 Eccere D^b ⟧ Ecce re N Ecce rem CT (illeg.) D
perdant ⟧ perdunt Y

340 Lep. Perii. Tib. O noctem bellam J^b ⟧ Lep. Perii perii,
plane perii, nunc vale Tiberi J

343   tu $\bigtriangledown$ tum NJ
haberes $\bigtriangledown$ habeas N
Cyathum CYNLJT^c $\bigtriangledown$ Ciathum PD Cythyacum T

345   est J^c $\bigtriangledown$ est Tiberi N erit est J

346   Quin $\bigtriangledown$ Quid Y
bibes $\bigtriangledown$ vides N

348   Nequicquam ne vis, i $\bigtriangledown$ om. Y
ne vis $\bigtriangledown$ novis D

350   <u>Lep</u>. Venio $\bigtriangledown$ <u>Luc</u>. Venio CT

Finis Actus Tertii $\bigtriangledown$ Actus Tertii Finis CJT om. DL

42   Lepidam] lepidam N
miseram] inferam L
non T^a] sic NJT
dignaris] digneris CYT^c dedignaris NLJ   dedigneris T

Actus 4.   Scena 2.

Piedro] om. CYNLT
Grillus] Gryllus J

43   aedipol CDN^{c}LJT] aedi pol P aedepol YN
istum] ista N

44   Quam] Quem J cum N

45   amplecti] complecti L

46   Petre] petre L
hercle T^a] certe Y om. T
lepidum DYNJT^a] Lepidum PCL om. T

47   mihi] mi NJ
vitam sustineam] sustineam vitam CYT

49   Por mis peccados, por mis peccados]
                Por mi peccador, por mis peccados CT
                Por mihi peccador, por mes peccados Y
                Por miss peccado Por mois peccadois N
                por vis peccados: por vis peccados L

50   ] line om. L
ipse etiam] ipssam Y
iamdudum] iam dudum J
hic T^c] hic hic T

51   hanc, age] hanc Y

52   Petre] petre L patrem Y

53   tu] te Y
hanc tibi in uxorem T^c] tibi hanc in uxorem L hanc in
      uxorem tibi N hanc tibi uxorem T

54   Petre] om. N
intolerabil CYNT] intollerabil D intollerabili P
      intolerabile L intollerabilis J

55   ] line om. L
    Y mortall] y mortal N y imortal T immortall C
                immortal' Y
    consuma] consumat CYT
    nolle] nolo NJ
    •tuam filiam] filiam tuam CYT

56   culinariam] culinarem CYNJT
    Grille] Grylle J

57   Petre] petre N

58   Ha ha he CYNT] ha ha ha PDLJ
    <u>Hor.</u> Atque D^c] <u>Hor.</u> <u>Hor.</u> Atque D atque L
    eccum T^b] om. NT
    percommode] percomode N procommode L

      Actus 4. Scena 3.

Lucretiae] Lucretius N om. Y
Tiberius] Tiberio D

61   id] is CT^c

62   Quin] Quin adesdum CYT

63   Aedipol] Aedepol YL
    est] om. N
    Horati, plurimum] plurimum Horati CY

64   est opus] opus est Y
    maxime] maximum CYT
    ocyus] ocius DN

65   perturbate haec C^{b}T^b] perturbata haec CT perturbat;
       haec Y haec perturbate PDNLJ
    invito T^c] invita NT
    aegre] agere L

66   me] te Y

67   interroga] interoga N

68   liquido N^c] liquide N
    modo] om. N
    Lepidam] lepidam T

69   gnatam] natum L
    Aecastor] Ecastor CYL
    honestam] honestum C

narras_7 narras et N[b]
et probam_7 om. N

71   Hor. Quin L[b] _7 Quin L

72   invicem T[a] _7 (illeg.) T

73   Annon CDNLJT / An non FY

74-5   ipsus, quorsum ego id nunc_7 ipsus quorsum id nunc N
        id ipsum, quorsum ego nunc CY id ipsum; Quorsum
        id ego nunc T[b] id ipsum; Quorsum id nunc T

76   Viden' T[a] _7 Videte T
        quomodo_7 quam CYT
        fassa_7 falsa CYNT
        ha ha he CYNT_7 ha ha ha PDLJ

77   Quin J[c] _7 Quid Quin J

78   Hor. Responde sis mihi_7 om. CYT

79   *In CYT lines 79 and 80 appear after line 82.
        dividit_7 dividet Y
        amplexus_7 amplexos L

80   Lepida_7 Lydia N
        Nu. Non tu id nosti?_7 om. CYT

82   Aut affirma_7 Et affirma CYT

83-4   _7 lines om. L

83   Nempe ita est_7 Ita est nempe CYT
        narrat J[c] _7 ait narrat J

84   O T[c] _7 om. CYT
        ego T[b] _7 om. T
        audio T[c] _7 audii T

85   Numquid_7 Nunquid YLJ
        facta CYT_7 om. PDNLJ

86   praedicat CYNJT_7 praedicant PDL

87/8   siccine senectutem solaris meam? sic me ante diem conficis?,
        Quid ego nunc faciam, Horati fili mi? O Lepida,
        Lepida! ⟧ om. Y

87   senectutem T^c ⟧ servitutem T
        ante J^c ⟧ ita ante J

88   mi ⟧ mihi CYLT
        deficiunt CDYNJT ⟧ dificiunt P   deficit L
        ah ⟧ oh CYT

89   Immo ⟧ om. Y
        bono ⟧ hercle L
        animo pater C^c ⟧ animo/animo pater C   pater animo Y
                                                     animo L
        huius ⟧ heus Y
        famam ⟧ om. N

89   resarciam CYNLJT^c ⟧ resartiam PDT

90   Quin etiam ⟧ Quinetiam C
        mea ⟧ om. N
        concubuit ⟧ occubuit N

91   me, morior ⟧ ne moriar Y

92   pater. Pater! pater! ⟧ pater pater pater mi N

93   mi ⟧ om. L
        animum CNJT ⟧ animam PDYL
        maerores N^c ⟧ mis maerores N om. L
        et miserias T^c ⟧ et miseriis T   om. L

94   prostibulum T^a ⟧ per posticum T

95   abeo. ⟧ abeo. Quin Lepida inquam. L

96   Tib. Nempe ⟧ nempe N
        mihi quam ⟧ quam mihi CYT   quam L
        Quin Lepida inquam ⟧ om. L   see l. 95

Actus 4. Scena 4.

Lepidus CL _/_ Lepida PC^bDY⁴JT
Tiberius CYNLJT _/_ Tiberio PD

97   nostin' _/_ nosti T
          hunc _/_ hanc J
          audi _/_ audin' CYT
          quae _/_ quod L

98   Vita _/_ O vita Y
          mea _/_ om. N
          expetivimus _/_ expetimus L expectavimus Y

99   libere _/_ libere Y

100   nunc iam _/_ iam nunc J nunc L huic Y

101   restat modo _/_ modo restat Y
          mel _/_ om. Y
          id T^c _/_ ita NJT
          audiat _/_ addiat L

102   Stultus _/_ Stultu L

103   fili mi _/_ mi fili CYT
          Fa la la; ha, ha, ha. _/_ fa la la la la la YJT
                fa la la la la C fa la la la N

105   istuc _/_ isthuc N

106-7   _/_ lines om. L

106   ac tua T^c _/_ atua T et tua CY
          ac seria _/_ et seria Y
          sic _/_ om. Y
          ludis T^c _/_ ludit T

108   Hor. Age _/_ Tib. Age C
          mea vita CYNLJT _/_ vita mea PD
          larvam _/_ lavam L
       *ne N _/_ nec PCDYLJT
          ac _/_ nec CYT

109   ex me T^c _7 om. T
    et CYDNLJT^c_7 esse P om. T
    te _7 om. Y

110   compressu _7 amplexu te compressam N
    haeres _7 heres D

112   gravida _7 gravidam N

113   Hor. Anima T^a _7 Anima CYT
    scio _7 Hor. Scio Y
    id negare _7 negare id CYT^c negare T
    postulaverim CLJT _7 postulaveris N postularem Y
       praestulaverim D praestolaverim P

114   A _7 Hor. A CT
    is _/ id L
    facile CYNLJT _7 facilis PD

115   tua fortassis _7 fortasse tua Y

116   tu concubitu usus es meo _7 usus es tu concubitu meo Y
        concubitu tu usus es meo N

118   Nonne his _7 hisce L

119   per T^b _7 om. T
    ceritus _7 certus CNLT caecus Y
    videns T^a _7 videris T
    vigilans _7 vigilansque Y
    somnias D^{c}T^a _7 somnias / somniabas ↵ somniavi T

120   quaeso _7 om. N

121   aedipol _7 aedepol L
    aliquanto _7 aliquando LT aliquid Y

122   hercle metuo _7 metuo hercle J

123   celes _7 caeles LJ

124   filium D^b _7 folium D
   *teipsam CT _7 teipsum PDNLJ te ipsum Y

125   agas _7 agis CYT

126   Numquid _7 Nunquid YLJ

128   Tib. Immo] Imo L
istuc] isthuc N istac CJ istoc Y
Horati D^b] (erased) D
age age Y^c] aeg age Y
tandem] om. CYT

130   sancte] fauste L

131   audi] audin' J
mas CYNLJT] mea PD
Lepida ^{Uc}] foemina Lepida C
haud quaquam] haudquaquam CYNJ nequaquam L

132   eam] eum J
autumas T^a] Hoc tua mas T
ut] om. N
praegnantes DNLJ] pregnantes P praegnantem CYT

133   et] om. CY
Horatium C^b] Lucretium C

134   Itane] Mane Y
huc T^c] huccine huc T
mi T^a] mihi N em T
hoc sis] sis hoc CYT
nunc] tum Y

135   Quin] om. N
ite intro ite intro] ite intro YN ite intro ite
                          intro ite intro L
nunc] nam Y om. N
uterum] verum L

136   mamillas] mammillas T
et] ac Y

137   Ite intro, ite intro] Iti intro Y
Lepida] Lepida N
duc] diu L
intro, ite] ite intro N

139   Lepide] Lepida N

140   Fiet] Fiat Y

141   honore nostro] nostro honore CYT
celare] caelare L

142   res est _7 est res Y res CN
       tota in _7 in tota N
       desponsetur _7 desponsatur CYT

143   uterum _7 verum L
       quaenam _7 quae N
       sunt _7 om. CYT

144   perfabricavit _7 fabricavit Y
       hoc _7 hic CY
       quomodo _7 quo modo J

145   forte _7 om. CYT
       illa CDYNLJT _7 et illa P
       supposuit _7 proposuit Y
       egreditur _7 aegreditur D   aggreditur T

147   etiam _7 om. N
       credis _7 credes Y
       nihil _7 nil Y
       mentitum _7 mentium L

149   aliquo NLJ _7 aliqua PCDYT
       Ah quam _7 aliquam L

150   Facito _7 Facito iam Y
       aut corrigas aut feras C^c _7 aut feras aut corrigas CY

Actus 4. Scena 5.

152   hoccine T^a _7 hoc T
       est _7 om. Y

153   sanum atque sobrium _7 sobrium atque sanum Y
       noctes N^c _7 die noctes N

154   pene T^a _7 porro NJT
       cum _7 om. N
       versatum _7 versari L

155   Aut _7 At CT om. Y
       sumne _7 sum ne L
       ego _7 om. Y
       ibi ubi _7 ubi ubi YL
       numquid _7 nunquid YLJ nunoquid N
       ego N^c _7 perii ego N
       hic T^a _7 tibi T

156   numquid ... numquid ... numquid _/ numquid ...
        numquid ... nunquid N numquid ... nunquid ...
        nunquid C nunquid ... nunquid ... nunquid YLJ

157   •Num _/ Numquid CNT Nunquid YJ
    aliquando virginem _/ virginem aliquando CYT
    scilicet _/ scil: C scit Y

158   vero _/ om. N
    immutato CYLJT _/ imutato N mutato PD
    sexu Y^c _/ sexei Y

159   O _/ Proh Y
    me Lucreti _/ me CYT
    pessundedit perfidia _/ perfidia pessundedit CYT^c
        perfidia pessundedit perfidia T

160   Hominemne _/ Hominem ne CDYNLT
    decuit $N^c T^a$ _/ decuit/decuit N (illeg.) T
    pro _/ per L

162   Ah _/ At Y
    revoca _/ reprime Y
    erat _/ erit L
    profecto _/ perfecto L
    illaec C^bNLJT _/ illa Y istaec P isthaec D om. C
    mollis _/ mollis et CYT
    delicatula T^a _/ delicata YT

163   eloquio _/ alloquio Y

164   certe _/ certae N
    multum _/ non multum CNT non Y

166   Neque quid _/ Nec quid YN
    neque quacum _/ nec quacum YL
    intelligo $D^c N^c$ _/ scio intelligo DN

167   gerit _/ gerit gerit CT

168   tu tu _/ tu CYNJT
    rem istam inultam non _/ non istam inultam me Y
    amittere DYNLJT _/ &amittere C omittere P

169   perdidit _/ prodidit L
    sentiet _/ sentit Y
    inimicus CDYNLJT _/ amicus P

170 Quinimo C] Quin imo Y Quin o PDNLJT^c Quin T
meus iste mihi nunc] mihi meus iste nunc Y meus
nunc iste N iste mihi nunc L

171 perfido] perfidum Y
cor T^b]·om. T

172 Crispine] crispine T
nunc] nunc iam Y
consilium tuum] tuum consilium Y

Actus 4. Scena 6.

174 impetum T^a] metum N ipsa ___ (illeg.) T
hunc] om. Y
neque] meque T

175 Quin etiam et Lepidam CT] Quinetiam et Lepidam Y
Quin et Lepidam etiam PDNLJ

177 perimus T^c] primus T
suffocasses] suffocasset L

178 Caelia] Celia N

179 Cui nec CNLJT] Cui neque PD Tui me Y
quicquid CYJT] quicquam N quid PDL
est reliquum] reliquum est CYT
miserrimum] miserimum C
specula] spicula Y

180 modo J^b] (illeg.) J

181 quaerit T^c] quaeret T
interimat] interimit C
ecquid C^c] quicquid C
esse] est Y
porro] om. L
quod D^b] cur CDLT^b quam T
cupiam] cuipiam N

182 illa CDYNLJT] illam P

183 millies] om. Y
mortem T^a] vita T

184   es CYNLJT] esse PD
        mea filia] me filla L
        fortuna et T^c] fortuna te et J te fortuna et T

185   Aut] et N
        aliquid nobis] nobis aliquid Y
        adferat] aderat Y

186/7   Nutrix?/Rescivit] rescivit nutrix N

187   nostrae] nostra T
        consilia] concilia Y

189   <u>Nu</u>. Quid] quid L
        <u>statuis</u>] statues CT om. N

190   <u>Luc</u>. Horatius T^c] Horatius LT
        <u>interminatur</u> T^c] interminantur T

191   Quin T^c] <u>Luc</u>. Quin T Quem Y Cum L
        ego, ubi ubi occurrerit CNJT] ego ubi occurrerit PD
           ego ubi accurrerit L ubi occurrit ego Y

192   Ibi] Ubi <u>Y</u>
        congressu] congressa C
        ferocior utrinque] ferocior utrimque N utrinque
                                   ferocior Y

193   hostilem] hostile Y
        morti occurram meae] mortem occurram mihi CYT

194   illa eius dextra] eius dextra, illa Y
        arcte] recte CYT
        amplexata est] est amplexata Y

195   configet C^c] continget et configet C configat Y
        mortuam ubi] ubi mortuam CT mortuum ibi NJ ubi
                                        mortuum Y

     *rescivit] rescibit DJ

196   Oh CYNJT] om. PDL

197   mortem] noctem N
        adeo optabilem] mihi optabilem CYT
        gratam] gratum C

198   invideas] invideat N

200   meam ⟋ meum Y
hanc ⟋ om. Y
omnem fraudem ⟍ fraudem omnem CYT

201   fortuna etiam ⟋ etiam fortuna CYT

202   absque ⟋ abs CYNT
hoc fuit CYNT ⟋ fuit hoc PDLJ

203   luam ⟋ luum T tuum CY
nolentem ⟋ nocentem CY (illeg.) T

204   addecet ⟋ decet YL
adire ⟋ om. L

205   cum CDYNLJT ⟋ dum P

206   malo inveniat ⟋ inveniat malo CY

207   hinc ⟋ hic Y
mala ⟋ malo L
sinas D^{b} ⟋ serius D

208   cupio T^{c} ⟋ cupeo D cupis T cupiam C
peream ⟋ moriar C morior peream Y pereo L
Horatio T^{c} ⟋ Horatius T

209   suadeas ⟋ ut suadeas CYT
se afflictet CDYNJT ⟋ seafflictet P seafflicte L
adeo C^{c} ⟋ misere adeo C

210   prorsus ⟋ prius L

212   et ⟋ ut C o YL

214   tuae N^{c} ⟋ tui N om. Y
altrices J^{c}T^{c} ⟋ attrices altrices J alterius altrices T
                                    nutrices Y

215   Enecas ⟋ Necas L
semel satius ⟋ semelsatius NL

217   Abeo ego ne T^{a} ⟋ Abeam nec NJT Abeo ego nec L
videam ⟋ video L

219   commendo me ⟋ comendo me N me commendo CYT commendo L

220   Hei oi ei ⟋ Hei oh hei CY hei hei hei N hei ei ei L

Actus 4. Scena 7.

Lucretia CYNLJT] Lucretius PD

221   lucescit CYNLT] lucessit PDJ
       iam] iam iam L
       eccum] om. Y
       aecastor] ecastor DYLJ eccastor T
       occidi] occide L

222   certe] om. L
       ei] is Y
       de sponsalibus] desponsalibus T

226   tun' CY] tune PDNLJT

227   rei] hoc rei Y

228   Aliud] Quid Y

229   est] om. Y
       sic te] te sic CT te Y
       afflictat] afflictatur Y

231   meae T^a] meae ut N (illeg.) T
       sient T^a] fierent T

232   mitte] mitte mitte N

233   Hui! an] om. Y

234   Luc. Hercle vero J^c] Luc. Hei mihi Hercle vero J
       vero] viro L

235-8 In J lines 237-8 are written out of place before
          lines 235-6 and again after them. The first
          set has been deleted.

235   Quippe] Quippiam N
       quae] om. CY
       eo] om. N
       intraveras] intra eras Y
       antehac] adhuc N

237   Quae haec CDYNJT] Quae hac L Quae est haec F
       redit D^b] redet D

238   o hominum] oh hominum CY atque N

239   mutationem] narrationem L

241   Lyd. ... Y^b] Lu. ... Y
            Hanccine] Hancine GL   Hanc ne Y
            fidem tuam] foedera tua Y

245   Plus quam CYLJT] Plusquam PDN

246   Quin] Qui CYNLJT
            es] est L

247   Si quidem] Siquidem CDNLJT
            delecteris] om. L
            in somniis] insomniis N
            erit T^a] est Y   exiit T
            iterum] item Y

248   aut nunquam] nunquam CYT
            pro te amans] amans pro te L   te amans Y
            me somnus nunc] nunc somnus me N   me somnus L

249   incumbunt] occumbunt Y

250   o anima] oh anima C
            ut quid] et quid CT   o quid Y
            etiam CYJT] om. PDNL
            e] ex Y

251   movet $CDNLJT^c$] movit PYT

254   foeminam amantem] amantem foeminam Y
            credulam] crudelem Y

255   simplicem] Nympham Y

256   dederat] dederit N

257   quæras] queras D
            tibi] om. CYN

258   est C^b] om. CY

259   finge] affinge L
            potes rationem T^c] potes cui excusatio nulla est
               reliqua rationem T

260   Perfide] Porperde L

262   falsiloquam] falsiloquum L falliloquam J

263   dolis] dolos YN

264   profecto] profecta YN

266   scires Y^b] scieres J scis Y

Actus 4. Scena 8.

Horatius. Lucretia. NLJ] Horatius. Lucretius. PCDT
      Lucretius. Horatius. Y

267   Hanccine] Hancine C
     perfidiam T^c] perfidam T
     velo] volo YNL

269   mihi] mi L
     vitam et mortem] mortem et vitam N

270   Hor. Atque] Crisp. Atque Y

271   Habes] Hor. Habes CYT
     imperes C^c] impares CT imopares L

272   Hor. Quid] Quid CYT
     admisi] commisi Y

273   sic] sit Y
     omnem] omnem adeo L

274   ut CDNLJT] at Y om. P

275   haec fides] om. N
     eloquere CY^bT] loquere PDNLJ (illeg.) Y
     Taces etiam] quid taces Y

276   intelligo] om. Y

277   Eccere] Ecce re CNT
     Istuc] isthuc N istud Y

278   vel] ut J
     suspicari CDLJT] suspicare Y suspicar N suspirari P
     odium N^b] (illeg.) N
     causa] om. N
     siet] fuit L

279   me amare] amare me L

280   quam] quem NJ quae L,

281   gnarum] ‾gratum T gratam CY
        mei] mihi CYT om. N

281-2   An tu hoc non intelligis, perfide?/Luc. Lepidam
                             marem! T^c] om. T

282   Lepidam] Lepidum CY
        quid audio T^c] om. YT quid audeo D
        at] et N
        et] est Y
        modestiam] modestam C

283   ense hoc] hoc ense CYT

286   Quodnam] Quod N

287   tu id] id tu Y

288   utrumque] utrunque Y

289   reperisse CDYNLJT] reperiisse P

290   eam nunc N] eam N^c

291   At] An Y
        vilem] vitam Y
        pauperculam] paupertatem Y

292   dixerim C^c] dixeram C
        est ementita D^b] ementita est CDLT commentita est Y
        ignoto ignota C^c] ignota ignota C ignota ignotus Y
        consuesceret] consuescerit DYT

293   hanc] om. N
        ac] et YNJ
        aequiparabilem] aequiperabilem N
        tibi] tibi esse L

294   Quaeque] Quae L
        ipsa] ipsum NLJ
        tu teipsum] tute ipsam Y
        eius fuit] fuit eius Y fuit CT

295   ut] unde L
        habeas odio] odio habeas L

296   istuc] isthuc N istaec Y

297   semetipsam_/ semet ipsam DJ seipsam NL
perdidit_/ prodidit L

298   illa est_/ est illa N
foemina_/ foeminae T

301   Et amplecteris, at fugis, et aspernaris cognitam; quam_/
                                                 om. L
amplecteris J^c_/ amplecteres J
at_/ et Y
larvatam, et sub alio_/ om. YL
larvatam T^b_/ om. T

302   _/ line om. Y
at_/ ut T
praesentem CDNLJT_/ presentem P

303   contumeliis_/ contumeliosis L
afficis._/ afficis: ohime! L

305   Aut_/ Et Y
praesente CDYLJT_/ presente PN

306   me_/ meipsa L

307   Atqui_/ Atque NL

308   <u>Luc.</u> Atque et_/ <u>Luc.</u> At CYN^{c}LJT <u>Hor. Luc.</u> At N
aderam_/ altera Y una aderam L

310-15 T^b_/ lines om. T

311   mulier_/ foemina NJ

313   fortassis_/ fortasse CY
te et me_/ me et te N

320   ingratitudinem_/ ingratutidem D

321   videre vult_/ vult videre YN
idipsum T^c_/ ipsum T
aspicit_/ videt CYT

322   agnoscere_/ cognoscere CY
ut CDYNLJT_/ om. P
misere_/ miserae CYLT

324   emittunt] emittit $C^b Y$
         Viden' YNLJ] Vidin' PCDT
         lachrymas] lacrymas L   lachrimas YN

325   aliud N^b] (illeg.) N
         lachrymae] lacrymae L   lachrimae N

326   caecus] ocyus L
         ac] et N
         at T^c] et T
         brevi manibus] manibus brevi N

327   interfeceris] interficeris Y
         ostendet] ostendit NJ
         .denique] om. Y
         forte] forsan N
         exosculabere D^b] osculabere CDYT

328   amplexabere L^b] amplexere L
         o] oh Y

330   sorore tua] Lydia L
         nunc] num L

331   appellans] appelles N

332   hoc est] est hoc N

333   Hor. Quid L^c] Hor. Ecquid CYT   Quid Hor. Quid L
         nunc tu C^c] tu nunc CY
         vir] vix CT

334   mitto] mitte CYT
         Quid quod] quid quid Y

335   meae] mea Y
         dum] dic Y
         hae sunt] sunt hae N   haec sunt L

336   nusquam factum hoc a me, neque cogitatum] om. N

338   Nihil] Nil NJ
         negat CYNT] neget PDLJ

339   prius qui] qui prius NLJ
         fefellit] fregit L
         hunc L^b] quid L

340   insimulaverit] simulaverit Y

341   dic tu _] tu dic J

342   hisce _] his N
    cum _] om. Y
    tecum _] te cum CDNJT te ad L
    Lydiam _] Lydia CDNJT

346   me novisti _] novisti me Y

348   alloquutus _] allocutus YL

349   mellitis _] mellitus Y

350   pellexeras J^c _] pellixeras J pollicebaris Y

350/1 postea **vero ex** hoc ipso loco vi multa invitam/In
                     aedes compuleras? T^b _] om. T

351   ei N^c _] et ei N

352   Quanta _] Manta Y
    o _] oh Y

353   Accerse _] Accerce D
    Lydiam _] Lepidam N

354   Accerse _] Accerce D
    genus _] genas CYNLJT

355   hic CYNLJT _] hinc PD

357   qua cum _] quacum DNLT

358   te _] me YJ

359   eccam _] eccum YN

Actus 4. Scena 9.

Lydia Horatius NLJ _] Horatius Lydia CYT Lydia Horatio PD
Lucretia _] Lucretius DYN

360   ut T^c _] et T
    atque _] et L

361   proxima _] postrema L

363   Hunc _] nunc L
    medullitus L^c _] medullis CT medulli Y medulli ___ (illeg
                                   medullitus L
    nempe virtutes _] virtutis nempe CYT

364   lepidos] Lepidos CT
tute ipse] tuteipse N tute ipsus Y

365   Praedicare] Praedicari J

366   pater] om. N

367   Synesium] Sinesium L
aliquandiu] aliquam diu T

368   mens] meis CYT
Postea ubi Lepidam (dulcissimam meam Lepidam)] om. L
Postea CYNJT] Post PD

369-71] lines omitted L

369   Hesterno] Histerno D

370   de] eo Y

371   veniam amori CYLT] amori veniam PDNJ

372   Et iurat nuptias] om. L
ah] at L

373   Perge] Ah perge Y

374   eum] eam Y
osculatur] deosculatur Y

375   et] est CYT

378   solent] solet Y soleat L
et] ac Y

379   Censeo] Credo Y Sentio DNLJ
amici T^c] amice T
extitisse] extetisse N existere CYT

380   denique] domi N

381   Quin] om. Y
gestio] gesto N

382   transfigere] trans figere T configere NLJ

385   O] Oh Y

386   te T^{a} _/_ rem T
nolo C^{c}T^{c} _/_ volo C (illeg.) T

388   Ahime _/_ Ahi me NJ   Ahine L   Ohime CYT
fugiam _/_ -fugam D
non _/_ num L
fero _/_ feram N

390   te _/_ om. Y

391   obtectam _/_ oblectam L
viden' YNLJ _/_ vidin' PCDT

393   ecce C^{b} _/_ ego C

394   Hic CT _/_ Huic PDNLJ   Haec Y

399   lubet _/_ libet N

Actus 4.   Scena 10.

401   O _/_ Oh Y
ego _/_ om. CYNT
sumne _/_ somno L

404   provocaveras _/_ provocaveris Y

407   nempe _/_ vero N
mamillas _/_ mammillas Y   mammas NLJ
pectore T^{c} _/_ pectori T

408   mamillas _/_ mammillas YN   mammas L

409   mamillas _/_ mammillas YN   mammas L
litem _/_ rem L
diremptam _/_ direptam CYT
istuc _/_ isthuc N

410   Iupiter _/_ Iuppiter L

411   hunc _/_ hanc N

412   mamillas illas _/_ illas mamillas N   mammas ullas L
        mamillas illi CT   mammillas illi Y

413   viderim D^b] videram D
tune] tum Y
ullas] illas NLJ

415   Mamillam-] Mammillam Y
conspexisse] aspexisse CYT
nunquam] umquam N

416   consimilem vidisse] conspexisse consimilem N

417   ira] irae L

418   vindictae] vindicta C
rabies] rabibies L

419   furor] fateor CYT

420   foemina] foeminae L

421   marem] mare L

422   Tu i intro] tu, et intro T tu, et ideo CY om. L
decretum] deoretum L

423   Ubi, ubi] Ubi CT Abi Y ubicunque N
Proteum T^b] prolea T

Finis Actus Quarti] Actus Quarti Finis J om. CDL

Actus 5. Scena 1.

Actus 5 _⁊_ Actus 4 Y
Synesius _⁊_ Synesii N
Faustulus L^b _⁊_ Faṡtulus L
Cassander _⁊_ om. YN
Puer _⁊_ om. N

1   sat bene, sat est D^b _⁊_ sat bene CDYT^a sat est N om. T

2   O _⁊_ oh Y
    Iupiter _⁊_ Iuppiter L
    servassint illam CT _⁊_ illam servassint DNL^b J illam
       servassent PL servassent illam Y

3   praedicas _⁊_ praedices L
    nutrix _⁊_ nutrix/nutrix L

4   Rem tibi omnem ordine et minutim feci palam _⁊_ Rem tibi
       ordine omnem et minutim feci palam L Rem omnem ordine
       et minutim tibi palam feci CYT
    quod _⁊_ quid Y

5   potes _⁊_ potest NLJ
    vitae _⁊_ vitam L
    male _⁊_ mali Y mele J

6   Ni CYNJT _⁊_ Ne PDL
    <u>Syn.</u> _⁊_ Synesius N
    <u>Me</u> _⁊_ O me N
    miserum et _⁊_ om. N

7   primum T^a _⁊_ (illeg.) T
    querar _⁊_ quaerar CLT quaeras N
    Lucretium _⁊_ Lucretiam NLJ
    quem _⁊_ quam NLJ
    crediderim CYNJT _⁊_ crediderem D credideram PL

8   invenerim _⁊_ inveneram L
    insuper _⁊_ in super NL

9   violaverit _⁊_ violavit L
    et _⁊_ om. CYNT
    vitam _⁊_ vita N

10   An] Aut Y
potius nunc] nunc potius L
cui in] an in NJ
tot] om. Y
sunt CYNLJT] sint PD

11   Nu. Vin' L^c] Vin'/Nut. Vin' L Nut. vin vin N^a Vim T
Non non non non] Non non Y
maneo] mane CY
vero] vel L

12   admixta sunt] sunt admixta CYT
filiam quod] quod filiam Y filiam N
habeas] habes N
Syn. Ocyus, ocyus Y^b] Syn. Tantis virt Y

13   Faust. Tantis] Crisp. Tantis D
praeditam CDYNLJT] praditam P
cedat] cedit CYT
vincat virtute] virtute vincat N

14   aliud] aliquid L
peccatum N^a] paratum N

15   admissum] admissam N
praestantia CYLJT] constantia PDN

16   cuiusvis] cuius vis YL cuisvis T
obfirmatae] obfirmatam Y
pudicitiam] pudititiam T
nedum] ne dum NJT
puellulae] puell/lulae T^a

17   si] sin Y
unquam] om. CYT
satis_tutae] satis factae Y
sunt] sint Y

18   amicorum] amatorum NJ
iniuste] inuste N

19   ipse] ipsa Y
periculis] periclis L

20   scipionem] Scipionem CYT
at] et Y
propera C^b] propere C

21   te id] id te CYT

22   ac ⨆ et YL
        uteretur ⨆ viteretur L
        fieri potuit ⨆ potuit fieri L
        here ⨆ om. CYT

23   Syn. Tace CDYNLJT ⨆ Tace P
        sis ⨆ sit N
        Faustule ⨆ Fastule T
        fidei ⨆ fides CT fide Y
        abs CYT ⨆ ab PDNLJ
        Ersilia ⨆ ersilia L Ersilla J

24   commissa CDYLJT ⨆ conmissa PN

25   tua ⨆ om. N
        at ⨆ om. Y
        hucusque ⨆ huc usque CYNLJ

26   Ahime! Ahime! ⨆ ehi me ahi me N Ahi me ahi me me T
        Ahine ahine L Ahime C ahi me JT[c] ohime Y

27   quam ⨆ om. N

28   dissuasi ⨆ desuasi N

29   aperturam ⨆ aperturum L
        incepto ⨆ incaepto D incoepto LJ instituto CYT
        desisteret ⨆ desisteris L
      *Illa ⨆ Illam PDYNLJT Illum C
        ibi ⨆ ubi YT[c]
        lachrymis ⨆ lacrymis L lachrnis N

30   totum ⨆ totam N

31   Mihi vita ⨆ vita mihi CYNT
        hac ⨆ haec L hoc CYT huc N
        non N[a] ⨆ (illeg.) N
        insana CYT ⨆ insanam PDNLJ

32   districto ⨆ destricto CJT distracto N
        minata sibi est ⨆ minata est sibi CYT minatam sibi esse PDNJ
        minatam sibi esset L

33   illi ⨆ om. L
        adiuvantem ⨆ adiuvante N

35   satis nunc est, ego eo ⨆ om. CYT
        ego eo ⨆ egero L

36   Verum *7* om. N

38   imprimis *7* inprimis CYJT

39   nuptias *7* nupties T

40   Fiet *7* Fiat N
         abite ergo *7* quo L

41   Cass. Satis *7* Satis CYJT
         quota *7* quarta Y
         diei *7* dies Y

42   At hem *7* Ahem L
         redierit *7* rediret CYT

44   quaeso *7* queso L
         siet *7* fiet N sciet T

Actus 5. Scena 2.

Cassander. Synesius. *7* Synesius. Cassander. Y

45   Abi *7* Ab Y
         me *7* om. L
         Signior *7* Senior N Sigor L Sig^{or} DJT Sg^{or} CY

46   Nuntium CDY LJT *7* nuntium N^a numbium N Nuncium P
         apporto CDYNLJT *7* opporto P
         tibi *7* om. N
         te fieri participem *7* participem te fieri N
         velles *7* velis L

47   summe CDYNLJT *7* sumne P

48   filius *7* fillius L
         tuus T^c *7* tuum T
         Lucretius. Syn. Oh./Cass. Non CYNJT *7* Lucretius. Syn. Oh.
            Lucretius/Non PD

49   *7* line om. L
    *fecit insigniter *7* insigniter fecit CYT
         iniuriam *7* iniuiriam T

50   supposuerat CYT *7* supposuerit PDNLJ
         ipsus CDYNLJT *7* ipsius P

51   Lydiam] Lepidam N
vitiavit N^c] vitiabit L violavit N
pernegat] denegat CYT

53   aliud D^b] illud DL
signior] Sg^{nior} Y senior L sigor L sig^{or} DJ T Sg^{or} C
Cassandro CYNLJT] Cassander PD

55   audacter] audaciter N

56   poenam DT] paenam PCYNLJ
censeas] censes YT censeo C^b sentio C

57   ut] et N
iudice T^c] iudicem T

58   ibi] ibit N
quae capitalis sit necesse est T^a] om. T

59   ] line om. CY
illum] om. L

60   inultum T^a] multo N om. T
patiamur] patiemur CYT
dedecus C^b] facinus C
An existimas igitur T^a] Quid si tuus hoc ipsum T
igitur] Sigor L

61   patraverit] pratraverit J perpetraverit N

62   et] ut L
maiore CT] maiori PDYNLJ

63-4   T^a] lines om. T

63   num] om. N
hoc] haec L om. CYT^a
serio] scio Y
me J^o] om. J

64   dico] dic Y

65   Quid] Quod NLJ

66   admisisset] admississet J admiserit Y
filius T^a] om. NLJT
numquid] num quid CT nunquid YL quid N
tam T^a] om. T

67 hercle _/ hercule CT

68 istuc _/ istoc Y

69 ament T^c _/ amant LT

70 Persancte N^c _/ Persantte N
deiero _/ diero L

71 eo igitur _/ igitur eo CT igitur Y
fiat _/ fiet Y
filium _/ fillium L ffiliam C
rapiamus _/ capiamus J eripiamus CYT

74 tu quod _/ quod tu L
praestes DYLT^c _/ prastes P praestas CNJT
meam T^a _/ om. T

75 Poh _/ Puh NJT om. Y
Istoccine _/ Istoc ne CYT Istaccine L
pacto _/ facto J
putas _/ putes C
te me posse CYN^{c}JT _/ me te posse N te posse me PDL

76 hercle _/ hercule CT
rem _/ te L
non gnatam tuam _/ gnatam tuam non Y cum gnatam tuam L

77 est nunc facta _/ facta est CYT est facta N

78 tu filiam CYT _/ filiam tu PDNLJ
ut _/ et L

82 plane est CJ _/ plane et T^a plane PDNLT est Y
memoras L^c _/ memores L

83 Lydiam _/ Lidiam N
perdidit T^c _/ prodidit LT
audi T^c _/ audivi T

84 sic tu CYT^a _/ tu PD sic NLJT
educasti _/ eduxisti CYT
Ersilia _/ Ersillia N Ersilla J Erissilla T Erysilla C

85 quidem _/_ om. CYT
  hodie nunc _/_ nunc hodie CYT
  ipsus _/_ ipsum YL
  nimis T^a _/_ om. T
  iam nunc _/_ nunc iam CYT
  esset _/_ est YL

87 imprimis _/_ inprimis CYJT

88 commendavi _/_ comendavi N[b] commendam YN
  natura _/_ naturae T

89 officio N[c] _/_ officia N
  functa _/_ functi L
  misere deperiit _/_ deperiit misere N
  nec _/_ neque N
  tamen T^a _/_ tam T
  ausa est CDYNLJT^a _/_ ausa P est T

90 aperte _/_ apertam CYNT
  eloqui _/_ elloqui L
  hanc _/_ hunc T
  ergo N[c] _/_ ego ergo N
  ergo technam CYNJT _/_ technam ergo PDL
  Lepidae _/_ Lepida T

91 potiretur CDYNJT _/_ poteretur P potireretur L
  factum et CT^a _/_ factum ut D factum PYNLJT
  saepius _/_ saepe Y

92 tandem _/_ tamen Y

93 mirum T^a _/_ multum T

94 Proculdubio CDYLJT _/_ Procul dubio PN
  hanc _/_ hunc T
  meditatur T[c] _/_ mediatur T

95 Ut pote _/_ Utpote CNLJT
  prorsus T^a _/_ om. T
  prorsus de salute C[c] _/_ de salute prorsus CY
  desperet _/_ desperit D desperat CYT
  perquirit _/_ perquirat N

96 fabulae T[b] _/_ fablae T

97 Estne T^a _/_ Est ne L om. T

98 <u>Cass.</u> O _/_ O Y
  O nobile _/_ ah nobile Y
  par T[c] _/_ per T
  amantium CYLJT _/_ amantum PDN

99   quantum N^c _7 quanta NJ

100   mihi nurum _7 mihi mirum N mihi miram T meo miram CY
nostrae _7 vestrae L om. N

101   dominam _7 dominum N

103   Quantas CDYNLJT _7 Quantus P
possem _7 possum Y
lachrymae _7 lacrymae L lachrimae N^cJ lachrima T
(illeg.) N
obortae _7 abortae CT
intercluderent CYNLJT _7 intercluderint PD

104   magis _7 modo CYT

105   Serva _7 serio Y
eam _7 om. Y
Horatium placabo _7 placabo Horatium Y

106   *Syn. Metuo _7 Metuo CYT
hercle _7 sane N
metuo ne _7 ne CYT
tarda _7 Sy. tarda N

107   propero _7 propera CYT
Vale. Cass. _7 Syn. Vale. Cass. CYT

Actus 5. Scena 3.

Horatius. Cassander. _7 Cassander. Horatius. CYJT

108   Qua _7 Quo Y
nunc me CYNJT _7 me nunc PDL
inferam _7 miserum CYT
quo fugiam CDYNLJT _7 om. P
pudeo _7 pudet Y

109   Et doleo _7 Ita nunc doleo CYT
irridiculo _7 deridiculo CYT

110   stupendi amoris _7 amoris stupendi Y
exemplum _7 exemplar CYT

111   multo me _7 me multo CYT^a me T

112   tam C^b _7 om. C
latitabit T^c _7 latitabat T lalitabat N
condignum ad CYNLJT _7 ad condignum PD
supplicium CDYNLJ _7 supplicum P suppliciam T

113 delusum ⌐ delusam C

115 angit ⌐ augit N angis L

116 haec est ⌐ est haec N
tute Tᵃ ⌐ -tu LT

117 dic clare ⌐ declare N
te sic ⌐ sic te J
vexant ⌐ vexent CT

118 ira, odium Lᶜ ⌐ ira/Crisp. Quid in te tuus Lucretius/
                                     Odium L
infamia ⌐ insania Y

119 istoccine Tᵃ ⌐ istoc T

120 Quid in ⌐ Quidni L
Lucretius ⌐ Lucretus N

122 utrumque ⌐ utrunque CN

123 Primo ⌐ primum NY
Lydiae Tᵃ ⌐ Lidiae N om. T

124 Deinde ⌐ Dein L
me ⌐ om. CYT
circumvenit ⌐ cercumvenit T circum venit L
ut Nᵇ ⌐ et N.

125 nescio Nᶜ ⌐ et nescio N
supposuerit CDYNLJTᶜ ⌐ supposuerat PT
scortum Nᶜ ⌐ scortam N
exoletum Nᶜ ⌐ exoletam N
illa ⌐ illi N

126 eo ⌐ illo Y
tamen Tᵃ ⌐ om. T
desponsata mihi ⌐ mihi desponsata CY mihi disponsata T

128 Lydia ⌐ Lidia T
hercle manifeste quidem CYT ⌐ hercle quidem manifeste PDNJ
                        quidem hercle manifeste L

129 talem Tᵃ ⌐ om. T
supposititiam Nᶜ ⌐ suppositiam LT suppositionem Y
                        suppositam N
tuam ⌐ tibi L

130 eam Tᵃ ⌐ om. YT
erat Cᵇ ⌐ erit CTᶜ
fuerit ⌐ fuit CYNT

131   T^a ⏚ line om. T
      esset CYNLJT^a ⏚ si esset PD
      depraehendisses ⏚ deprehendisses CNLJ   deprehensisses Y

134   Verum ⏚ Tam Y
      etiam ⏚ om. CYT
      nobilitate ⏚ nobilitati Y^c
      dote par CYNLJT ⏚ par dote PD
      sit T^a ⏚ om. NLJT

135   hanc ⏚ om. N

136   Hor. Nostin' T^a ⏚ Nostin' T

137   Fortasse ⏚ Fortassis CT

138   Hor. J^b ⏚ Cass. J

139   Tace ⏚ om. Y

140   Lucretius N^c ⏚ Lucretias N
      ut ⏚ om. CYT
      intulerit ⏚ attulerit CYT

141   istum T^a ⏚ hoc T
      ingratum N^c ⏚ ingratam YN

142   ac ⏚ at Y
      unico CYNLJT ⏚ uno PD
      verbo expedi ⏚ expedi verbo N

143   est tua CYT ⏚ tua est PDNLJ

144   noli ⏚ nolo Y
      mi CYT ⏚ te PDLJ om. N
      pater ⏚ om. N
      perfidiam ⏚ praefidiam T
      mihi T^a ⏚ om. T

145   quam ⏚ quem Y
      causa T^c ⏚ (illeg.) T
      amicitiae N^c ⏚ amiti amicitiae N   amicitia T

146   Oblivione ⏚ in oblivione Y
      sepultam ⏚ sepultum CT

147   Lucretii T^c ⏚ Lucretiis T
      dehinc deletum ⏚ deletum dehinc T dehinc deletam N
                                                  deletum CYT^c
      siet ⏚ sit CYT^a

148 loco *J* hoc loco Y
  tibi imposuit *J* sibi imposuit Y

149 iste *J* ille CYT
  deliquit *J* reliquit N

150 <u>Hor.</u> Quaenam *J* Quaenam L
  est haec *J* haec est CYT
  quam *J* quae N

152 Advorte *J* Adverte CLT

153 is *J* om. Y
  cluit *J* cluet YL
  et est *J* et et L
  annos *J* anmos L

154 tuasque ...virtutes *J* virtutesque ... tuas CYT
  suspiciens *J* aspiciens Y adspiciens CT

155 flagravit *J* flagrabit L
  cumque T^a *J* tuque T
  Lepidam *J* Lepidum T

156 aditum *J* additum T
  praeclusum *J* perclusum N proclusum L
  perspiceret *J* prospiceret CYNL

157 illius *J* illis Y
  et *J* ac Y
  sui *J* om. Y
  fieret *J* fiat CYT

158 es *J* is L

159 T^a *J* line om. T
  Lucretia Lucretia *J* Lucretia Y
  cumulasti *J* cumulastis Y

160 instituisti *J* constituisti N

161 omnes superasti *J* superasti omnes Y
  pericula *J* peritula L

162 caute T^a *J* tecte T
  scriptis *J* scriptos Y

163 fictis *J* fiictis T fictisque CY
  narrationibus *J* rationibus Y

164   non *]* cum Y
       Quin *]* quem T

165   ingratus T^c *]* ignarus T
       tibi *]* om. NL
       inhumanius *]* inhumanus L inhumaniter CYNJT

166   mea manu *]* manu mea CYT
       maximopere *]* maximo opere L magnopere CYT
       oppetere *]* appettere T

167   fortassis L^b *]* fortasse L
       conciliasti *]* conscivisti CYT
       misera *]* miseras L miser L^c
       tunc L^c *]* hunc L
       perii *]* pereo L

168   hoc T^a *]* haec L om. T
       continuis *]* contumeliis CYT
       suspiriis *]* susperiis T
       contabescet N^c *]* contabescit CNJT

169   fundent T^c *]* fundant T
       ipsi *]* ipsam L

170   siem T^a *]* om. T
       infame *]* insaniae N

171   et *]* atque NJ

172   hunc T^a *]* nunc T
       lachrymas *]* lacrymas L lachrimas NJ

173   Et *]* om. CYT^c
       potest *]* potes CYT^c
       illac C^c *]* illam L
       quaeritatum C^{c}N^c *]* quaeritatam C utatum N queriturus L
       Lucretiam *]* Lucretium N

174   bonum animum *]* animum bonum J
       eamus, eamus, eamus *]* eamus eamus CYT

175   Eo *]* Eio J

Actus 5.   Scena 4.

Lucretia _⃦ Lucretius CYT

177   obtulisti _⃦ dedisti CYT
        tua T^a _⃦ om. T
        neve CYLJT _⃦ neque PDN

179   Ecce _⃦ Quae L
        deliciae _⃦ delitiae DL   delicias CY   delitias T

180   interlucent T^c _⃦ interlucet Y   interluceret   interlucent T

181   Eximia N^c _⃦ opimia N
        pulchritudo Y^c _⃦ pulchretudo DY
        indicia _⃦ inditia N   iudicia L   indicium CY   iudicium T

182   O _⃦ O me Y
        hanccine _⃦ hancine CT

183   ex sententia succedat _⃦ ex sententia succedit N
                      succedit ex sententia CYT
        bene N^{b}T^b _⃦ pene T   bee N

184   Quod _⃦ Quid CT
        si _⃦ om. N
        ille _⃦ illa C
        usque D^c _⃦ usquam D

185   ipsa _⃦ ipse Y
        beneficium hoc _⃦ hoc beneficium CYT
        ingratiis _⃦ in gratiis D

187   haud CY _⃦ aut N   non PDN^{b}LJT
        minitatur _⃦ meditatur CY   mediatatur T

188   quassat CYNLJT _⃦ quassit PD
        ex CYNLJ _⃦ et PDT

189   multae certe _⃦ certe multae CY   certe multa T
        insunt _⃦ sunt N

190   exanimales NLJ _⃦ exanimantes PDYT   exaninantes C
        Me _⃦ ne D
        conspexit _⃦ aspicit CYT
        atque _⃦ et Y
        prout _⃦ pro ut T
        meritus _⃦ meritras T^c (illeg.) T

191   aggreditur L^b ⨼ agreditur L
      contollam T^c ⨼ attollam T convellam L

192   adhuc ut potero C^{b}T^c ⨼ ut potero adhuc CY adhuc ut
                                                        poterem T
      aegritudinem CDYNLJT ⨼ aegritudine P

193   Horati ⨼ Sigor Horatio L

194   D^b ⨼ line om. ↙
      prosequutus ⨼ prosecutus YN persecutus CLT
      es N^c ⨼ est L et N
      conviciis ⨼ convitiis CYNLJT
      et ⨼ ac L
      interminaris ⨼ interminatur J interminatus J^b
                                              interminatus es L

195   pulchra ⨼ pulchrae T
      praebet ⨼ prebet ↙ probat N
      occasio ⨼ occosio N
      decernendi ⨼ discernendi NJ

196   experiemur T^a⨼ expedi T

197   Lucreti ⨼ Sigor Lucretio L
      tu me nunc J ⨼ nunc tu me N tu me PDL me nunc CYT

198   Luc. Siccine T^c ⨼ Lucretius siccine T

199   extimescis ⨼ ex timescis D extimescas CYT
      inquam ⨼ in quam N
      sic te ⨼ te sic N sic Y
      perdidi ⨼ prodidi NLJ   pdidi D

200   En ⨼ Et CYT
      cessas ⨼ recusas Y
      hasce ⨼ hasle T husce N

201   Qui ⨼ Lucreti Y
      tam repente teipsum ⨼ teipsum tam repente CT^a te tam
                      repente T te ipsum repente iam Y
      incuses T^c ⨼ recuses T

202   sis ⨼ om. CYT
      cessas ⨼ restas Y
      percute ⨼ parate Y
      insta N^b ⨼ om. N
      nequibis N^c ⨼ nequibas T nequis Y neque iubis N
      pectori ⨼ pectoris L

203 doleat CYNLJT] dolet PD
  quo] quod Y

204 me vis N^c] nescis me vis N
  duellum] duelli L
  homine] om. N
  imbecilli] imbelli CYNLJT

205 inexperto] in experto CNJT
  nosti] possis L
  assentatiunculis] assentationibus T osculationibus CY

206 vi N^c] ni vi N
  experiri] expetiri T^c (illeg.) T

207 noli] nosti Y

208 interimamus] interminamus T interminemus C
              intereamus Y

209 putas] putes T
  fiet C^b] fiat Y om. C
  priusquam D^b] praeterquam D
  experimur] experiamur CYJ experiemur NT

210 eramus antehac amici DYLJ] eramus ante hac amici PC
    eramus antehoc amici T amici eramus antehac N
  atque CYT] et PDNLJ
  causa iam CYT^a] causa PD^{b}NLJ casa D iam T

211] line om. L
  amplexemur] amplectemur Y
  ac CDNJT] at PL et Y
  deosculemur] diosculemur T

212 conficiemus] conficiamus CY

213 libitum tibi C^{c}T] libitum est tibi C tibi libitum PDYNLJ

214 abiicio] deiicio YN

215 meae] mea L
  o vita] oh vita Y
  qua] quam YN
  vita] om. CYT
  multo] mea L

216 tibi mortem] mortem tibi N
  ut T^a] om. T
  vitam dedisti] dedisti vitam L

217 vivere N^c ⟧ vivire N
    taedio ⟧ in taedio Y
    poeniteret T^a ⟧ peniteret N poenitet T

219 errore hóc T^c ⟧ errore hoc errore hoc T
    genua tua CYNJT ⟧ tua genua PDL
    meam CDYLJT^c ⟧ mea P om. NT

220 rogarem N^c ⟧ rogare L om. N

221 sis ⟧ sic L
    machaeram ⟧ macheram T
    infamem ⟧ infaelicem N
    atque ⟧ et YN

222 intentare T^a ⟧ interminare T
    meum D^c ⟧ mecum D

224 Quod si ⟧ Quodsi N
    mens mihi T^c ⟧ mihi mens NLJ mens haec Y mens mea mihi T
    integerrima N^cT^a ⟧ integerrimu N om. T
    dictaret ⟧ dictitaret J distaret CT
    ignorantia ⟧ ignorantiae L

225 persancte C^b ⟧ persanctam C
    deiero CDYNJT ⟧ deiiero P diero L

226 ut ⟧ et L

227 condignas ⟧ condignis D^c
    meis ⟧ meas D

229 siem ⟧ sim CYT
    meo patrono ⟧ patrono meo N mei patroni Y
    antehac CDNLJT ⟧ ante hac PY
    ignotam ⟧ ignota J ignato L

230 poenae ⟧ penae N pene C paene T
    agnitam T^c ⟧ agnotam T
    me T^a ⟧ ne L om. T
    redames T^a ⟧ redamus T
    in posterum CDYNLJT ⟧ imposterum P

231 te sciam hoc ⟧ hoc scirem te CYT
    praestiturum ⟧ prestiturum NT praestitutum L

232   mihi res posthac potest intervenire] res mihi potest
       intervenire post hac C res mihi potest intervenire
       post haec T res potest mihi intervenire posthac Y

233   adferat CYNLJT] afferat PD
       conceditur T^c] concederetur T

234   amplexari C^c] amplectari CT

235   falsas] falsus Y

236   et T^a] est T
       percipere] procipere L
       Jupiter J^b] Juper J

237   gaudia] Luc. gaudia N

238   an] aut T om. Y
       inferos CYT] mortuos PDNLJ
       sim] sum N imo Y
       inopinato] inopinata N inopinate L

239   oborta CYNLJT] aborta PD
       mihi est CYT] est PDNLJ
       mihique] mihi N
       adhuc ante oculos] ante oculos adhuc CT^a ante
          oculos Y ante ___ s (illeg.) T
       obversatur CDYNLT] ob versatur P observatur J
       imago mortis L^{b}T^a] ante oculos L (illeg.) T

240   etiamdum] etiam dum CNLJT
       videor] videar C

241   amplexari D^{c}T^a] amplexare D ample ___ (illeg.) T
       tamen T^a] om. T

242   Annon] An non CJT
       me satis] satis me CYT
       noveras] noveris L

243   Lucretia T^a] Lu. T
       mihi credere] credere mihi Y
       ausa T^c] ausus T
       quae] quod CY

244   haec neutiquam] haec neutequam D neutiquam haec N
       evenissent T^c] evanissent T

245   tuas virtutes T^a] om. T

246 eximias N^b ⟧ opimias N

247 propterea ⟧ praeterea Y
ausa ⟧ om. Y
eram ⟧ erat ❧

248 et T^b ⟧ est T ac J om. N
animum L^c ⟧ animam L

249 mihimet ⟧ mihi met J

250 succenseo C^c ⟧ succenseo merito succenseo C succenseas L
radiantium ⟧ radiantum Y
oculorum ⟧ occulorum L
coeleste N^c ⟧ scaeleste NT

251 tuto L^b ⟧ toto L
omnis est ⟧ est omnes N

252 quodque ⟧ quod CYT^c

253 Ahime ⟧ Ahi me NJ Ohime Y

254 est ⟧ om. Y
commutatus ⟧ conmutatus T connutatus N
color ⟧ calor N
numquid ⟧ nunquid YNL
male ⟧ mali N
est ⟧ e L

255 Calor CDYNLJT ⟧ Color P
insuetus ⟧ desuetus N dissuetus J
mihi T^a ⟧ om. T
artus C^c ⟧ arctus CT
occupat ⟧ ocupat T

256 symptomata ⟧ sumptomata D
sentio ⟧ senteo D sensio L

257 Dicam gaudio provenire ⟧ Gaudio provenire dicam Y
ac ⟧ an N et CYT

258 Ne quid ⟧ Nequid YN
metuas T^a ⟧ met ___ (illeg.) T
mea T^c ⟧ meas T
aedes nunc tuas ⟧ aedes tuas NL^{b}J nuptias L

259   actutum N^C ⟧ actu tum N
      abscesserit ⟧ abcesserit L   abcescerit T   discesserit Y
      Quin ⟧ Quum L

260   Ahime ⟧ Ahi me NJ

                    Actus 5. Scena 5.

261   virginis ⟧ verginis ?
      quae ⟧ qui CYT

262   Hesterno me vesperi CNJT ⟧ Hesterno me vespere PDY
                      Multo me heri L
      maximo ⟧ maxime CT
      oravit ⟧ me oravit N om. Y

263   darem T^C ⟧ dat ___ (illeg.) T
      orator ⟧ oratus NJ

264   Lydiam T^C ⟧ Lepidam T
      uti ⟧ ut L
      det coniugem ⟧ congugem det L
      Lepido ⟧ Lepidam NL

265   Perfabricavit ⟧ perfabricabit T   perfricavit Y
      etiam nomine ⟧ nomine etiam CYT

266   succenseam ⟧ succenserem NJ   succensirem L
      Poh ⟧ o poh T   proh Y   puh NLJ

267   lenem ⟧ levem CT

268   ingenium ⟧ genium Y
      adolescentum ⟧ adolescentium Y
      novi novi ⟧ novi novi novi CYT
      qui C^C ⟧ quid C

269   nunquam boni frugi ⟧ nunquam frugi boni CYT   boni
                           nunquam frugi N

270   cuius ⟧ eius Y
      olim ⟧ om. Y

271   adhuc ⟧ ad huc C
      Tiberi T^C ⟧ Tiberii T
      aliquantum ⟧ aliquentum N   aliquid Y
      humorisque ⟧ hummorisque T
      tuo ⟧ tui N

272 Etiam ⏋ om. N
corpore ⏋ pectore NLJ
Hey ⏋ He CYT
fa la la la CJ ⏋ fa la lala L fa la la FDT
          fa la la la la YN
lyra ⏋ lyra etc. NLJ

273 quem 1ª ⏋ om. T

274 illius ego CLJT ⏋ ego illius PDYN
hilaritudine ⏋ hilaritate L

276 Cassander ⏋ senior Cassandro N Sig^or Cassandro LJ
vales T^c ⏋ valeas LT

277 Tib. Quid C^b ⏋ Tib. ut C

278 An ⏋ Ah CT At N om. Y

279 Quid tua id ⏋ Quidnam ita Y

280 Tib. Ah! ⏋ Tib. Oh N Hor. Ah CT
Quin ⏋ Tib. Quin CT^c quia N
hancce ⏋ hance C hanc se NLJ
habere oportet bene ⏋ oportet bene habere Y
hilariter ⏋ hila/lariter L

281 vitae quod ⏋ quod vitae CYT
vino ⏋ vivo N
et CYNLJT ⏋ om. PD

282 Quid ⏋ Cass. Quid CYT
puh NLJ ⏋ pugh PD Tib. Phh CYT

283 fecimus ⏋ facimus L
si ⏋ om. Y

284 Sin ⏋ quin Y
sinapi ⏋ synapi CL

285 ⏋ line om. Y
Apage ⏋ apage sis N
tristitiam ⏋ tristitiam et N
serena vultum ⏋ sereno vultu CT

286 sunt ⏋ om. N
Hey ⏋ hei CLT Hem Y

287 habes Lepidam ⏋ habes lepidam NL Lepidam habes CT

288 Ha ha he *⸗* ha ha ha LT
     quid N^c *⸗* quod N

289 bellam *⸗* bellum L

291 foemina foeminam *⸗* feminam feminam N

292 scis *⸗* sis N
     •loquor CDNLJT *⸗* loquar PY

293 venditasti *⸗* vendicasti Y
     luxuriosus *⸗* luxuriosus est Y
     Lydiae *⸗* Lidiae T Lidae N

294 iam quod *⸗* quod iam N
     Nam *⸗* Num NJ
     nunc mos *⸗* om. L (six dashes show the position of the
                                                    words)

295 Quid D^cN^c *⸗* Quod D quod quid N
     fecit *⸗* facit
     homo si amet *⸗* homo CY homo si T^b phrase cut off
                                    bottom of page in T

296 potiatur suis *⸗* suis potiatur Y
     Lydia *⸗* Lydiam Y Lydiae CJ
     per CDYNLJT *⸗* pro P
     vim *⸗* unum Y
     intulisset CDYNLJT *⸗* obtulisset P

297 esset *⸗* est YNJ

299 fecere *⸗* facere L
     tale *⸗* tale autem N
     antehac *⸗* ante hac Y

300 etiam CDYNLJT *⸗* et iam P

301 Verisimile *⸗* Veri simile N
     pol est *⸗* est pol N
     nunc *⸗* om. Y

302 *⸗* line om. L

303-9 The order of lines is disturbed in L; lines 308 and
          309 precede line 303.

303 Tib. Fortasse *⸗* om. L

304   meo vitio vertis, potius *J* meo potius vitio vertis J
vitio J*c J* ut vitio J
tuae *J* meae N
cum *J* tum N

306   Ha ha he CYT *J* Ha ha ha PDNLJ
mi *J* me N

307   Verum si sapis, tu istuc insipienter factum *J* om. L

308   illisque *J* aliisque Y
ignoscas *J* agnoscas C

309   Animi T*c J* animis T
resarciamus CYNJT *J* resartiamus PDL

310   Atque qui CYT*c J* Atque T Atqui L At qui PDNJ
placet N*c J* pat placet N

312   contracta *J* contructa C

313   oblatam *J* ablatam N

314   Nam *J* Num L

315   tum *J* tunc Y om. N
innui *J* inivi Y munum N

317-19   *J* lines om. L

318   verbo *J* om. Y
quando *J* quondo D
hoc in *J* in hoc CY

320   is rei *J* rei is CYT
prospexit *J* perspexit J

322   desponsavit *J* desponsabit L
verum *J* virum DNLJ

323   nunc restat *J* restat nunc Y nun restat L

324   nuptias *J* om. N
Restituetur T*c J* Restituitur T

325   evanescet *J* evanescat YT evanescere L
Quanquam *J* Quamquam LT

326   Quanquam J Quamquam LT

327   illam D^b J illum C om. D
         uxorem J uxorēs T

328   <u>Tib</u>. Nunc J Nunc CYT
         Hah J <u>Tib</u>. Hah CYT^c

329   amplexer J amplecter CT^c amplectar Y^b plectar Y

330   Signior J Seguor Y Senior N Sig^{or} DLJT Sg^{or} C
         Tiberio J Tiberie C Tiberi Y

331   qui T^c J quae T
         sint J sunt N

332   imprudentius J impudentius CJ
         <u>Tib</u>. Quin J <u>Cass</u>. Quin C Quin L
         ergo J om. Y
         nunc J om. LJ

333   Cupio mehercule D^c J Cupeo mehercule D Cupio me
            hercule L Cupio me hercle N Mehercle cupio CYT

334   utcunque J utrunque CD utrumque YT
         difficilem N^b J diffilem N
         intuli J vitali Y

335   cum J quum Y
         feceras verba CYT J verba feceras PDNL verba faceres J
         simul J semel NLJT semel simul C om. Y

337   non igitur J non CT tu Y

339   <u>Cass</u>. Boni J <u>Tib</u>. Boni Y

340   Immo J Immno et N Ino et N^c
         summi J suavis Y
         et J atque J om. CLT
         insperati J in sperati L sperati N

342   Optime J om. CYT
         immo? ha ha he regie J imo? ha ha he regie CYJT
            imo ha ha ha regie NL ha ha ha immo regie PD
         pollucibiliter J pollucebiliter N
         dic amabo J amabo dic N

343 Ut *]* Ut a Y
   secum *]* sexu Y
   Lepida T^c *]* Lepidae T
   commutavit *]* comnnutavit N commigravit CYT

344 Synesii *]* Sinesii
   transiit *]* transit CYT

345 Whaw *]* Whaio J ie haud C id haud T id autem Y
   ha ha he CYNT *]* ha ha ha PDLJ

346 perfruitur *]* perficiuntur Y

347 gravida N^c *]* graviter N
   fiunt *]* fiant T

348 festus CDYNLJT *]* festos P
   dies *]* diee L
   quam me *]* om. Y
   dicent *]* viderint Y
   lepidum DLJ *]* Lepidum PCYNT

349 ridendo, saltando *]* saltando ridendo Y

350 sumam *]* summam N
   convivas C^cT *]* cives convivas C in convivas L in Camaenas N
     in caminas J in convivos PD comicos Y

351 *Valerium *]* Synesium CYLJT Sinesium N
   Areotinum CDLT *]* Areolinum J Aretinum PY Ariclanum N
   Quintianum *]* Quintinianum CT Quintilianum Y
   Aemilium T^a *]* Armilium Y om. T
   et *]* om. NJ

352 Quique T^c *]* Quisque T
   etiam *]* om. Y
   in CDYNLJT *]* om. P
   nos nuptias *]* nuptiis nos CT nuptiis vos Y
   imprimis *]* inprimis CYJT

353 suum *]* om. N

354 Illumne *]* Illum ne CT Illum me Y
   foelicem *]* infoelicem CYT
   Cocalum *]* Coculum L

356   ridicule *]* ridiculi NJ
agit *]* agat L
ac *]* et Y atque CT

357   Vale, vale, vale; *]* vale vale N

358   nimio *]* nimium CYT
aliquid *]* aliquod Y

359   comparetur *]* comperetur L

360   duc *]* duce Y

361   prospectum *]* perspectum L
cum illo *]* cum illa N Camillo Y

362   mutabit *]* mutavit Y
iam tum antea, nunc huic rei *]* cut off the bottom of
    the page in T iam tum nunc rei T^c
tum antea *]* tum T^c dum CY
huic *]* om. CYT^c

363   Iustae *]* Iuste L
seriae *]* serio L

364   lepidum CDLJ *]* Lepidum PYNT
o *]* et Y

365   ego *]* ergo N
posticum *]* posticam DNJ
iamdudum *]* statim D^{b}NLJ
Lepidum *]* Lepidum senem CYT
edamus *]* edemus CLT om. Y
iam *]* nunc iam Y
bibamus *]* bibemus CYLT

366   obsequamur *]* obsequemur CYLT
splendeant aedes *]* aedes splendeant N

367   hilaritudine *]* hilaratudine L
nos *]* vos Y
risu *]* rem L
fa la la lyra CJT *]* fa la la la lyra PDN fa la la la L
                                            ha ha he lyra Y

Actus 5. Scena 6.

Crispinus. Cassander.] Chrispinus Cassander L
Cassander Crispinus N

368   here] bene NJ
        tune] tue Y

369   quod] quid CL
        dii Y^b] om. YN
        quid] quod Y

370   apporto] opporto T
        nuncium] nunceum D multum Y
        *laetificabilem] laetificabile CYJ letificabile NT

372   Hae] Illae NJ
        toto totae] totae toto C totae totae NJ totae YL

373   Numquid] Nunquid YNLJ
        At] om. NJ

374   istuc] istoc C hoc Y om. L
        noveris CYNJT] noverit L noveras PD
        nuperrime] nupperrime N nupperime Y nuperime CDLT

375   summe T^c] om. LT
        boni] bonae rei Y

376   Cass. Quid illa?] om. CY
        illa DNLJT] alia P

377   Eloquere, cito. Crisp. At enim placide volo. Lucretia
        iam nunc $_b$ - D^b] om. CDY
        Cass. Quid D^b] om. D

378   ignoscitur] ignoscit L cognoscit Y

379   transis] transfers Y

380   male] mali Y
        conqueritur] conquaeritur T

381   Dumque] Denique Y deinde L
        sedulo CYT] sedulam PDNLJ

382   potuit *J* poterint CYT
    foras *J* om. L

383   priusquam *J* prius quam CT
    advenire *J* advenire/advenire N
    putuit *J* poterat NLJ

384   puerum *J* purum N
    venustulum L^c *J* venustulum venustulum L venustatum T
                                              venustum CY

385   O *J* Oh L
    bonis T^c *J* donis L hodie T

386   Atque *J* Atqui L
    hunc *J* hoc C^{c}Y
    nuncium *J* nuntium YNT^c nuncyum T
    exoptabilem *J* exoptabile C^{c}YT^c

388   Observabo *J* obsecrabo Y
    agat *J* agit CY

Actus 5. Scena 7.

Synesius *J* Sinesius N Synesyus T
Crispinus *J* Chrispinus L

389   et N^c *J* om. N
    incertus CDYNL^{b}JT *J* in certus P (illeg.) L

390   Qui *J* Quae CT

391   abiit *J* abeat Y

392   metu *J* melu N
    hoc *J* hunc L
    eximam *J* eximiam N

393   Synesi *J* senior Synesi N Sig^{or} Synesio LJ
    maximo C^c *J* maximum C maxime Y
    opere *J* o here Y
    ut ad illum *J* ad illum ut Y

394   Numquid ⟧ Nunquid YNLJT
        Lucretia ⟧ Lucretio J
        apportas ⟧ opportas T
        hic te expectant ⟧ hic te exspectant.D te expectant
                                 hic CLT te expectant Y

395   Syn. An ⟧ An NL
        rediere ⟧ redire N

396   Admodum ⟧ Ad modum C

397   etiam hac nocte ⟧ hac nocte etiam Y
        fient CYNLJT ⟧ fiunt PD
        ac ⟧ et CYT
        herilem ⟧ hercle Y

398   Lepidum ⟧ Lepidam CYN lepidam T
        est ⟧ om. Y
        e ⟧ a YNJ
        sicuti ⟧ sicut Y

399   e ⟧ a N
        facta ⟧ om. Y

400   istoc ⟧ isthoc T

401   Crisp. Immo ⟧ Imo L

403   deinceps T^c ⟧ deinceps esse T
        animo aequiore ⟧ animo aequiori L aequiori animo N

404   filiam ⟧ filium NL
        utrumque T^o ⟧ utrunque CYNL (illeg.) T

405   filio ⟧ filia NJ
        bellulum CYT ⟧ bellum PDNLJ
        nepotulum peperit ⟧ peperit nepotulum Y

406   Peperitne ⟧ Peperit Y

407   olim ⟧ etiam Y

408   vidisti ⟧ vidi L

409   hinc ⟧ huc CY hic T

410   ut ⟧ ni T
        insperati ⟧ in sperati N

411   manta modo _J_ modo manta Y   mane modo N   maneto modo L

414   potius _J_ om. Y
O benedetto Iddio L _J_ O benedicto Iddio PD^b J
O bene dicta N   om. CDYT
quantis T^c _J_ quanta NT
es N^c _J_ es es N

Actus 5.   Scena 8.

Scena 8 _J_ Scena ultima N
Crispinus. Grillus. _J_ Crispinus Gryllus T   Grillus Crispinus NL
Gryllus Crispinus J

415   Crisp. _J_ Gril. Nemo me insequitur? Crisp. NLJ
Ecce _J_ Eccum N
Grillum _J_ Gryllum JT

416   _J_ line om. L
Ah _J_ om. NJ
vamos, Petre vamos DJ _J_ vamos, Petre vamo P   vannos
petre vannos N   vamos, oh Petre vamos CT   vannos
ah petre vannos Y
etc. _J_ eh T   oh Y   om. NJ

417   Grille _J_ Grylle JT

418   istic _J_ isthic T   istuc Y
Grille _J_ Grylle J

421   ut T^b _J_ om. T
excluderet _J_ excludat N

422   indiget N^c _J_ eget indiget N
nummus _J_ munus YL
est _J_ om. N

423   Nec ... nec CYJ _J_ nec ... ne T   neque ... neque PDNL
cibus _J_ cybus T
ego T^c _J_ ergo T

424   recepisse CYT _J_ recaepisse L   recipisse PDNJ
mei NLJ _J_ me PCDYT

426   Ha ha he CYNJT _J_ Ha ha ha PDL
alias _J_ alios J
habet _J_ habeat N
quas _J_ quos J
Gril. Ne T^c _J_ Grylle Ne T

Ne *J* Ille Y
pannum *J* parvum L primum Y

427 Qui *J* Quin Y
es N^c *J* es es N

428 praeterierat *J* praeterirat T^b praetereat YT

429 me *J* ego N
primum CYT *J* primus PDNJ primis L
ad *J* in N
illum *J* illam N

430 Haec *J* Hac T
ut T^c *J* cur T
liquerat DNLJ *J* reliquerat PCYT

431 proprietaria *J* proprietoria CT propriataria N
fuit *J* sint CT om. N
protelata *J* protelatu L cum celata Y

432 locationis *J* vacationis N
pretium *J* precium CYT
cum *J* in N

433 rapi se *J* se rapi CNT rapi Y
solutione *J* solatione N

434 Ego, quam habui, dedi *J* om. N
quam *J* quod L
Ha, ha, he C^cYJT *J* Ha he C Ha ha ha PDNL

436 intravimus *J* intrabamus Y

437 *sella Y *J* cella PCDNLJT
nec cistula *J* aut cistula NJ
nec quicquam *J* nequicquam NJ necquicquid L

438 aliquantulum YN *J* aliquantum PCDLJT
thorum *J* torum NLJ
appellavit *J* appellabat L

439 Incipit *J* Incepit CYT Infit L

440 animalia *J* animalla C
memorare *J* memorat Y
perpinguia N^c *J* perpingua N

441   Quae _⁊_ Qui J
inquit nunc N^c _⁊_ nequit nunc N nunc inquit Y nunc C
                                           inquit J

442   Grille _⁊_ Grylle J

443   Verum _⁊_ om. NJ
decubuerat _⁊_ discuberat L
quin _⁊_ quim N

444   id _⁊_ id ego N
persentisceram _⁊_ persentiscerem CNT praesentiscerem L
fideiussor D _⁊_ fide iussor PCYLJT fideiusor N
qui _⁊_ quin N
prima _⁊_ om. L

445   iustitiam N^c _⁊_ iustitiae N
Petri N^c _⁊_ petri NL
liberavi _⁊_ liberavit Y

446   Ha, ha, he YJT _⁊_ Ita ha he C Ha ha ha PDL om. N
dii _⁊_ om. CT
ament _⁊_ amant NL
eiectus _⁊_ om. YL
iam aedibus _⁊_ om. Y

447   obambulat _⁊_ obambulabit YN
Pacheco _⁊_ Pachecho N Bache Y
D'Alcantara _⁊_ d'Alcantara CYLT don Alcantare N

448   historia haec _⁊_ haec historia NJ haec Y

449   restitutis _⁊_ restituas Y
vestitus _⁊_ vestitus Y

450   nobiscum D^b _⁊_ om. D

451   anui _⁊_ amicis Y
satisfiat _⁊_ satisfaciat L
huic _⁊_ hanc Y
sit _⁊_ hic Y

452   prandio N^c _⁊_ prandeo N praedam Y

453 Cedo ⟋ Cede Y
   quid ⟋ quod N
   si T^b ⟋ om. T
   Grille ⟋ Grylle J
   huc ⟋ hic C
   recipiam ⟋ eripiam Y

454 in hisce ⟋ hisce in N
   suppromum ⟋ subpromum Y^b

456 enim ⟋ nunc N

457 servorum ⟋ servire N
   e ⟋ a Y te L
   servum ⟋ servus Y

458 nihili ⟋ nihil Y
   hic est CYNLJT ⟋ est hic PD
   qui ⟋ om. N
   poscit ⟋ posset N

459 hominum ⟋ horum Y

460 nam exedit mihi paene ventris medullam fames / om. N
   paene ⟋ pene CT

461-4 ⟋ All four lines are written in large letters in CYT.
   Spectatores Labyrinthus only is written in large
   letters in N.

462 unusquisque ⟋ unus quisque YN^{c}J unus et quisque N

464 lychni C^c ⟋ lychyni Y lychno C
   optime ⟋ optime/Plaudite YJ

Finis ⟋ Actus Quinti Finis CT om. J

Stage Directions

position
in this
text

$\lfloor$ •-indicates that the manuscript is marked
to show the exact point for the insertion of
a stage direction. $\rfloor$

I.1. 1.1 Horatius, Crispinus e domo Cassandri Baccalaureorum. J $\rfloor$
Horatius et Crispinus egrediuntur e domo Cassandri. =
Horatio et Crispinus egrediuntur e domo Cassandri. D

1.1 Don Piedro aedes Lepidi venerans fugit conspecto
Horatio. $\rfloor$
Don Piedro aedes Laepidae venerans fugit conspecto
Horatio. L^c
Don Piedro passeth on the stage. CY
Don Piedro must passe over the stage. D
Don Pedro passes out the stage. L
Don Piedro passe over the stage. J
Don Piedro passeth over the stage. T^b
Don Piedro ad Dominae fenestram. T
Exit viso Horatio. PD^b

$\rfloor$ A letter J (1.5)

1.14 He puts on his cloake. L (1.16) $\rfloor$
puts on his cloake. J (1.14)

1.19 He knockes. D$^{b.}$ (•tick tock) $\rfloor$

1.33 Lepidus' window must be open $\rfloor$
Lepida's window must be open. J (1.30)
Lepidaes windowes must be open. D
Epidas window must be open. L

I.2.1.70 Grillus a foro Decani superioris. N (sp.h.) J (sp.h.) $\rfloor$
Grillus a foro Decani. PD

1.116 Exit Grillus per forum Decani. D$\rceil$
Horatius abigit cum fuste. D^b $\rfloor$
Horatius abigit eum fuste. Exit Grillus. P
Gryllus is beaten out ad forum Decani. J
Horatius Gryllum expellit foras. CT
Horatius Grillum expellit foras. Y
Grille beate. N (part of text)
Exit Grillus. L

I.3. 1.120 Crispinus conscendit fenestram Lepidi. ⌐
           Crispinus conscendit fenestram Lepidae.
                            C (1.121) T (1.121)

1.121 Tiberius e domo sua Decani. N (sp.n.) ⌐
           Tiberius e domo suo Decani. J (sp.n.)
           Tiberius e domo propria. D
           Tiberius e domo propria ingreditur cantans. P
           Tiberius ... propria. Ingreditur cantans ad
              cytharam Buon di Buon di, Madonna Modina etc. D[b]

1.121 Cantat ad cytharam. C Y (1.123) T⌐

1.169 ⌐ Aliquis pulsat fores. T

1.176 Cantus. Buon di, buon di, etc. D[c] (* Stava) ⌐
           Buondi, buondi - Cantus. P (part of text)
           Iterum cantat. CYT

1.177 Crispinum vidit a tergo ad fenestras. PD[b] ⌐
           Crispinum vidit à tergo ad fenestram. CYT
           Videt Chrispinum a tergo trementem et minatur
              sub dolus senes inspectoribus ut Chrispino
              metum incuperet. L

1.178 Confodit sedile pugione. CYT⌐

1.188 Lepidus e fenestra videt Crispinum. ⌐
           Lepida e fenestra videt Crispinum Y T (1.187)
           Lepida e fenestra vidit Crispinum C (1.187)
           He spies Crispinus in the window. D (1.189, deleted)
           Lepida e fenestra alloquitur. PD
           Lepida e fenestra. N L (sp.h.) T (sp.h.)
           e fenestra Lepida. J (sp.h., 1.184 deleted and
                               rewritten at 1.188)

1.188 Desilit Crispinus. PD[b]T (1.191)⌐

1.214 Pecunias offert Crispino. PD[b] ⌐
           Pecunias affert. T (1.212)

1.216 Exit Tiberius in aedes suas Decani. J ⌐
           Exit Tiberius in aedes suas. CDN
           Exit Tiberius. PL

I.4. 1.217   Lucretia et Faustulus e domo Synesii. DN⏋
          Lucretia Faustulus e domo Synesii. J

     1.220   She spies Horatius and nods to him to be gone.⏋
          She spies Horatio and nods to him to be gone. D^b

     1.224   Exeunt Horatius et Crispinus ad forum Baccalaureorum.
                                    NJ⏋
          Exeunt Crispinus et Horatius per forum
                               Bacchalaureorum.
          Exeunt Crispinus et Horatius. P
          Exeunt Horatius et Chrispinus. L

     1.432   Ostendit Faustulo gravidum uterum. T⏋
          Ostendit ventrem. PD^b
          Gravidam se narrat Faustulo. C (1.435)

     1.434   Synesius e fenestra. CYT⏌ (sp.h.) ⏋
          Synesius in domo. D

     1.436   Exit Faustulus in aedes Synesii. C Y (1.435)
                             D(insuper*) T⏋
          Faustulus in aedes Synesii. J
          Exit Faustulus. P

I.5. 1.437   Lysetta e domo Cassandri Baccalaureorum. N J (sp.h.)
          Lysetta e domo Cassandri. D

          ⏋ A payre of hangers. J (1.438)

     1.497   Exit Lucretia ad forum Decani. J⏋
          Exit Lucretia. L

     1.501   Lucretia steps back againe on the stage. J(sp.h.
                                 1.502) ⏋
          Lucretia steps back on the stage. L^b
          Lucretia steps back into the stage. C Y (1.502)
          Lucretia stepps back into into the stage. T(1.502)
          Lucretia steps back againe. D^b (1.502)

     1.502   Exit per forum Baccalaureorum. ⏋
          Exit per forum Bacchalaureorum. D
          Exit Lucretia. P
          Revertit Lucretia. CT

     1.502   Lysetta going towards Cassanders house returnes back
          at her call.⏋
          Lysetta going towards Cassanders house returnes
                     back at his call. L^b (*Lys.)

Lysetta goes out towards Cassanders house.
    shee returnes. C (1.503)
Lysetta goes out towardes Lysanders house,
    she returnes. Y (1.503)
Lysetta goes toward Cassanders house. Shee
    returnes. T (1.503)
Lysetta goes towards Cassanders house
    Baccalaureorum she returnes straight. J

I.6. 1.504 Lepidus e fenestra Tiberii Decani. N J (sp.h.) T_/
            Lepida e fenestra. CY
            Lepida e fenestra loquitur. D

    1.514 Descendit Lepidus e domo Tiberii Decani. N(1.517)
                                                J (1.515)_/
            Descendit Lepida e domo Tiberii. C (1.515) YT
            Lepidus descendit e domo Tiberii. P D (1.515)
                                                L (1.515)

       _/ A pockett with gold. J (1.519)

    1.523 Lepidus diffingit collare Lysettae. _/
            Lepida diffingit collare Lysettae. CT
            Lepidus diffundit collare. Y (1.520)

    1.532 Refingit denuo. C (1.530) T_/
            Refringit denuo. Y (1.529)

    1.540 Lepidus harkes in her eare. J_/

    1.585 Dat plures nummos. PD^b _/

    1.587 In aurem Lysettae insusurrat Lepidus._/
            In aurem Lysettae insusurrat Lepida. C(1.586) T
            In aurem Lysettae insurrat Lepida. Y(intus*)
            aurem Lysettae insuserat. D^b

    1.625 Vidit Lepidus patrem egredientem. P D^b (1.623)_/

    1.625 Exeunt Lepidus et Lysetta per forum Baccalaureorum._/
            Exeunt Lepida et Lysetta per forum
                                    Bacchalaureorum. D
            Exeunt ad forum Baccalaureorum. N
            ad forum Baccalaureorum superiorem. J

I.7. 1.626 Tiberius et puer e domo Tiberii. PD _/
            Tiberius e domo sua Decani regina Cypri. J (sp.h.)

1.626   Tiberius with a hawke. L⟋

1.626   Spaniels. J⟋

1.629   Alloquitur accipitrem pugno insedentem. CT⟋
         Alloquitur accipitrem pugno insidentem. Y

1.631   Columbam dat accipitri in cibum. CYT (1.632)⟋
         He gives him the pigeon. D
         he gives him a pigeon. L (1.633)
         The boy gives a pigeon. J (avem*)
         Reddit puero. P

1.659   Cassander e domo propria consulens horologium. PD^b ⟋
         ingreditur Cassander consulens horologium.
                                      C (1.658) T
         Intrat Cassander horologium consulens. Y
         Cassander e domo propria Baccalaureorum.
                                      N (1.658) J (sp.h.)
         Cassander e domo propria. D
         Cassander de domo propria. L(sp.h.)

         ⟋ A watch. J(1.661)

1.671   Ostendit ei Cassandrum. PD^b ⟋

1.672   Cantat et ingredientem revocat Cassander. PD^b ⟋
         Ingredientem revocat Cassander. CYT

I.8. 1.675   Exit puer in aedes Tiberii. PD (bene*)⟋

1.718   Intrat puer cum cyatho vini quem domino porrigit.
                             C (1.719) T (1.720)⟋
         Intrat puer cyatho vini quem porrigit
                             domino. Y (1.717-19)
         Intrat puer cum vino. N (1.718) J (1.719 minus*)
         Puer cum vino. L (1.719 *hem)
         Puer vinum ministrat. P
         The boy gives him a boule of wine. D (1.719
                                               minus*)

1.719   Propinat Cassandro ille recusat. P⟋
         propinat Cassandro, ille vero recusat. D^b

1.721   Tiberius bibit C (1.719) Y (1.722) T⟋

1.732   Exit puer. PD^b (pipere*)⟋

1.759   Exit Cassander in aedes suas. PDN (1.757)
                             J (1.759 *Cass.) $\rceil$
      Exit in aedes suas. CYT (1.754)
      Cassander exit. L (1.758)

1.764   Lepidus, Lydia et Lysetta e foro Baccalaureorum
            .superiore. J (1.765 *Atque) $\rceil$
      Lepida, Lydia, Lysetta e foro Bacchalaureorum. D
      Led. Lydia Lysetta a foro Baccalaureorum. N (1.765
      Enter Lydia; Lepida; et Lysetta a foro. CT
      Intrant Lydia, Lysetta, Lepida a foro. Y (1.765)

      Lepidus osculans Lydiam. $\rceil$
        Intrat hic Lepida osculans Lydiam. P_b
        Inerat hic Lepida osculans Lydiam. D^b

1.778   Exit Tiberius ad suam domum Decani. J $\rceil$
      Exit Tiberius in aedes suas. P
      Exit Tiberius in aedes proprias. D
      Exit. L^b

I.9. 1.859   Osculatur Lydiam. CYT (1.860) $\rceil$
      Osculatur eam. P_b
      He kisses her. D^b

1.864   Exit Lydia in aedes Cassandri Baccalaureorum. $J^b \rceil$
      Exit Lepidus in aedes Cassandri
                        Baccalaureorum. J
      Exit Lydia in aedes Cassandri. D (1.863)
      Exit Lydia. L

I.10. 1.890 Dat pecunias. $PD^b \rceil$

1.893   Exit Lysetta in Cassandri aedes Baccalaureorum. NJ $\rceil$
      Exit aedes Cassandri. D
      Exit Lysetta. PL
      Exit. CYT

1.895   Exit Lepidus in Tiberii aedes Decani. J $\rceil$
      Exit Lepida in aedes Tiberii. D
      Exit Lepidus. P
      Exit. CYT

II.1. 1.1   Horatius a foro Baccalaureorum, Lucretia a foro
                   Decani simul. J $\rceil$
      Horatius e foro Bacchalaureorum, Lucretius e
           foro Decani. CD

Horatius a foro Baccalaureorum. Lucretia
a foro Baccalaureorum simul. N

1.11   She sighes. D $\rfloor$
       Lucretia sighes. J
       Suspirat. CYT

1.17   She sighes. D (est*) $\rfloor$
       He sighes againe. J (1.16)
       Suspirat iterum. C (est*) YT (est*)

1.18   She sighes. D (dies*) $\rfloor$

1.19   She sighes. D (hercle*) $\rfloor$
       Lucretia sighes. J
       Suspirat iterum. CY (1.21) T

1.86   Exit Lucretia maesta et plangens ad forum Decani. $\rfloor$
       Exit Lucretius maestus et plangens ad forum
                                    Decani. D^b
       Exit Lucretius maestus et plangens. PT^a
       Exit Lucretius ad forum Decani. D (ha*) J (1.87)

II.2. 1.96   Crispinus a foro Baccalaureorum cum armillis. J $\rfloor$
       Crispinus a foro Decani. D

1.186 Exeunt Horatius et Crispinus in aedes Cassandri
                             Baccalaureorum. J $\rfloor$
       Exit Horatius et Crispinus in aedes Cassandri
                             Baccalaureorum. N
       Exeunt in aedes Cassandri. D
       Exeunt. P

II.3. 1.187 Omnes a foro Baccalaureorum $\rfloor$
       Omnes a foro Bacchalaureorum. D
       Don. Grillus a foro Baccalaureorum. NJ

1.221 Citharaedus canit ad citharam stava la gentil
                             dama etc. D^b $\rfloor$
       Citharaedus canit ad citharum stava la gentil
                                    dama. P
       Citharaedus canit citharae. C
       Cytharaedus canit cytharae. Y

1.225 Cytharaedus. Don et Grillus cantant. N $\rfloor$
       Fidler Don and Grillus all singe. J
       They all singe. D (deleted)

1.243   Exit Citharaedus ad forum Decani. NJ $\rfloor$
      Exit in forum Decani. D
      Exit. P

    $\rfloor$ A capons leg. J (1.247)

1.253   Grillus furtim femur caponis edit. P $\rfloor$
      Depascit crus gallinaceum Grillus. CT (1.254)
      Grillus depascit crux gallinaceum. Y
      Grillus is eating a capons. legg. D

II.4. 1.276 Tiberius ex aedibus propriis. D $\rfloor$

1.276   Tiberius in genua. P $\rfloor$
      Tiberius falls on his knees. D (Oh.*)
      Tiberius genu flectit. CYT } (sp.h.)

1.342   Exit Tiberius in aedes proprias. D $\rfloor$
      Exit Tiberius. P

1.348   Don et Grillus exeunt ad forum Baccalaureorum. NJ $\rfloor$
      Exeunt in forum Decani. D (mihi*)
      Exeunt. P

II.5. 1.349 Horatius e domo Cassandri. Lucretia e foro Decani. $\rfloor$
      Horatius e domo Cassandri. Lucretius e foro
                    Decani. D
      Horatius a Cassandro Baccalaureorum. Lucretia
           a foro Decani. J

1.381   Lepidus singes within. $\rfloor$
      Lepida singes within. D^{b}N (1.379) J
      Lepida intus cantat. CYT

II.6. 1.387 Lepidus e fenestra Tiberii Decani. J (sp.h.) $\rfloor$
      Lepida e fenestra Tiberii. D
      Lepida e fenestra. N

1.400   Lysetta starchinge a ruff at the window Cassandri
               Baccalaureorum. J $\rfloor$
      Lysetta starching a cuf out of the window.
                            N (1.397)
      Lysetta e fenestra Cassandri starching a
               bande. D^b (1.396)
      Lysetta e fenestra Cassandri. D (1.399 Lysetta*)
      Lysetta e fenestra starching. CY (1.399 Lydia*)
      Lysetta in fenestra starchinge. T (1.399)

1.455   Horatius incedit Synesii domum Decani. J (1.456) $\rfloor$
        Horatius incedit in Synesii domum Decani.
                                     N (1.452)
        Horatius incedit domum. D^b
        Exit Horatius. PT

1.455   Lysetta, Lydia at the window. C (amicitiam*) $\rfloor$
        Lysetta et Lydia at the window. T (1.457)
        Lydia Lysetta at the window. NJ (1.457)
        Lysetta Lydia ad fenestram. Y (1.456)
        Lysetta Lidia in fenestra. D (1.456)

1.496   Descendit Lepidus e fenestra in interiores
                aedes Tiberii. D^b (Vale*) $\rfloor$

1.501   Descendunt Lydia et Lysetta e fenestra Cassandri. PD
        They shutt their windowes. J

II.7. 1.502   Horatius ex aedibus Synesii Decani. J $\rfloor$

1.553   Lucretia exit in aedes Synesii Decani. J $\rfloor$
        Exit Lucretia in aedes Synesii. PD
        Exit Lucretia. CT
        Exit Lucretius. Y

II.8. 1.561   Nutrix Horatium alloquitur e fenestra ex
                      aedibus Synesii. D $\rfloor$
        Nutrix e fenestra Synesii. NJ (sp.h.)
        E fenestra. CT

1.564   Lucretia e fenestra eadem. D (1.563) $\rfloor$
        Lucretia e fenestra. T (1.565)
        Lepida e fenestra. Y (1.562)
        Lucretia ad fenestram. NJ (1.565 Vita mea*)

1.596   E fenestra. CT $\rfloor$

1.599   Lucretia ac nutrix abscedunt a fenestra.
                    D (Venio*) $\rfloor$
        Lucretia et nutrix abscedunt e fenestra. J (1.600

II.9. 1.601   Crispinus a foro Decani. D $\rfloor$
        Crispinus e foro Decani. J (sp.h.)

II.10. 1.614 Don, Grillus a foro Decani. J $\rfloor$
        Don Grillus e foro Decani. D

1.645 Exeunt Horatius et Crispinus in aedes Cassandri.
                                    D (Decimam*) ⨼
       Exeunt Horatius et Crispinus. P
       Horatius Crispinus ad forum Baccalaureorum.
                        N (1.647) J (1.647)

1.647 Exeunt Don et Grillus in forum Decani. D ⨼
       Don Grillus ad forum Decani. NJ
       Exeunt Don et Grillus. P

III.1. 1.1 Horatius et Crispinus e domo Cassandri. D ⨼
            Horatius Crispinus a foro Baccalaureorum. J

III.2. 1.19 Don et Grillus e foro Decani. D ⨼
             Don. Grillus a foro Decani. J

III.4. 1.92 Nutrix e domo Synesii. CYᴺJT (sp.h.) ⨼
             Nutrix e fenestra Synesii. D

1.99 Lucretia e fenestra Synesii Decani. J ⨼
      Lucretia ex eadem fenestra. D (probe*)
      Lucretia in Lepidas apparel playe out of the
                        windowe. J (1.100·Luc.*)

1.112 Horatius et nutrix ingrediuntur domum Synesii. J ⨼
       Exit Horatius in domum Synesii. D (1.114)
       Exit Horatius. P (1.115)

III.6. 1.123 Lepidus e domo Tiberii Decani ⨼
             Lepidus e domo Tiberii Decani habitu Lucretiae. J
             Lepidus sub habitu Lucretiae ex Tiberii
                                        aedibus. D

1.155 Don Grillus ad forum Decani. J (1.152) ⨼
       Don et Grillus ad forum Baccalaureorum. N
       Exeunt in forum Decani. D (1.157)
       Exeunt. P

III.7. 1.162 Lysetta et Lydia e fenestra loquuntur ex domo
                                    Cassandri. D ⨼
             Lysetta et Lydia e fenestra. P
             Lysetta Lydia e fenestra. J (1.163)
             Lysetta Lepidus e fenestra. N

1.217 Lydia comes downe on the stage. N(1.218)J(1.218 *Hem)
        Lydia on the stage. D^b
        Lydia descendit e domo Cassandri. P (1.214)
                                   D (1.214)

1.226 Lepidus carryes Lydia into Cassanders house
                   Baccalaureorum. J⟋
        Lepidus carieth Lydia away in domum Cassandri
                 Baccalaureorum. N (1.223)
        Lepidus cum Lydia ingrediuntur in aedes
                        Cassandri. PD
        Ingrediuntur. CYT^a

III.8. 1.233 Tiberius puer a domo Tiberii Decani. J⟋
           Tiberius Puer e domo Tiberii. N
           Tiberius et puer ex aedibus Tiberii. D

1.238 Exit puer in aedes Tiberii. D (intro*) ⟋
        Exit Puer. P

III.9. 1.244 Horatius e domo Synesii Decani. J⟋
           Horatius e domo Synaesii Decani. N
           Horatius e domo Synesii. D

III.10 1.258 Lucretia e fenestra Synesii mox descendit ad
                       ostium. D⟋
           Horatius Lucretia e domo Synesii Decani. J
           Lucretia e fenestra. J (sp.h.)

1.258 Horatius draws her out at the doore. J⟋

1.274 Exeunt Horatius et Crispinus in aedes Cassandri.
            Lucretia in aedes Synesii. P D (est*) ⟋
        Horatius Crispinus Cassandri Baccalaureorum.
                           J (1.276)
        Lucretia Synesii domum Decani. J (1.278)

III.11 1.279 Lysetta et Lepidus in fenestra Cassandri. D⟋

1.280 Lepidus desilit e fenestra. D (*O bene)⟋

1.350 Exeunt in aedes Tiberii. D⟋
        Exeunt. P

IV.1. 1.1   Horatius ex aedibus Cassandri Baccalaureorum. NJ^b⟋
           Horatius aedibus Cassandri Baccalaureorum. J
           Horatius ex aedibus Cassandri. D

1.8   Tiberius ex aedibus suis Decani.   J (sp.h.) _/
             Tiberius ex aedibus propriis.   D

1.40   Don Grillus a foro Decani.   N (1.43) _/
             Don Gryllus a foro Decani.   J (1.43)
             Don e foro Decani cum Grillo.   D (*Atque)

IV.2. 1.57   Don et Grillus exeunt per forum Decani.   D _/
             Don Gryllus ad forum Decani.   J
             Exeunt Don et Grillus.   P (1.58)

IV.3. 1.60   Nutrix e domo Synesii Decani.   J _/
             Nutrix e domo Synesii.   DN

1.95   Exit in aedes Synesii.   D _/
             Nutrix ad aedeis Synesii Decani.   J
             Exit.   P

IV.4. 1.97   Lepidus e domo Tiberii Decani.   J _/
             Lepida ex aedibus Tiberii.   D

1.140   Horatius Lepidus in aedes Tiberii Decani.   J (1.139)
             Lepidus Horatius in aedes Tiberii.   N (1.138)
             Exeunt in aedes Tiberii.   PD (Fiet*)

1.146   Horatius ex aedibus Tiberii Decani.   J(*At) _/
             Aegreditur Horatius.   D (Lepida*)

1.150   Tiberius in domum suam Decani.   J (1.151) _/
             Exit Tiberius in aedes suas.   P D (vale*)

1.173   Horatius exit in domum Cassandri Baccalaureorum.   J _/
             Exit in domum Cassandri Baccalaureorum.   CT
             Exit in domum Cassandri.   Y
             Exit in aedes Cassandri.   PD

IV.6. 1.174   Nutrix Lucretia a domo Synesii Decani.   J _/
             Nutrix et Lucretia ex aedibus Synesii.   D

1.220   Nutrix exit in domum Synesii.   J _/
             Exit in aedes Synesii.   PD

IV.7. 1.221   Lydia e domo Cassandri Baccalaureorum.   J _/
             Lydia ex aedibus Cassandri.   D

1.263   Exit in domum Cassandri Baccalaureorum.   N(1.262) _/
             Lydia in domum Cassandri Baccalaureorum.   J (1.266)
             Exit Lydia in aedes Cassandri.   D (mihi*)
             Exit.   P

IV.8. 1.267   Horatius ex aedibus Cassandri Baccalaureorum. J ⌐
          Horatius ex aedibus Cassandri. D

     1.328   Crispinus ex aedibus Cassandri Baccalaureorum ⌐
          Chrispinus ex aedibus Cassandri Baccalaureorum.
                                     J (1.320)
          Crispinus ex aedibus Cassandri. PD (vivam*)

IV.9. 1.360   Lydia ex aedibus Cassandri. D ⌐

     1.388   Lydia exit in domum Cassandri Baccalaureorum. NJ ⌐
          Exit Lidia in aedes Cassandri. D
          Exit Lydia. P

     1.400   Exit Lucretia in forum Decani. ⌐
          Exit Lucretius in forum Decani. D
          Lucretia ad forum Decani. N (1.398) J
          Exit Lucretius. P

     1.423   Exit Crispinus in aedes Cassandri. Horatius in
               forum Decani. D ⌐
          Crispinus in aedes Cassandri. Horatius ad
               forum Decani. N (1.422) J
          Exeunt. P

V.1. 1.1   Synesius, nutrix, Faustulus e domo Synesii
                              Decani. J ⌐
          Synesius, nutrix et Faustule ex aedibus
                            Synesii. D
          Faustulus a domo Synesii. N

     1.20   Faustulus exit in aedes Synesii petitum scipionem.
                         PD (obsecro*) ⌐
          Faustulus fetcheth a Synesii domo. N (1.19)
          Faustulus fetcheth a staffe a Synesii domo.
                              N^b (1.19)
          Faustulus fetcheth a staff a Synesii domo
                          Decani. J

     1.22   Faustulus regreditur. PD (1.24) ⌐
          Faustulus with a staffe. J (1.25)

     1.40   Cassander et puer ex aedibus Cassandri. D (1.39) ⌐
          Cassander e domo sua Baccalaureorum. J (1.45)

1.44   Exeunt nutrix, Faustulus in domum Synesii
                                    Decani. J (1.41)
        Exeunt nutrix et Faustulus in domum Synesii.
                                        PD (1.41)
        Exeunt. D (siet*)

V.2. 1.107   Synesius in forum Decani. J 7
             Exit ad forum Decani. N (1.106)
             Exit Synesius ad forum Bacchalaureorum. D (Vale*)
             Exit Synesius. P

V.3. 1.108   Horatius a foro Decani. DJ 7

     1.174   Cassander exit ad forum Baccalaureorum. N 7
             Exit Cassander per forum Bacchalaureorum.
                                        D (eamus*)
             Cassander exit ad forum Decani. J
             Exit. P

V.4. 1.178   Lucretia a foro Decani. D (1.179) 7
             Lucretia e foro Decani. J (1.179)

     1.260   Horatius Lucretia in aedes Cassandri
                                   Baccalaureorum. J 7
             Exeunt in aedes Cassandri. CYT
             Exeunt in Cassandri aedes. D
             Exeunt. P

V.5. 1.261   Tiberius e domo sua Decani. J 7
             Tiberius ex propriis aedibus. D

     1.272   Cassander a foro Baccalaureorum 7
             Cassander a foro Bacchalaureorum. D (1.273)
                                             J (1.273)

     1.367   Exit Tiberius in aedes proprias. D (lyra*) 7
             Tiberius exit in aedes proprias. CT
             Exit. P

V.6. 1.368   Crispinus ex aedibus Cassandri. D 7

     1.387   Exit Cassander in aedes proprias. D (macerat*) 7
             Cassander exit in aedes Decani. J
             Exit. P

V.7. 1.389   Synesius e foro Decani. D_/
                Synesius a foro Decani. J

     1.414   Synesius in aedes Cassandri Baccalaureorum. J_/
                Exit Synesius in aedes Cassandri. PD

V.8. 1.415   Grillus e foro Decani. PD_/

Changes in Punctuation

Act 1.

Line Number	This Edition	Base Text
24	Herculem	Herculem,
52	abstines	abstines;
53	oportet magis,	oportet, magis
137	(hah), rem	(hah) Rem
176	ceperit. Stava	ceperit (Stava
231	nuptiis.	nuptiis,
336	denique.	denique
410	tuli	tuli,
499	faciam.	faciam,
525	exemplum	exemplum.
598	caverem.	caverem
627	crocitant.	crocitant
659	diu gravidam?	diu? Gravidam?
660	praedam.	praedam
661	erat,	erat.
672	Cancro.	Cancro?
696	potus.	potus

Act 2.

Line Number	This Edition	Base Text
42	tuo,	tuo;
73	tibi?	tibi.
119	abest	abest.

135	credas?	credas.
152	periurii huiusmodi,	periurii, huiusmodi
205	iam,	iam
	me.	me
234	Pacheco	Pacheco,
	vestra.	vestra
328	arbitratu.	arbitratu
459	dare.	dare
503	vitae,	vita!
513	sim	sim;

Act. 3.

13	hoc est,	hoc, et
26	nominare.	nominare
62	appetitus	appetitum,
74	naribus,	naribus
85	mi	mi,
108	ardet	ardet,
179	amor.	amor,
214	Lyd. Certe?	Lyd. Certe
225	perperam.	perperam
232	spectate	spectatum,
246	hercle,	hercle
291	Hei.	Hei
333	iniquum est,	iniquum est

Act. 4.

15	vim	vim,
18	tempus	tempus.
19	Tiberius,	Tiberius
64	testimonium,	testimonium
141	Lepidae;	Lepidae,
157	certe:	certe,
179	specula.	specula,
182	illa	illam,
224	ubi ubi	ubi, ubi
349	mellitis	mellitis;
422	pugnare	pugnare --
423	invenero.	invenero?

Act. 5.

80	Syn. Foeminam.	Syn. Foeminam?
122	indignum	indignum,
144	obsecro, mi	obsecro te,
224	ignorantia	ignorantia,
230	posterum,	posterum.
310	Atque qui	At, qui
346	Lepidae	Lepidae,
355	illum	illum!

TEXTUAL NOTES

Dramatis Personae	**Baccalaureorum** The abbreviation has been expanded according to the spelling in the texts of <u>Leander</u>, as the full form is not found in the manuscripts of <u>Labyrinthus</u>.

Act I.

58   **herus tibi**   The base text has been followed here as there are no criteria by which to determine originality, the readings of both groupings, CYT and PDNLJ, being equally appropriate, and neither likely to have been derived from the other. Such evidence supports the theory that there may be two authorial versions, see Editorial Introduction pp 227-8. For similar instances in Act I see ll. 165, 173, 214, 231, 302, 336, 466, 469, 652, 743.   See also II,10; III,26; IV,55; V,49, below.

70   **Hypocrassum**   The name is spelt with a <u>y</u> in all texts of <u>Labyrinthus</u> but with an <u>i</u> in the cast lists of <u>Leander</u>, including those MSS which contain both plays.

121   <u>Stava la gentil dama, buon di, buon di; Madonna Modina</u> There is some confusion as to the song which Tiberius sings here.   The texts are divided into their typical groupings in a way which suggests that a choice of songs may have been given originally: CYT support <u>Madonna Modina</u>,

NLJ _Stava la gentil dama_, and PD reproduces both with the
addition of _buon di, buon di_. Compare I,176 where the
stage direction in D seems to divide the song into two:
Stava la gentil dama. _Cantus_. _Buon di, buon di_ etc.
In the absence of evidence for the existence of any
Italian songs which begin with these words, it seems best
to adopt the collective reading of PD.

Modina   Modena is used in modern Italian for an inhabitant
of the town of the same name, but there is no such
adjective as _modina_. This form may have stemmed from a
confusion between Modena and the latin name Mutina,
although it is not found elsewhere in contemporary
literature.

163   _permanesceret_   The adopted reading is supported by only a
single manuscript, and that generally unreliable. However
a simple misreading of _sc_ as _ss_ produces the majority
reading _permanasseret_, a hybrid form of the pluperfect
and imperfect subjunctive of _permanare_.

169   _crepuerunt fores_   The minority reading has been adopted here
In Roman comedy the formula of the creaking door is spoken
by a character on stage (c.f. Plautus, _Amphitruo_ 496;
Aulularia 665). It seems likely that the phrase was
understood to be a stage direction and removed to the
margin as in T, or omitted altogether as in CYNLJ.

177   **praehenderem**   Manuscript support is equally divided between the two tenses of the subjunctive. Reference to Hawkesworth's style elsewhere shows that he often uses an imperfect subjunctive with a future sense, rather than an orthodox conditional construction.

298   **commodam**   It is uncertain whether Lucretia speaks of herself as male or female. As she has already revealed her secret to Faustulus by this time, there is little sense in continuing the deceit. It becomes clear later in the play that Lucretia has no doubts about her gender, c.f. II.59.

321-2   There is no obvious reason for the omission of these lines in the majority of MSS. Stylistically and dramatically however these lines in PD^b are satisfactory and have therefore been adopted.

331   **prohibessit**   The conjectured reading accounts for the forms of the unknown verb _prohibesco_ by a misreading of ss as sc (c.f. I,163 above). It is also the _lectio difficilior_: "prohibessis pro prohibueris antique" (Cooper, _Thesaurus_) c.f. Plautus, _Pseudolus_ 13-4 "Id te Iuppiter/Prohibessit".

340   **amoris venis**   This conjecture accounts for the reading of PDNLJ by an error of word division. The reading of CYT appears to be the result of an attempt to make sense of

amor invenis by simplification, in the substitution of
the verb to be.

342   mediam per parietem   The minority reading of PD^b is
likely to be an interpolation by a scribe, who knew
Hawkesworth's earlier play, Leander, in which the lovers
meet this way (II.1), or who remembered what was to come
in Labyrinthus (I,375). That Horatius saw Lepida through
an adjoining wall is, of course, impossible as a passage
was never constructed except in Lucretia's lies.

364   e Neapoli   The ablative of names of towns and small
islands is used without a preposition. None of the
alternative readings is grammatically correct.

398   pudentiae   This reading is most likely to be authoritative
because of majority manuscript support, although it is a
rare and non-classical word, not found in Cooper's
Thesaurus.

418   perceperam   Licet should be followed by the subjunctive
as in T (perceperim), but all manuscript evidence supports
the indicative, as T is changed to a less correct reading.

437   Signior Lucretio   According to the O.E.D. the title was
spelled signor, signior, signiour, signier, as the variant
readings of the MSS reflect. I have adopted the spelling
Signior as the form most frequently employed by editors of

sixteenth and seventeenth century texts. It appears from
instances elsewhere in the play (II,276; V,45, 330) that
Hawkesworth generally used the Italian form of the name
with Signior, the Latin form when the name is used alone.
I have standardized the readings in such cases.

456   possit   Quando in this case should take an indicative,
as the clause represents Lucretia's own opinion not an
hypothesis. The majority of the MSS however have a
subjunctive (a more difficult reading), the present tense
being best supported and most suitable in the context.

476   resiste   The adopted reading is supported by only a single
manuscript, and that generally unreliable, but its use is
supported by Roman comedy, compare Terence, Andria 344.
The synonym resta makes good sense but does not explain
the more difficult reading of PDLJ restiti.

496   Quin etiamdum   There is confusion among the variants between
quinetiam (not spelled as one word in classical Latin)
(c.f. I,494) and etiamdum.

563   vivit   The reading of the base text has been adopted as
both variant readings are grammatically incorrect. In
an ideal condition both verbs should be subjunctive and,
generally, in the present tense.

589   <u>iudicaram</u>   Hawkesworth normally uses the subjunctive in such emphatic wishes (c.f. I,546-7), but this contracted form of the pluperfect indicative is the more difficult reading and also has majority support.

608   <u>creveram</u>   The perfect indicative and not the pluperfect is generally used in a temperal clause introduced by <u>ut</u>, if a single act in the past is referred to. The pluperfect is used to express the repeated occurrence of the act. The imperfect supported by CYT makes the construction into a final clause, but although grammatically unorthodox, the adopted reading makes clear sense: 'when I had grown up."

617   <u>amplectar</u>   There is no such form as <u>amplecter</u>, although it is the majority reading. It presumably stems from a confusion of first conjugation <u>amplexor</u> with third conjugation <u>amplector</u>, and misreading of <u>a</u> as <u>e</u>.

623   <u>curassis</u>   A Plautine form of the perfect subjunctive (c.f. <u>Mostellaria</u> 526) and therefore a more difficult reading even than the abbreviated form of the pluperfect subjunctive. It also provides a parallel to <u>fueris</u>.

628   <u>Canace</u>   Most readings preserve the sound if not the correct spelling of the dog's name, taken from Ovid's <u>Metamorphoses</u>.

663   **adibo**   The reading of CYT is so easy that it is unlikely to be original, there being no reason why it should have been corrupted into the unsatisfactory variants of the other texts. In the context, however, it makes perfect sense and has therefore been adopted.

732   **chelidonia**   The adopted reading is supported only by J but is the correct biological name for the ingredient in question.

749   **condormierint**   *Difficilior lectio* which may easily have given rise to the majority reading by a confusion of minims, and to the reading of NL by transposition.

755-7   The misplacement of these lines in CYT cannot be explained by the physical features of the texts as they now stand, and presumably occurred at an earlier stage of the tradition. The variant may have arisen as a result of haplography, the scribe's eyes jumping from one of Tiberius' speeches to the next. The omission may have been subsequently noticed and the missing lines added at the bottom of the page with a mark to call them back to their proper place. If the next scribe failed to see the mark he would copy out the verses as they stood. Alternatively this variant may be due to scribal emendation, confusion stemming from the word **natum**, which may have been taken to

refer to Lepidus, and the speech moved accordingly. In
fact the words obviously refer to Cassander, whose
indignation has had Tiberius roaring with laughter
for half a scene.

875   Regina   The rejected reading here is the more difficult
reading, but compare the passage in Plautus' Cistellaria,
from which Hawkesworth took these lines. See Commentary.

Act II.

10   hercle   The base text has been followed here as there
are no criteria by which to determine originality. For
similar instances in Act II see ll. 46, 171, 173, 391.

36   illum quem   The adopted reading is not only the more
difficult, as Lucretia in her male persona would naturally
speak of her lover as female, but is supported by the
majority of texts. Hawkesworth may mean Lucretia to err
subconsciously here (c.f. II,59), but it is strange that
she does not correct herself, nor does Horatius comment
on the incongruity.

41   me   The minority reading of L^a is grammatically correct
as contingat should take an indirect object in the dative.
However the overwhelming support for me makes it likely
that Hawkesworth here used an accusative and infinitive
construction in error.

50   inter   The only criterion to determine originality here is that of difficilior lectio, as one reading has not obviously arisen from the other. The adopted reading is most likely to be authoritative as it involves the use of the sophisticated stylistic device of tmesis, whereas the reading of CYT probably represents an attempt to make sense of the scribal interpretation of inter as a preposition without an object.

72   ipse ut   Grammatically ut is redundant but the majority reading is adopted here, as the addition of a word is unlikely to have occurred independently in so many MSS.

87   resiste   c.f. I.476 above. The reading of PDLJ probably results from transposition.

174   suspicarier technas   The unusual archaic form of the passive infinitive of CYT is adopted together with the more difficult word order of PDNLJ.

187   villiaco   The word is found spelled both villiaco and villaco in P, DNLJ have villaco fairly consistently, and CYT always have villiaco. The latter form has been adopted throughout because of its similarity to the Italian vigliacco, although it was also spelled villacco (see John Florio's Queen Anna's New World of Words (1611) s.v. villacco).

190 <u>mondo</u> The rejected reading is the easier because it is a Latin form. However John Minsheu points out in his <u>Dictionarie in Spanish and English</u> (1623) that the Spaniards often use one letter for another, and among examples gives "o and u, as Mochacho, Muchacho, a boy, a lad" (A6v).

234 <u>buon giorno</u> <u>Buon</u> is a conjecture which accounts for the readings of NJ and L by simple misreading of letters. The unexpectedness of finding an Italian phrase mixed with Spanish probably accounts for the omission in CYT. The reading of PD seems to represent a separate version altogether but has been rejected here as a slightly easier reading because of its similarity to Latin.

238 <u>respexis</u> Archaic form of the perfect subjunctive and therefore the more difficult reading.

290 <u>E iuro</u> The reading of PDY is rejected here as the Latin <u>eiuro</u> is obviously the easier reading. The reading of CT represents the two word form supported by all the other texts, and makes sense in context. However <u>e</u> is Italian rather than Spanish and <u>iuro</u> is not found in either languag

339 <u>non? Don? Sane</u> The minority reading of L accounts for the other variants. PNJ omit <u>Don</u> as a result of haplography. D confuses the vocative with the speech heading for Don Piedro, but the following speech which is

patently Tiberius' in style and content shows this to be an error. CYT also read <u>Don</u> as a speech heading but carry corruption one step further by adding a speech heading for Tiberius before <u>egregius</u> to avoid incongruity.

405   <u>illum</u>   All the texts are obviously wrong here. "Lepida" is about to go up to "Lucretius", who, as far as he knows, is a man. The confusion in the texts is natural in the convoluted plot, especially as a feminine pronoun <u>hanc</u> is found in the previous line. The error must stem from the archetype but the absence of scribal emendation is unusual.

466   <u>quaecunque</u>   Again a question of Lucretia's gender. The minority reading is adopted here as it supports an ironic construction of Lucretia's words: no woman would be successful in wooing Lucretia, because she is a woman herself. Presumably the reading of the groupings NJ and CYT occurred as a result of convergent variation.

<u>amet</u>   The indefinite relative normally introduces a clause whose verb is indicative. The subjunctive is the more difficult reading here and fits into the context. "Lucretius" does not know whom "Lepida" is talking about and expresses the opinion that, whoever it is who <u>may</u> love him (according to Lepida), is doing so in vain.

490   adferres   The majority reading is incorrect in sequence after the primary rogandus es. It is more likely however that J has been emended to correctly read adferas, than that the seven other texts erred independently.

540   occisam   All texts are incorrect here, as a supine is necessary after both iri, to represent the future passive infinitive, and ire, to express the purpose of the motion. The word is obviously meant to agree with the feminine subject of the sentence, Lucretia. The incorrect reading is retained because the majority support of the texts make it likely that this is an authorial error.

548   abrepat   The majority reading but not a recognized Latin word. It is probably based on abripio, to carry off and obrepo, to take by surprise.

631   apertissimamente   A conjecture which accounts for the odd use of the adjective apertissima with mente found in all texts. It is a pseudo-Spanish adverb formed from the Latin aperte by adding mente to the feminine of the superlative, c.f. John Minsheu, A Spanish Grammar (1623) on Adverbs "whereof some in the Spanish tongue are formed of Nownes of the feminine gender in a, as are almost all the Adverbs of Qualitie, as Alta, high; Altamente highly" (S s iv).

635   <u>coragio</u>. The adopted reading accounts for the latinized readings of P and CYT, and for the emendation of NLJ to make the word fit into the context, where it seems to be used as an adjective. It is also nearest the Spanish <u>corage</u> or <u>corajo</u>, courage.

Act III.

26   <u>hercle est</u> The base text has been followed here as there are no criteria by which to determine originality. For similar instances in Act III see ll. 74, 84, 105, 137, 147, 200, 214, 258, 271.

31   <u>Hisios del</u> The adopted reading seems to be a corruption of <u>hijos del</u>. The reading of CYT is accounted for by confusion of <u>ca</u> with <u>io</u>. See Commentary for further discussion.

38   <u>pransus fuero</u> The verb after <u>perinde ac</u> should be subjunctive because the comparison is something imaginary, and the tense is usually determined by the rule for normal sequence. The minority reading of C is most correct, but has been subsequently changed and <u>fuero</u> is, therefore, the best reading available.

Act III.   Scene 3.   Generally a new scene is begun with the entry or exit of a character. A new scene is technically unnecessary here, as all the characters that take part are already on stage in III.2. N omits the scene division but the majority reading is adopted here. Perhaps the distinction is that Horatius and Crispinus have hidden themselves and do not participate in the action on stage until l. 80. C.f. I.7. and 8., in which Cassander enters twelve lines before the end of Scene 7, the scene changing when he addresses the other characters.

91   whew whew   The majority of texts support a repetition of the whistle and this has been adapted to the spelling of the base text. The minority reading of L seems to have come directly from La Cintia (D11r), where the same formula for the whistle is used, but it must be rejected unless convergent variation is assumed in all the other texts.

104   pertinget   Although the minority reading is grammatically more correct, as the verb of both protasis and apodosis is generally present subjunctive in an ideal condition, the reading of the majority is adopted, the future indicative representing colloquial usuage.

150   **ast**   Although a minority reading, the archaic spelling of _at_ is the more difficult.

158   **annon**   The rejected reading is that normally used in a question expecting an affirmative answer, but for Hawkesworth' unorthodox usage of interrogative particles see section on style and language p.143 . c.f. also III,45.

195   **nisi ne**   The adopted reading presents an unusual grammatical construction, perhaps a colloquialism: **nisi ut** + negative. The reading of CYT is easier, makes less sense, and was probably produced by the proximity of **me** after **velint**.

279   **desaltus**   Neither this word or the alternative reading **desultus** are normally used as nouns, the latter being the past participle of **desilio**. **Desaltus**, however, is supported by the generally reliable MS J as well as by the grouping CYT, and presumably is based on **saltus**, a leap.

306   **hoc noctis**   A minority reading supported by normally unreliable texts (YN), but c.f. Plautus, **Amphitruo** 154.

Act IV.

55   **tuam filiam**   The base text has been followed here as there are no criteria by which to determine originality. For similar instances in Act IV see ll. 103, 157, 363, 415.

79-83 There are no criteria to determine originality here. The variant readings do not seem to stem from scribal errors, and are well-integrated into the text. The reading of PDNLJ seems superior dramatically as the nurse's delaying tactics increase suspense, and it is slightly more "difficult" as there are several changes of speaker and an extra speech by the nurse included.

108 **ne** A minority reading supported by only one MS, and that normally unreliable, is grammatically more correct. When a subjunctive prohibition follows another prohibition **neve** should be used rather than **nec**. For a similar case c.f. V,177 where **neve** has been corrupted to **neque** in PDN.

124 **teipsam** A minority reading but obviously correct. Horatius addresses "Lepida" supposing him to be a woman. c.f. II,405 for a similar confusion of gender.

157 **Num** **Num** in a question expects a negative answer, but the answer here is affirmative, qualified by **aliquando**. Nevertheless the majority reading **Numquid** is rejected because it is probably affected by the occurrence of the word four times in the preceding two lines.

195 **rescivit** The rejected reading **rescibit** obviously arises from a misreading of v as b. Grammatically the verb should be in the future perfect as it refers to an action which,

although genuinely future, is also prior to the action
of the main verb.

Act V.

29   <u>Illa</u> All the texts read <u>Illam</u> here, as if Hawkesworth
were using an accusative and infinitive construction in
<u>oratio obliqua</u> instead of the historic infinitive more
suited to the nurse's description of a series of actions.
The grouping PDNLJ is consistent in error, while CYT change
the construction in mid-course with <u>insana</u> (1.31) and
<u>minata est</u> (1.32).

49   <u>fecit insigniter</u> The base text has been followed here
as there are no criteria by which to determine originality.
For similar instances in Act V see 11. 51, 85, 166, 358.

106-7   There are no external criteria for determining originality
here. The speech divisions in CYT are supported by slight
changes in the text, e.g. <u>propera</u> for <u>propero</u>, but the
arrangement of speeches in PDNLJ seems better dramatically,
the pessimistic and emotional line <u>Metuo, hercle</u>
<u>metuo, ...</u> being much more in character with Synesius
than with Cassander.

292   <u>loquor</u> The minority reading is most correct grammatically,
i.e. subjunctive in indirect speech, but the reading of the

majority is adopted here. Hawkesworth varies in his
use of mood in such cases, c.f. I,479-80 and II,153
where the indicative is used; V,136 and I,373 where the
subjunctive is used.

351   Valerium The majority reading is rejected as the easier
        reading as it is obvious that Synesius would be invited to
        his own daughter's wedding. There is, however, no reason
        why Valerius should have replaced Synesius in PD, but
        compare the cast lists in LJ, which read Valerius senex
        alias Synesius.

370   nuncium laetificabilem The minority reading is adopted
        here, but compare V,386 where the majority of texts support
        the masculine adjective. In classical Latin nuntius
        and nuntium are interchangeable although Servius
        specifies "'nuntius' est qui nuntiat, 'nuntium' quod
        nuntiatur" (on Virgil, Aeneid XI.896). In V.386
        Hawkesworth uses a Plautine phrase from Stichus 395.

437   sella The minority reading supported by an untrustworthy
        manuscript is adopted here. The other texts all support
        the homynym cella whose meaning does not fit the context.

COMMENTARY

Title page   LABYRINTHUS   A situation of bewildering intricacy, as well as a maze.

Prologue   Hawkesworth has rejected Della Porta's introduction a eulogy of the city of Naples spoken by the River Sebeto, and replaced it with a shorter prologue which follows the conventions of Terentian comedy, asking for the attention and favour of the audience.

5-6   Vos, o Florentiae/summi et magnates viri   The scene of the play is set in Florence and Hawkesworth addresses his Cambridge audience as if they too are included in the illusion on stage.

Dramatis Personae   Decani superioris   See pp. 78-82 for a discussion of the significance of this and also of Baccalaureorum in Medecina and Decani inferioris. When these terms are used in the stage directions with reference to houses they are omitted from the translation, as they appear to have no meaning outside the specific production to which the text of the play originally referred.

__Mr__   The prefix __Mr__ denotes a Master of Arts or a
Fellow-Commoner, __Ds__ a Bachelor of Arts, and the
absence of a prefix an undergraduate not in
Fellows' Commons.

__Mr Verney__   The earliest record of this name at
Trinity College is in 1608 when George and Richard
Verney matriculated, five years after the first
production of __Labyrinthus__ in 1603.

__Goldingham__   Edward (?) Goldingham became a Scholar
of Trinity College in 1601, B.A. in 1605/6, Fellow
in 1608, M.A. in 1609. He played Mincio in the
1603 production of __Leander__.

__Ds Taverner__   John Taverner was the second son of
Peter Taverner of Hexton, Herts. and the grandson
of Richard Taverner, clerk of the Signet to Henry VIII
He matriculated pensioner from Trinity c.1597,
became a Scholar as John Tavernor in 1599, B.A. in
1601/2, M.A. in 1605. He played Flaminia in the
1598 production of __Leander__ and Rhinoceron in the
1603 production of the same play.

Taverner was incorporated at the University of
Oxford in 1606. He later became Professor of Music
at Gresham College (1610-1638). He was ordained

deacon in 1620 and priest in 1624/5. He was Vicar of Tillingham, Essex from 1624 to 1629, and then became Vicar of Hexton, Herts. and Rector of Stoke Newington, Middlesex, which positions he held until his death in August 1638.

Cassander   The name is given to one of the characters in Zelotypus produced at St John's, Cambridge in 1606: "Cassander maritus Laviniae et Zelotypus".

De Forrest   Miles Forrest was admitted Pensioner t Emmanuel College in April 1595. He migrated to Trinity and became a Scholar there as Emilius Forrest in 1599. He received the degree of B.A. in 1599/1600. He played Fabritius in the 1598 production of Leander, and spoke the prologue in the second production in 1603. One of his name was admitted to the Middle Temple in 1602 as son of Miles Forrest of Morbourne, Hunts.

Bing   William Byng matriculated from Trinity in 1602. He became a Scholar in 1605 but did not graduate. He played Ardelia in the 1603 production of Leander.

Crispinus   A character of this name is found in
Ben Jonson's _Poetaster; or, His Arraignment_, acted in
1601 and printed in the following year.

Thwaites   Mark Thwayts received his B.A. from Trinity
in 1603/4, his M.A. in 1607. He played Spinetta in
the 1603 production of _Leander_.

Cademan   Thomas Cademan was born in Norfolk c.1590.
He matriculated from Trinity c.1601, became a Scholar
in 1605, received the degree of B.A. in 1605/6, and
of M.A. in 1609. He also appeared in the part of Motus
in _Locus, Corpus, Motus_, probably performed at Trinity
in 1604/5. He later studied abroad and received the
degree of M.D. from the University of Padua in 1620.
He became physician to Queen Henrietta Maria. Cademan
died in May 1651.

Blaxton   Joshua Blaxton was admitted as a Scholar to
Trinity from Westminster in 1600, although there is no
record of his matriculation. He received the degree
of B.A. in 1603/4, became Fellow and M.A. in 1607, B.D.
in 1614 and D.D. in 1619. He played Vulpinus in the
1603 production of _Leander_.

Synesius   Texts L and J of Labyrinthus read Valerius
senex alias Synesius. There is no further mention of
Valerius except in PD, which read Valerius for
Synesius at V,351. A character called Valerius appear
in Leander but Blaxton did not play the part. In
Zelotypus one of the characters is named as "Phanio
alias Florio" and Churchill and Keller remark, "Dieser
Doppelname hatte wahrscheinlich in der Quelle (which
is unknown) einen bestimmten Sinn, in Zelotypus nicht
mehr" (Shakespeare Jahrbuch, p. 314 n.1). This is
obviously not the case in Labyrinthus where there is
no mention in the source La Cintia of Valerius, but
similar circumstances in the early stage of the
composition of Labyrinthus may account for the origin
of this discrepancy.

Ds North   There were two Norths at Trinity at the time
of the production of Hawkesworth's play. Thomas North
and John North both received the degree of B.A. in
1602/3 and of M.A. in 1606. Cooper (Athenae, I,446),
and Venn after him, name the latter as the North who
participated in College dramatics, taking the part of
Flaminia in the 1603 production of Leander as well as
acting in Labyrinthus. John North was ordained priest
in 1603 and was the author of Latin verses in Threno-
thriambeuticon. Academiae Cantabrigiensis ob damnum
lucrosum, et infoelicitatem foelicissimam, luctuosus
triumphus (Cambridge, 1603).

Ds Simpson   Edward Simpson, born on May 9, 1578, son
of Edward Simpson of Tottenham, was admitted to Trinity
as a Scholar from Westminster in 1597. He received
the degree of B.A. in 1600/1, became Fellow in 1602,
M.A. in 1604, B.D. in 1611, and D.D. in 1624. He
played the part of Lucianus in the 1603 production of
Leander. Simpson was chaplain to Sir Moyle Finch from
1611 to 1614, and became Junior Dean in 1617/8, and
Tutor in 1635. At the same time he was Rector of
Eastling, Kent from 1617, Rector of Pluckley from 1628
to 1649, and became Prebendary of Lincoln in 1628. He
was the author of Chronicon historiam Catholicam
complectens. Simpson died in 1652.

Nidd   There is no record of the matriculation of
Leonard Nidd. He became a Scholar of Trinity in 1602,
and received the degree of B.A. in 1603/4. He
migrated to Clare College where he became M.A. in 1607.

Don Piedro Pacheco D'Alcantara   Alcantara is a town in
Western Spain on the left bank of the Tagus. It became
famous about 1215 as the stronghold of the Knights of
Alcantara. The long name was supposed to be typically
Spanish. In Della Porta's La Trappolaria (III.1)
Trappola meets Dentifrangolo and introduces himself as

"Nullacredimi, Tuttagabbali, Ororuballi, Donnascamballi
explaining, "Non e maraviglia son di razza spagnuola,
e ho nome per quattro". (Le Commedie, ed.
V. Spampanato, 2 vols, Bari, 1910-11).

Mr Kitchin Thomas Kitchin became a Scholar of Trinity
in 1591 from Westminster. He received the degree of
B.A. in 1595/6 and of M.A. in 1599. He became Fellow
in 1597, Junior Bursar in 1609/10, Junior Dean in
1611/12, and Proctor in 1614/5. He played Gerastus in
both productions of Leander. Kitchin was ordained
deacon and priest in June 1606 and became Vicar of
Trumpington, Cambs. in 1611, of Bottisham in 1612,
and Rector of Grundisburgh, Suffolk in 1617.

Mr Freeman George Freeman matriculated Pensioner
from Trinity c. 1592. He received the degree of B.A.
in 1594/5 and of M.A. in 1598. He played Grillus in
both productions of Leander as well as in Labyrinthus.

Citharaedus In College Plays (p. 32) Moore Smith notes

  The music a t a performance seems generally ... to
have been provided by the waits of the town. But at
Queen's on 1 March 1541, we have a payment of 12d to
one Tusher 'qui pulsabat organa in agendis comoedijs'..
The dramatis personae of Senilis Amor (1635/6)
includes 'Tibicines'.

Music in Labyrinthus is provided by the lute-player
who has a small speaking part in II.3, and by Tiberius

who plays a harp in I.3. Certainly Wilkinson, who took the part of <u>Citharaedus</u>, was a member of the College, but professional musicians may have been employed also to play incidental music.

<u>Wilkinson</u>   Thomas Wilkinson matriculated Sizar from Trinity in 1601, and received the degree of B.A. in 1605/6 and of M.A. in 1609. He was ordained deacon and priest in 1611 and became Vicar of Langtoft, Lincs. in 1613.

<u>Mr Hassall</u>   Thomas Hassall matriculated Sizar from Trinity c.1591 and became a Scholar in 1593. He receive the degree of B.A. in 1594/5 and of M.A. in 1598. He played the part of Alphonsus in both productions of <u>Leander</u>. He became Vicar of Great Amwell, Herts. in 1599, which he held together with St Alphage, London by dispensation as chaplain to Lord Hunsden. He died in September 1657, aged 84. It is interesting to note that he acted in <u>Labyrinthus</u> after he had been ordained, c.f. John Milton, <u>An Apology against a Pamphlet</u> (1642), B3v.

<u>Scena est Florentiae</u>   It was the vogue in academic dram to have a continental setting: c.f. <u>Loiola</u> set in Amsterdam (acted at Trinity, 1622/3), <u>Versipellis</u> set

in Antwerp (Queen's, 1631/2), <u>Senile Odium</u> set in

Frankfurt (Queen's, 1628/9?).

Act 1. Scene 1. The characters that will appear throughout the

scene are listed in the heading of each scene without

regard for the moment of entry. This continental/

classical mode of massed entry, used in the printing

of Latin drama in the Renaissance, is employed alongside

the usual procedure in English printing of marking

each entry at the place within the scene where it is

specifically required.

This scene is original with Hawkesworth.

1   <u>O hermosa</u> (Spanish) "Oh lovely".

3   <u>Ha ha he</u>   Method of recording laughter, together with

the Italianate sigh <u>Ohi me</u> (I,220), the song <u>La la la</u>

(I,216), and the exclamation <u>pugh</u> (I,445) and <u>pish</u> (I,

5-6   <u>Quem ego, si hasce per plateas rursus prodeambulantem</u>

<u>offendero,</u>

<u>Nihili bestiam, Hispanum inaniloquum</u> —

c.f. Terence, <u>Eunuchus</u> 1064-5: Phaedria, the

adulescens, threatens his rival, the soldier Thraso,

"Si te in platea offendero hac post umquam, .../...

periisti".

6   Hispanum inaniloquum   Pistol, in Shakespeare's
        Henry IV, Part 2 speaks of "the bragging Spaniard"
        (V.3.124), and Don Armado in Love's Labour's Lost takes
        the grandiloquence associated with the Spanish to its
        extreme. In fact, despite this epithet, Hawkesworth
        chose not to exploit this aspect of Don Piedro's
        character, although there is a firm basis for it in
        the bragadoccio of the Capitano in La Cintia.

19   (tick tock)   Taken from the sound of knocking. Similar
        stage directions are also found in Leander, Club Law,
        Byrsa Basilica, as well as in Lingua, which F.G. Fleay
        notes in his Biographical Chronicle of the English
        Drama 1559-1642 (II,261).

24   Illarum queis ferunt Iove prognatum Herculem   Alcmena,
        wife of Amphitruon, was visited by Zeus during her
        husband's absence in the wars, and subsequently gave
        birth to twin sons, Heracles to Zeus and Iphicles to
        Amphitruon. Zeus was said to have been employed for
        three nights in forming the child, whom he intended to
        be the greatest hero the world had seen (c.f. Ovid,
        Heroides X,9-10). In Plautus' Amphitruo Jupiter prolong
        the night for the purposes of pleasure.

Mercury explains on the eve of the birth of Hercules:

> Et meus pater nunc intus hic cum illa cubat
> Et haec ob eam rem nox est facta longior,
> Dum cum illa quacum volt voluptatem capit.   (112-114)

Horatius too imputes the long night to motives of pleasure rather than of procreation.

30   ego solem Iovi non crederem hisce conditionibus   In case the god was so loath to leave Lepida that he would never allow the sun to follow its course, and thus plunge the world into perpetual darkness.

42-3   Crisp.   At here.

Hor.   At here; quid here?   c.f. Terence, Andria 889-90.

Act 1.   Scene 2.   This scene is original.

70-3   Ut illum dii omnes infaelicitent Hypocrassum, miserum
                                                    senem;

Qui postquam Flaminia se emunctum viderat, et ab Ardelia

Mulctatum male, ...

These lines refer to Hawkesworth's Leander, performed in 1598, and for the second time the day before Labyrinthus in 1602/3. Hippocrassus is an old doctor and Grillus is his servant. Flaminia, the heroine, is promised in marriage to Hippocrassus by her father Gerastus. Ardelia is a courtesan, mistress of Alphonsus. Hippocrassus is tricked out of marriage with Flaminia by Alphonsus and Cocalus/Leander, who discredit the old doctor in the eyes of his future father-in-law by arranging that Hippocrassus be seen entering the house of the courtesan on the eve of his wedding. Hippocrassus is persuaded to dress himself as the soldier Rhinoceronte, Alphonsus' rival for Ardelia, and in this disguise he receives a beating at the hands of the courtesan who has promised Alphonsus to show her contempt for his rival in this way. Gerastus cancels the match and Flaminia is finally married to her childhood sweetheart Leander, who, as the foolish Cocalus, has been acting as servant to Gerastus.

79-80   Ecquis est iam omnium qui unico panis frustulo
In perpetuam me recipiat servitutem?   There is a similar incident in which the parasite offers himself for sale in Plautus, Stichus 171-2. c.f. also Labyrinthus V,457-8. In Adagia Erasmus explains: "Frusto panis pro re quantum-libet pusilla ac vili, nostris quoque temporibus vulgo dictitant" (col. 151).

100   Per supremi regis regnum iuro   c.f. Plautus, Amphitruo 83

106   deluctari   Used only by Plautus among classical writers.

116   (Tiff, taff, toff.)   The sound of beating.

118   <u>Ad diurnam stellam crastinam</u>   Lucifer i.e. until

daybreak. c.f. Plautus, <u>Menaechmi</u> 175.

<u>At sumne ego miser</u>   c.f. Plautus, <u>Casina</u> 303, <u>Bacchides</u>
623.

Act 1. Scene 3. This scene is original with Hawkesworth.

121   <u>Stava la gentil dama, buon di, buon di, Madonna Modina</u>.

Presumably the first line of an unknown Italian song:

"The fair lady was standing there; good day, good day,

my lady Modina". <u>Modena</u> is used in modern Italian for an

inhabitant of Modena, and this may be the meaning of

<u>Modina</u> here, although it is not generally spelt with an <u>i</u>.

122   <u>O quam luculentum focum! Renidet pol tota domus</u>

c.f. Erasmus, <u>Adagia</u> (col 1003) "Primum domus ornamentum

est, ut luceat focus, proinde qui in aedes immigrant,

novas, aut in diversorium ingrediuntur, ante omnia

iubent ignem incendi".

133   <u>Musas meretriculas</u>   c.f. Boethuis, <u>Consolatio</u>

<u>Philosophiae</u> I.Prose 1. 27-8 "has scenicas meretriculas

⎣Musas⎦ ".

135   <u>Sat est in vita aegritudinum, solae quae obveniunt ultro</u>

c.f. "Mala ultro adsunt" (Hans Walther, <u>Proverbia</u>

<u>sententiaeque Latinitatis medii aevi</u> (Göttingen, 1963-9),

14302c)

136-7   ... vitam aequam, certam, mediam, nec luxu obsitam,/

Nec depressam sordibus (hah), rem ego (Iupiter)

quantivis duco pretii.

c.f. Horace, Odes II.10.5-8

       auream quisquis mediocritatem
       diligit, tutus caret obsoleti
       sordibus tecti, caret invidenda
       sobrius aula.

144-5   Amore, comitate, et benigna imprimis opera

Res agi satius est, quam lite et querimonia

c.f. The Civile Conversation of M. StephenGuazzo,

Divided into Foure Bookes, the First Three Translated ...

by G. Pettie ... the Fourth ... Translated ... by Barth.

Young (1586), III, Yyr "threatning words, wherewith they

make all the house to shake: not knowing that (as the

Poet saith) 'Great force lies hid in gentle

Soveraigntie'".

147   Lepidum senem   Plautus uses this same epithet several

times of Periplectomenus in Miles Gloriosus, e.g. 135,

155, 649. Periplectomenus may well have provided a

model for Hawkesworth's Tiberius, for the two

characters have much in common in their philosophy of

life, their good humour, their understanding and

indulgence of the young, and Hawkesworth in fact borrows

some of Periplectomenus' words, e.g. V, 271-2. The
adjective lepidus occurs frequently in Miles Gloriosus
and may have provided a hint for Hawkesworth's translation
of the Italian name Amasio as Lepidus.

154   amatorculos   Found only in Plautus among classical writers,
        e.g. Poenulus 236.

155   obstipare Not a classical word although found in some old
        editions of Plautus. It was first used to mean "stop or
        block up" c.1256.

158   tara tantara farara   A fanfare, the noise of a trumpet or
        a drum, c.f. Ennius, Poesis Reliquiae 452. See also I, 766;
        I, 778.

169   Crepuerunt fores   Such an interruption of a soliloquy is
        a stock device in Roman comedy, c.f. Plautus, Miles
        Gloriosus 410, Curculio 486, Poenulus 741.

170   barbiton   "An instrument of musike, called as I thinke,
        dulcimers: some think it a kinde of harpe." (Cooper,
        Thesaurus, s.v.). The stage direction at the beginning of
        Scene 3 introduces Tiberius singing "ad cytharam" -- a harp,
        so that the second definition of barbiton is probably the
        one meant here.

172   retia   Nets were used in fowling, c.f. Thomas Middleton

The Wisdom of Solomon Paraphrased Chapt. IV, 12

        The fisher hath a bait deceiving fish,
        The fowler hath a net deceiving fowls;

(The Works of Thomas Middleton. Edited by A.H. Bullen

8 vols. London, 1885-6.)

177   So ho!   "This is the cry of sportsmen when the hare is

found in her seat"(T.F.T. Dyer, Folk-Lore of Shakespeare,

New York, 1966, p. 498.)

185   Deum Fidium   Fidius is a surname of Jupiter, c.f.

Plautus, Asinaria 23.

189   eccere   Exclamation of surprise, found only in Plautus

and Terence among classical writers.

197   callidus   Crispinus is here acting as the servus

callidus of Roman comedy, fooling the senex with his

quick wit, and extricating himself and his young master

from a difficult situation.

214   nevis   for non vis, c.f. Plautus, Trinummus 1156,

Mostellaria, 110.

Act 1. Scene 4. This scene is closely based on I.1 of

Della Porta's La Cintia.

256 Totiesque infantem manibus gestavi meis? c.f. Terence

Adelphe 563.

262 Et in scena ac si foret Is the following passage to be

acted out? Hawkesworth here translates literally from

the Italian, La Cintia I.1, "come se haveste à

raccontarlo in una scena" (A7r).

266-7 Proin largiendo hic prudens affectat viam. Servi primo

capti,/(Uti est ingenium) cognati mox, mox nutrix, mox

perviam fecit domum. c.f. Plautus, Miles Gloriosus 105-8:

  Insinuat sese absentis ad illam amicam eri:
  Occepit eius matri suppalparier
  Vino, ornamentis opiparisque obsoniis:
  Itaque intumum ibi se miles apud lenam facit.

273 aureos "A peece of gold money: a noble: a croune"

(Cooper, Thesaurus, s.v.) The general term aureus for a

gold coin is used several times in Labyrinthus (I,575;

I,623; II,125), together with denarius and mina which

are units of ancient currency.

374-5   ... Ego qua pateret commeatus amantibus

       ... perfodi parietem censui

       c.f. Plautus, Miles Gloriosus 142-3

          In eo conclavi ego perfodi parietem,
          Qua commeatus clam esset hinc huc mulieri.

Act 1.   Scene 5.   This scene is loosely based on La Cintia I.2.

437   Signior Lucretio   Italian.

444   subcingula   Found only once in classical Latin in

       Plautus, Menaechmi, 200 (under-girdle). In the sixteenth

       century the word was used for "a bracing-girdle; a

       girdle to hang a woodknife by" (Cooper, Thesaurus, s.v.).

       A marginal note in J (I,438) specifies the gift as a

       "payre of hangers" i.e. sword carriers.

447   nunc dierum   now-a-days. A non-classical phrase

       common in the Latin of this period, c.f. Pedantius I.1.46

       (edited by G. C. Moore Smith, Louvain, 1905), Fucus

       Histriomastix I.2.13 (edited by G. C. Moore Smith,

       Cambridge, 1909).

466   personam hanc detrahe   Persona and its synonym larva

       are used frequently throughout Labyrinthus, (IV,41;

       IV,108; IV,301; V,234). Hawkesworth exploits for the

purposes of dramatic irony the dual meaning of the words, in their technical sense of the masks used by players in the Roman theatre and in the simple sense of role or character. Lysetta does not realize the aptness of her words when she urges "Lucretius" to remove the mask.

491   cum sola solo cum in loco   c.f. Terence, Eunuchus 579 "solus cum sola".

Act 1. Scene 6. This scene is based on La Cintia I.3. The first half of the scene (ll. 504-564) is expanded by Hawkesworth from the basic situation in his source. The second half of the scene is an almost literal translation from the Italian.

505   Ad sancti Laurentii The church of San Lorenzo on the west side of the Piazza San Lorenzo in Florence. This accurate reference to a place in Florence may indicate that Hawkesworth's knowledge of Italian and Italy was not merely academic. Information was, of course, available about foreign places from guide books such as Francesco Bocchi's Le bellezze della citta di Fiorenza (1591).

510-11   Lepida/Quae nomen ubi obtinet, curas et aerumnas, ubicunque eas invenit, fugat Lepidus; "Neate:

pleasaunt: polits: preatie: merie:" (Cooper, Thesaurus,
s.v.) This cannot be conveyed in English without changing
the name.

527-8 ... eone es oella? / Quia amatorem vestiarium habes?
The allusion here is not clear, and is obviously lost on
Lysetta. Lepidus is probably teasing the maid by saying
that she must have connections in the clothing-trade to
be so well turned-out.

582 Quae mihi si praestiteris, Fortuna faculam alluxit
lucrificam tibi C.f. Plautus, Persa 515 "Neque quam tibi
Fortuna faculam lucrifera adlucere volt".

600   **Genere de Malvezzi**   The name is taken from **La Cintia**:

> Tu sai, che siamo da Bologna della famiglia de'Malvezzi
> principal in quella terra, e siamo Ghibellini,
> nemici affato de'Guelfi, ... e principalmente
> ne'Mafolti (I.3, B3v).

The Malvezzi were supporters of the Bentivoglio, the
leading family of Bologna in the fifteenth century.
Jealous of their position in the city the Malvezzi plotted
to overthrow the Bentivoglio in 1488. The plot was
discovered, the ring-leaders executed and the rest of the
family sent into exile. The conflict however was not part
of the Guelph-Ghibelline feud which was a struggle between
supporters of the Empire and those of the papacy. The
Mafolti do not appear to be a real family. In making
Tiberius a native of Naples, Hawkesworth further confuses
the historical facts. Presumably to the University
audience the Malvezzi and Mafolti merely represented two
feuding Italian families no more based in historical fact
than Montagues and Capulets.

601   **Mafoltiam**   see note on l. 600.

624   **regina Cypri**   Venus, the personification of the power of
love. Legend has it that Venus landed at Paphos in Cyprus
when she first emerged from the sea. She was the chief
deity of the island. c.f. Horaces, **Odes** I, 30, 1-2.

Act 1. Scene 7. This scene is original with Hawkesworth.

627-8   <u>Vide quin ut cornices crocitant./Pluviae, puer, pluviae.</u>

Among the many omens attributed to the bird, the

foretelling of rain by its call is especially mentioned.

c.f. Horace, <u>Odes</u> III.27. 9-12:

      antequam stantes repetat paludes
      imbrium divina avis imminentium,
      oscinem corvum prece suscitabo
      solis abortu.

628   <u>hispaniolos</u>   The English name Spaniel comes from the Old

French adjective <u>espaignol, espagneul</u> "Spanish dog".

"Howe necessary a thing a Spanell is to Falconrie,

... I deeme no man doubteth, as well to spring and

retrive a fowle being flowen to the marke, as also divers

other wayes to assiste and ayde Falcons and Goshawkes".

("A Treatise and Brief Discourse, of the Cure of Spanels ...

devised and written by Master Francesco Sforzino Vincentino"

in <u>The Booke of Faulconrie</u> ... by George Turberville

(1575), Zvv-Zvi).

<u>Canace</u>   The name of a dog. One of Actaeon's hounds in

Ovid, <u>Metamorphoses</u> III, 217.

<u>Dorilas</u>   The name of a dog. A Greek name found in Ovid,

<u>Metamorphoses</u> V, 129 and 130; XII, 380.

637   **montis Lernii**   An imaginary place.

639   **lacum Lemnium**   An imaginary place.

641   **Signior Bentevoglio**   The name Bentivoglio was well known in the sixteenth century. Ercole Bentivoglio wrote verses and two comedies **I Fantasmi** (1544) and **Il Geloso** (1545), copies of which are in the library of Trinity College. Only a few years before the composition of **Labyrinthus** Gui Bentivoglio had been made Chamberlain to Pope Clement VIII at the age of nineteen. It is doubtful if an historical personage is being referred to here. The name was probably chosen as typically Italian, c.f. Shakespeare's Benvolio and Malvolio.

        Don Hernando Del Humore Hispaniolo   A typical Spanish name.

642   **Il Cavaliero Marte Bellonio di Mantua**   A stock type, the soldier as Don Hernando represents the Spaniard. A captain Martebellonio is one of the characters in Della Porta's **I due fratelli rivali** (Venice, 1601).

644-5   **Ipse princeps expectabatur, sed nullⁱs venit, Literae credo ex Hispania, aut aliquid certe inerat.** Although Hawkesworth sets his play in Florence and refers to landmarks of the city (I,505), the places and characters

mentioned in this scene seem to be fictional. The
reference to the princeps may be a topical allusion. The
Dukes of Florence owed their power to Spanish arms and
diplomacy, and although Ferdinand I, ruler of Florence
from 1587 to 1609, was relatively independent, the
Spaniards had held five fortresses on the coast of
Tuscany since 1530, and kept a military stranglehold on
the Duchy. "Letters from ⁰pain" may refer to some
contemporary intrigue between Florence and Spain, but it is
more likely that Hawkesworth has invented this plausible
reason for the celebrity-seeker Tiberius for the absence of
the Head of State from his hunt.

651   (cick). Hisp. Ah. Tiberius may be making soothing noises
to the bird which he is probably still holding. There is
no direction to indicate that the bird is to be removed
from the stage. Alternatively Tiberius may be providing
sound effects to illustrate his description of the hawk's
performance, c.f. I, 662 and 670.

659   Instat fere quinta The action in Labyrinthus takes place
in the course of a single night between about four in the
afternoon and eight or nine in the morning. Events are
arranged to reach a peak at ten o'clock in the evening, when
all the participants in the intrigue agree to meet (II,428;
II,494; II,643). Tiberius resolves to tell Cassander the

truth about Lepidus "ubi primum illuxerit" (IV,11), and
Synesius confronts Cassander with Lucretia's real identity
at seven o'clock in the morning (V,42).

661   Ubi esse hanc dicam tam diu gravidam?   Refers to Tiberius'
       "daughter" Lepida.

672   Madre ella amour   Presumably the first words of another
       Italian song, here somewhat garbled. "Amour" is French
       rather than Italian and "ella" makes no sense in this
       context. It may be a corruption of "Madre del amore";
       "O mother of love".

       Cancro   A corruption of the Italian Cancaro, an alternative
       spelling of canchero, meaning nuisance or pest, c.f. Leander
       V.9. (Bodleian MS, Rawlinson D 341). "Grillus: Cancaro".

Act 1. Scene 8. Loosely based on La Cintia I.4.

695-6   Risus seni est ignis in hyeme, est umbra in vere, et
              potus in febri
         Est vinum in convivio, est amor in vino, est lectus, est
              focus, est cibus, est potus
         c.f. Leander V.3. "Grillus: ignis hyeme, umbra vere,
              dulce/Scortum nota nocte, tirr ri ... " (Bodl. Rawl. D34?

710   basta   Italian, meaning enough.

700   si India mi- daretur   India was proverbial for its wealth of gold and precious stones c.f. Thomas Dekker's Shoemakers Holiday V.5: Lacie protests that he would not lose Rose "for all Indias wealth".
(Dramatic Works of Thomas Dekker. Edited by Fredson Bowers. 4 vols, Cambridge, 1953-61).

726   Dispennat adeo et pandiculatur "When you do perceive your Hawke to sit broodely and crowching, with her feathers displaied and open ... then you may be sure that she is not well in her body, and that shee is either troubled with wormes, or els with some other inward griping, or gnawing" (Simon Latham, Latham's Falconry (1615), O1v).

728   quinquaginta minae   "Decem minae. of our money 20 poundes" (Cooper, Thesaurus, s. v. mina), i.e. £100.

732   chelidonia cum pipere   Greater Celandine (in Latin Chelidonium maius). "The roote cut in small peeces is good to be given unto Haukes against sundry diseases whereunto they are subject, as wormes, craie, and such like" (John Gerard, The Herball; or, Generall Historie of Plantes (1597), Chapt. 419). Both pepper and root of celandine are recommended by George Turberville as emetics to clear

the bird's crop (The Booke of Faulconrie or Hauking, Qvv and Qiiiv).

752   Sannio   A buffoon and clown,but also the name of the pimp in Terence's Adelphi.

776-7   ... Vive dum est tempus. Solet brevis esse aetas

                                   eiusmodi virtutibus.

Vita est caduca, fruere aetate

A collection of common places about the transitory nature of human life, c.f. Horace, Odes I.11.7-8 "dum loquimur, fugerit invida/aetas: carpe diem quam minimum credula postero"; Seneca, Phaedra, 454 "aetate fruere: mobili cursu fugit"; Ulpian Fulwell, An Enterlude Intituled Like Wil to Like (1568), E1v "Take time while time is for time dooth flee".

Act 1. Scene 9. This scene is loosely based on La Cintia I.5.

787   Patrisque cum ancillis cubat nec metuitur Because "Lucretius" isn't man enough to take advantage of the situation.

844   Auxilium frustra rogat qui petenti negat c.f. Publilius Syrus, Sententiae 56, "Beneficium qui dare nescit, iniuste

petit" (ed. R. A. H. Bickford-Smith, London, 1895).

Act 1. Scene 10   Very loosely based on La Cintia I.6.

869   Non est hic locus, unde me/dem precipitem?

c.f. Terence, Andria 606.

875-80   ... Ita me Iuno Regina,

....

Ita quid dicam nescio; immo audi, iam scio - Dii me

omnes magni

c.f. Plautus, Cistellaria 512-521:

            At ita me di deaeque superi atque inferi et medioxumi
            Itaque me Iuno regina et Iovis supremi filia
            Itaque me Saturnus eius patruos et summus pater,
            ....
            ... Enimvero ita me Iuppiter,
            Itaque me Iuno, itaque Ianus, ita, quid dicam nescio .
            Iam scio - ...

876   Eiusque vir et frater, supremus Iupiter   Both Jupiter and

Juno were the children of Saturnus and Rhea and therefore

brother and sister, as well as husband and wife.

patruus eius Saturnus   The father of Jupiter and Juno and

Juno's uncle by marriage to her brother Jupiter.

877   Castor pater   One of the Dioscuri, sons of Jupiter by

Leda.   The Romans were fond of swearing by this divinity,

e.g. <u>Aecastor</u>. <u>Pater</u> is here used as a term of respect rather than as a genealogical designation.

895   Sum deus, sum deus, sum deus   c.f. Plautus, <u>Curculio</u> 167.

Act 2.   Scene 1   This scene is closely based on <u>La Cintia</u> II.1.

13   <u>o Dio</u>   (Italian) "O God".

14   <u>oppilationem</u>   Obstruction of the bowels i.e. constipation. c.f. Sir Thomas Elyot, <u>The Castel of Helth</u> (London, 1539): "oppilations or hard congeled matter in the inner partes of the body" (Liiiiv).

<u>aquam ... inter cutem</u>   I.e. dropsy, so-called because the disease is characterized by the accumulation of watery fluid in the serous cavities or in the connective tissue of the body. Symptoms of the disease are the swelling of the limbs and shortness of breath owing to pressure of fluid on the diaphragm and, therefore, Horatius' diagnosis of Lucretia's condition is quite plausible.

43-4   <u>Ut priusquam ego amor rerum quid esset noveram,</u>
<u>Amicitia haec omnis in amorem abiret mihi.</u>
c.f. Ovid, <u>Metamorphoses</u> X.637
      Quid facit, ignorans amat et non sentit amorem.

54   Facile decipitur dum sperat amantis animus

c.f. Virgil, Eclogues VIII,108, "qui amant, ipsi sibi
somnia fingunt", which Erasmus glosses "Nam quod quisque
sperat, facile credit" (Adagia, col. 561).

81-2   Qui amicam amplectitur cuius animus in alio abest

Cadaver ille, haud amicam, amplectitur

The soul contains the life of a man, c.f. Aristotle,
Metaphysica V.18.4 "ἡ γὰρ ψυχὴ μέρος τι τοῦ ἀνθρώπου,
ἐν ᾗ πρώτῃ τὸ ζῆν".

Act 2. Scene 2. This scene is closely based on La Cintia II.2.

99   mare mortuum   The lake or inland sea in the south of
Palestine, into which the Jordan flows. The same name was
given by the Greeks and Romans to the Arctic Ocean in the
North of Europe, c.f. Pliny, Naturalis Historia IV.13.94.

110   ultimo die Veneris   April 30. April was considered among
the Romans as Venus' month, the first day being set aside
as Festum Veneris et Fortunae Virilis. The month was
named by Romulus after Aphrodite the Greek equivalent of
Venus.

128-9   negat sibi quicquam commercii/Cum Lucretio fuisse unquam
This is a complete contradiction of Lucretia's words,
"Lepidae in amicitiam interius me statim intuli" (I,349).

136   Immo non credis, quia non placent haec tibi

c.f. Erasmus, Adagia col. 561, "Et tarde, quae credita laedunt, credimus, ut ait Ovidius".

151-2   ... Ipse cum perfidiae sis plenus

Et periurii, huiusmodi et illum reris consimilem tibi.

c.f. Shakespeare, Henry VI, Part 3, V.6.11 "Suspicion always haunts the guilty mind".

180   Et Lucretium illum pateris tibi glaucomam oboculos obiicere

c.f. Plautus, Miles Gloriosus 148 "Glaucumam ob oculos obiciemus".

Act 2. Scene 3   This scene is original with Hawkesworth

187   O per dios quae aquell villiaco m'a traydo (Spanish)

"Oh in the name of the gods, what's that scoundrel got me into". Villiaco does hot seem to be a Spanish word but a corruption of the Italian vigliacco, also spelled villacco. See Textual Notes.

188   Bide, bide, bide for Vide, vide vide. John Minsheu writes of Spanish pronunciation, "they confound and use one letter for another, as B for V consonant, and V consonant

for B; as ^Ballesta or Vallesta, a crossebowe" (A Dictionary in Spanish and English: First Published into the English Tongue by Ric. Percivale Gent. Now Enlarged and Amplified .. by John Minsheu (1623), A6v). See also l. 210 varvam.

190   Doh reniego, del mondo, ubi es villiaco? Holla mochacho (Spanish) "Oh damn the world, where is the scoundrel? Hey, boy!"

191   Burrachio (Spanish) "You drunkard". c.f. ^Shakespeare's Much Ado About Nothing (1600) which has a character named Borrachio.

193   Esclavo   (Spanish) "Slave!"

196-9 Hawkesworth appears to have taken this episode, satirizing the formality of the ^Spaniards, from the story of Lazarillo de Tormes. (The Pleasaunt History of Lazarillo de Tormes by David Rouland edited by J. E. V. Crofts. Percy Reprints 7 (Oxford, 1924) p. 53. All references are to this edition.)

196   Beso las manos dev merced   (Spanish) "I kiss your honour's hands". ^This was a well-known ^Spanish phrase c.f. George Ruggle, Ignoramus V.10. "bezo las manos"; Ben Jonson, The Alchemist IV.3.21 "Sennores, beso las manos, à vuestras mercedes".

197 <u>Las piernas villiaco</u> (Spanish) "My legs you scoundrel".

202-4 Grillus brushes down Don Piedro's clothing. A parallel

for these lines is to be found in <u>Lazarillo de Tormes</u>:

"I was his brushe" (p. 42).

204 <u>lindamente, lindamente. Doh mochacho</u> (Spanish)

"gently, gently. Hey boy".

211 <u>varvam</u> i.e. barbam. See 1. 188 above.

213 <u>Mal fuego os abrase villiaco</u> (Spanish) "May you burn in

hell fire."

216-7 <u>quid suavi cantu aedes hasce/Non concelebras</u>

c.f. Plautus, <u>Casina</u> 799, "Suavi cantu concelebra omnem

hanc plateam".

217 <u>bolo</u> i.e. volo

218 <u>Alla Hispaniece, alla gala, alla gala</u> (Spanish) "In the

Spanish fashion, merrily, merrily" - by serenading her.

222 <u>Oh galano, o gentil. Por dios olla maravilla gratiosamente,</u>
<u>doh.</u>

(Spanish) "Oh well done, oh fine! By the gods a marvell,

wonderful, ah." The form <u>gratiosamente</u> is strictly

Italian, the Spanish form being _graciosamente_. Don Piedro
is praising the musician.

226-7 _Buenos dias/Ala Senniora Lepida, hermosa, galana, gentil_
(Spanish) "Good day to the lady Lepida, beautiful, fine
and comely".

229 _O Burrachio_ (Spanish) "Oh drunkard!"

232 _Doh reniego los cielos_ (Spanish) "Oh damn the heagens".

233 _por estas varvas_ (Spanish) "by this beard". c.f. Ben
Jonson, _The Alchemist_ IV.3.91 "Por estas honrada's barbas".
It seems to have been customary to swear by the beard,
c.f. Shakespeare's _As You Like It_ I.2.75-7 "stroke your
chins, and swear by your beards that I am a knave".

234 _buon giorno ala senniora vestra_ "Lepida" speaks to him
in Italian: "Goodday to your Lordship".

236 _Malos annos_ (Spanish) "Really?" This is perhaps a
latinized version of the phrase _mal año_. The double _n_
represents the _ñ_ of modern Spanish.

237 _picaro vagamundo ministril_ (Spanish) "You rogue, you
vagabond, you minstrel."

238   **berbero**   i.e. verbero

240   **Al diablo**   (Spanish) "Go to the devil!"

241   **viginti minas**   Ten minae equalled £20, c.f. I,728. This is a ridiculous sum to pay a musician, especially for the miserly Don Piedro, even if he intends his servant to pay it. Hawkesworth was clearly using the term as a vague unit of currency without regard for its exact worth.

244   **Esclavo mio**   (Spanish) "Slave of mine".

246-7   **Hilaris ubi sum, hilaris et tu esto: cum irascor, treme,**

                                                    treme, treme.

Si quid affirmo de cavaliero, dejera tu, et si opus est pejer

c.f. Terence, *Eunuchus* 252-3

        Negat quis: nego; ait: aio; ostremo imperavi egomet mih. Omnia adsentari.

This type of scene between servant and master was very popular in academic drama. In Act 2, Scene 2 of **Hymenaeus** (performed at St John's College, Cambridge in 1578/9) Pantomagus and his servant Gothrio prepare themselves for dinner at Julia's house. Pantomagus instructs Gothrio on how he is to behave, "verbis fac meis vultus respondeat tuus" (1.6), and Gothrio affirms,

si quid tu nolis, id me nolle etiam,
tu siquid velis, id me sponte cupere. (11. 29-30)

(Edited by G. C. Moore Smith, Cambridge, 1908)

A similar episode is found in Act 1, Scene 1 of Pedantius (performed at Trinity College, Cambridge in 1580/1).

Crobulus lectures Pogglostus, "pendeas ex nutu, in verba iures, mandata celeriter exequare " (11. 73-4).

(Edited by G. C. Moore Smith, Louvain, 1905.)

247   de cavaliero   A hybrid of Spanish cavallero and Italian cavalliere, "about a gentleman".

248   Por dios por todos los santos, poh reniego del Emperador (Spanish) "By the gods, by all the saints, oh damn the Emperor".

Emperador   Probably Charles V, ruler of the Holy Roman Empire (1519-1558) and at the same time King of Spain as Charles I.   Charles was the last Emperor to be crowned by the Pope.   Rudolf II (1576-1612), ruler of the Empire at the date of the composition of Labyrinthus, was strictly speaking only a king of Germany.

249   alicunde corraseris   c.f. Terence, Adelphi 242.

253-60   This episode is based on Lazarillo de Tormes (p. 40).

253   <u>por tua vida</u> (Spanish) "by your life".

257   <u>por vida del Emperador</u>   (Spanish) "by the Emperor's life".

258   <u>Hoc tribus vel quatuor biris in Hispania nobilibus sufficere</u>

c.f. Thomas Heywood, <u>The English Traveller</u> I.1: "Spaine,

that yeelds scant of food; affords the Nation/A parsimonious

stomach".

(<u>Dramatic Works of Thomas Heywood</u>, collected by R. H.

Shepherd, 6 vols, London, 1874.)

<u>biris</u>   i.e. <u>viris</u>

261   <u>Una insalata, colta di mano di fanciulla</u>   (Italian <u>not</u>

Spanish) "A salad picked by the hand of a maiden". The

diet of the Spanish was largely made up of salads and

fruits and was despised by the English as meagre.

c.f. Peter Heylyn, <u>MIKPOKOΣMOΣ</u> (Oxford, 1627) "The Cattle

hereof are neither faire nor many; so that their fare is

for the most part on sallets and fruits of the earth"

(B8v-C1r).

267   <u>Vamos ... vamos</u>   (Spanish) "Let's go ... let's go". See

also II, 271 and II, 275.

Act 2. Scene 4   This scene is loosely based on La Cintia II.3.

289   por vida del Emperador   (Spanish) "by the Emperor's life".

290   E iuro a los cielos   (Spanish) "I swear to heaven".
         See textual notes for discussion of E iuro.

291-2   por dios/Por todos los santos   (Spanish) "by the gods, by
         all the saints".

301   expetissunt   A Plautine word.

308   pocas pallabras   (Spanish) "less talk": c.f. Shakespeare's
         The Taming of the Shrew, Induction, ll. 5-6, "paucas
         pallabris".

311   versiculos quosdam quos hodie composui   Don Piedro has
         literary pretensions like Don Armado in Love's Labour's Lost.

312   e mui gentiles   (Spanish)   "and very fine".

319   Archidux Mediolanensis   Presumably a fictitious character,
         as the last duke of Milan, Francesco Sforza, died in 1535,
         and Milan became henceforth a dependency of Spain.

321   Hoc epitaphium est Imperatoris Caroli quinti   Charles V,
         Holy Roman Emperor died in 1558.

322 <u>Vicerege Neapolitano</u> Naples was ruled by a Viceroy, appointed by the King of Spain, after the conquest of Naples in 1504.

325 <u>a coena</u> Nonclassical phraseology.

331 <u>Mala, pas qua del dios a quell villiaco</u> (Spanish) "God's curse on that scoundrel".

336 <u>Por il cuerpo santo de la Letania</u> (Spanish) "By the holy book of the Litany".

338 <u>malos annos</u> (Spanish) "really". See II, 236.

341 <u>Te risu interficere</u> c.f. Erasmus, <u>Adagia</u> (cols. 1033-4) "Emori risu. Proverbiales hyperbolae sunt et illae, Emori risu, Defluere risu, pro vehementer ridere ... ". Hawkesworth twists the usual saying.

346-7 These lines are based on <u>Lazarillo de Tormes</u> (p. 37).

348 <u>vamos, vamos</u> (Spanish) "let's go, let's go".

Act 2. Scene 5. This scene is closely based on <u>La Cintia</u> II.4., although Cintia's first speech in the Italian play is omitted and the end of the scene is slightly altered.

351   <u>Familiaritate fit lenior</u> c.f. Ovid, <u>Remedia Amoris</u>, 131 "Temporis ars medecina ferest", and Terence, <u>Heauton Timorumenos</u> 422 "diem adimere aegritudinem hominibus".

Act 2. Scene 6. The early part of this scene is closely based on <u>La Cintia</u> II.5. Towards the end Hawkesworth makes certain additions, and paraphrases and condenses the Italian.

470   <u>Catulli Lesbia</u> 25 to 30 of Catullus' poems concern the poet's affair with his mistress. Hawkesworth quotes from one of them at V, 252.

471   <u>Horatii Lydia</u> Horace addresses four poems to Lydia, <u>Odes</u> I, 8, 13 and 25, <u>Odes</u> III, 9.

485   <u>in usum scenae</u> Hawkesworth exploits the ambiguity of the phrase for the purposes of dramatic irony. The clothes will be used on the stage but as part of the plot of <u>Labyrinthus</u> rather than in imaginary amateur theatricals.

Act 2. Scene 7 Closely based on <u>La Cintia</u> II.6. with the addition of some lines spoken by Horatius (ll. 526-32).

514   <u>Magnam in me clusam partem latere tui</u> She is carrying his child.

529   lacteolas   Used in the double sense of "milk-white" and "full of milk" (as "Lepida" is pregnant).

556   suspicionum architectus   c.f. Shakespeare's Titus Andronicus, V.2.122. "Chief architect and plotter of these woes".

Act 2. Scene 8   Almost the whole scene is directly translated from La Cintia II.7.

580   **Te penes est cor meum**   It was a commonplace of Renaissance literature that the mind or heart of the lover dwells in the beloved. c.f. Erasmus, Apophthegmatum (Venice , 1577) V.39.

> Amantis animum dicebat $\underline{\mathord{\int}}$ Cato $\underline{\mathord{\int}}$ in alieno corpore viver
> quod hodie quoque celebratur animam illic potius
> esse ubi amat, quam ubi animat.

Act 2. Scene 9   This scene is closely based on La Cintia II.8.

Act 2. Scene 10   This scene corresponds to La Cintia II.9., Don Piedro and Grillus replacing the Captain. The plot content of the scenes are the same: a meeting is arranged for the rival suitor to witness Amasia/Lepida's acceptance of Erasto/Horatius as a lover.

615   O mi hermosa Lepida   (Spanish) "Oh my fair Lepida".

616 <u>Por dios nos derisit gallantamente</u> Grillus, speaks a mixture of Latin and Spanish: "By the gods she made fine fools of us".

620 <u>vamos</u> (Spanish) "let's go". See also II,623 and 626.

621 <u>screator</u> Found only once in classical Latin: Plautus, <u>Miles Gloriosus</u> 647.

621-2 <u>... canis tu famelice! Habeo hic epistolam</u>
<u>Quam ad Cerberum cognatum tuum deferas.</u>
Cerberus was a monstrous dog (and therefore a relation of "canis famelice") with fifty heads according to Hesiod (<u>Theognis</u>, 312), or three according to other sources, who guarded the entrance to Hades to prevent the living from entering and the dead from escaping. i.e. Crispinus is threatening to send Don Piedro to Hell.

631 <u>por mia vita</u> A mixture of Spanish and Latin: "By my life". Grillus' Spanish is even more idiosyncratic than Don Piedro's.

 <u>apertissimamente</u> (Spanish) "absolutely clearly". See also Textual Notes.

634-5 <u>por vida</u> / <u>Del cielo sois coragio y'honrado</u> (Spanish)

"In the name of heaven you are brave and honoured".

The grammar of this line is very peculiar; <u>sois</u> is

second person <u>plural</u> of <u>ser</u>, <u>coragio</u> is a noun, while

<u>honrado</u> is a singular adjective. See Textual Notes.

646 <u>Pocas pallabras</u> (Spanish) "Say no more".

<u>Adios</u> (Spanish) "Farewell". See also II, 647.

Act 3. Scene 1. This scene is closely based on <u>La Cintia</u> III.1.

2-3 <u>instat decima,</u> / <u>Praeterea dudum nox media</u> Hawkesworth

seems to contradict himself here, unless he is using the

Roman method of measuring time, dividing the day into two

parts from sunrise to sunset, and from sunset to sunrise,

and each part into twelve <u>horae</u>. If the sun set about six

o'clock the tenth hour would be four o'clock in the morning

and thus after midnight. Furthermore the word <u>conticinium</u>

(1.1) is used for the period between cock-crow and dawn

(c.f. J. Langius, <u>Polyantheae</u> (1681), p. 795). Another

plausible explanation for the discrepancy may lie in

confused adaptation of the source. In <u>La Cintia</u> Erasto

and Dulone are on hand to meet the Capitano at two

o'clock, and correctly say, "Gia deve esser la città
tutta sepolta nel sonno, e la meza notte passata" (D10r).

4   Animo cupienti here ipsa celeritas est mora
         c.f. Erasmus, Adagia (col. 709) "Etiam celeritas in
         desiderio mora est".

8   aspice despice circumspice   c.f. Plautus, Amphitruo 984
         "Concedite atque abscedite omnes, de via decedite".

Act 3.   Scene 2.   This scene is original.

22-3   Poh, illiberal'mente,/O baxo pensamento. Gril. Pensamento'
         (Spanish) "Oh how vulgar. O that's beneath consideration
         Gril. Consideration?".

25   o vil o ingentil   "Oh contemptible, oh mean!" Neither
         vil nor ingentil are found in contemporary Spanish
         dictionaries. The words may be inventions by Hawkesworth
         based on the Latin words vilis and ingentilis. In his
         Spanish Grammar (1623) Minsheu includes "Generall
         observations from the Latine for the framing of the
         Spanish" (Mm4r):

             The Latine ending in lis,) Materialis)   (Material
             by taking away is, as   ) Finalis   )Spanish(Final

27 servidumbre (Spanish) "slave". The word actually means bondage or servitude.

29 docente nemine In classical Latin nullo is used for the ablative of nemo.

30-1 villane esclavo / Hisios del capones; abaxati (Spanish) "You peasant, you serf, you son (?) of a chicken; humble yourself". Hisios seems to be a corruption of hijo, son. J was pronounced in Spanish as sh, c.f. Minsheu, Grammar Mm6v.

33-4 Docet herus, /Discit servus; uterque necessitatis est
discipulus
c.f. Xenophon, Cyropaedia II.3.13 οὐ γὰρ ἔστι διδάσκαλος οὐδεὶς τούτων κρείττων. τῆς ἀνάγκης.
Johannes Stobaeus, Florilegium 60.10 (ed. A. Meineke, Leipzig, 1855) Χρειὼ πάντ' ἐδίδαξε.

36 praxin From the Greek πρᾶξις ; by practice.

50 An pro camelionte me habes From their inanimate appearance and power of existing for long periods without food, chameleons were formerly supposed to live on air.

c.f. Shakespeare, Hamlet III.2.97-9

King. How fares our cousin Hamlet?

Ham. Excellent i' faith; of the chameleons dish
I eat the air promise-crammed.

54-5   longaeviores sunt multo qui parce, quam qui largiter edunt

Taken from Lazarillo de Tormes p. 42.

61-2   c.f. Erasmus, Apophthegmes, translated by Nicolas Udall

(1542) aiiir "mene should abstein from meates, whiche

might provoke a manne to eate, havyng no appetite, nor

beeyng houngrie".

63   acetum, sinapi   Like other condiments, with their

pronounced flavour, used to season or give relish to food,

or to stimulate the appetite.

65   peccata sua, quae ut nosti probe ieiunando expiari assolent

There is no command to fast in the New Testament, but

abstinence from food and drink was generally considered a

way to avoid or expiate sin.   C.f. Erasmus, An Epystell

unto ... Christofer Bysshop of Basyle Concernyng the

Forbedynge of Eatynge of Flesshe (c.1530), Aiiiv-Aivr.

68-9   Eam dum cogites facile fames excidit   C.f. Ovid, Heroides

XI.26-7 on the effect of love:

                    macies adduxerat artus,
            Sumebant minimos ora coacta cibos

73   _pomum quoddam Indicum_   Indian apple is another name for

the may-apple, an American herbaceous plant bearing

yellowish fruit, which resembles a pineapple in flavour.

There is a reference in Sir William D'Avenant's The Wits

to "soft Indian plum" (II,iii) i.e. _Flacourtia Cataphracta_.

However it is most likely that the fruit referred to here

is the orange for which Spain, especially Seville, was

famed.   It has a strong fragrance and appears to have

originated from the Northern frontier of India, although

it is not called an Indian fruit elsewhere.

78   _Esclavo!_   (Spanish) "Slave!"

Act 3.   Scene 3.   This scene parallels the action of _La Cintia_ III.2,
      the vital part of the scene (ll. 81-91) being translated
      literally from the Italian.

Act 3.   Scene 4.   This scene is closely based on _La Cintia_ III.3.

113   _Con il diablo, doh, malos annos_   (Spanish) "May the

devil take you, oh yes indeed!" Again Spanish and Italian

are confused: Italian _il_ is used for _el_.

Act 3.   Scene 5.   This scene parallels the action of _La Cintia_ III.4.

117   <u>meique Mavortis</u>   Mavors is an old and poetic name for

    Mars, god of war, and Don Piedro uses the word to represent

    his military career.   Love affairs and war cannot be

    reconciled, c.f. Shakespeare, <u>Love's Labour's Lost</u>

    I.2.188-90.

    <u>Don Armado</u>: Adieu, valour! rust, rapier! be still, drum!
              for your manager/is in love; yea he loveth.

Act 3.   Scene 6.   This scene parallels the action of <u>La Cintia</u> III.5.

132   <u>Malos annos</u>   (Spanish) "Indeed".

135   <u>Ve con dios, passate con dios</u>   (Spanish) "God be with you,

    pass with God's blessing".

142   <u>Etiamne hic stas? Hem tibi ubi es omnium?</u>

    A stage direction is needed here.   Don Piedro is hiding from

    Lepidus, while pretending to seek him out at the same time.

    The parallel passage in <u>La Cintia</u> elucidates the action

    here: "<u>Ama.</u> Dove fuggi.   <u>Cap.</u> Io fuggo? ahi Ciel traverso, io

    seguo te ... " (E2r).

146-7   <u>Don. Hem tibi, meum gladium, aggredere tu illum.</u>

    <u>Gril. Nunquam is mihi commovit bilem, quod scio.</u>

    Hawkesworth again uses the same situation originally found

    in <u>Leander</u> IV.9., <u>Hippocrassus</u>: Cape sis hoc baculum Grille./

    Grillus: Ah/Minime here.

152   hominum mendicabula c.f. Plautus, Aulularia 703.

153   Vamos ... vamos (Spanish) "Let's go ... let's go". See
also III,154 and 155.

Act 3. Scene 7. This scene is an almost literal translation of
La Cintia III.6.

172-3   Gratiae Veneres,/Et Cupidines Lepidus appeals to deities
who might be expected to favour lovers: Venus, goddess of
love, Cupid, her son, and the three Graces, personifications
of favour, lovlieness and grace. For the use of Venus and
Cupid in the plural c.f. Catullus, Carmina 3.1 "Lugete,
o Veneres Cupidinesque".

176-7   amorem iamdudum ipso hoc in pectore/Fecisse incendium mihi
A common conceit used several times by Hawkesworth, e.g.
III,107; III,181-2; III,186. c.f. Andreas Alciatus,
Emblemata (Leyden , 1551), p. 124 "In statuam Amoris";

        Igneus est, aiunt, versatque in pectore flammas.
        Cur age vivit adhuc? omnia flamma vorat.

179   Quippe faemineus raro solidus est et stabilis amor
c.f. Virgil, Aeneid IV. 569-70 "Varium et mutabile semper/
femina" and Seneca, De remediis fortuitorum 16.4 "nihil est
tam mobile quam feminarum voluntas, nihil tam vagum".

213   Fidem si fefellero, habeatur Lucretius mortalium perfidissimus

This device was originally used in Plautus, Amphitruo

9_33-4 when Jupiter, disguised as Amphitruo pledges

Id ego si fallo, tum te, summe Iuppiter,
Quaeso Amphitruoni ut semper iratus sies.

See also Labyrinthus III, 138; III,312.

220   Quam sit hic locus metuo pudicitiae lubricus, nox,

tenebrae atque amor

c.f. Terence, Adelphi 470 "Persuasit nox amor vinum

adulescentia".

Act 3 Scene 8.   This scene is original with Hawkesworth, providing

a parallel to La Cintia III.7.

Act 3. Scene 9. This scene is loosely based on some lines in the

second part of Act 3, Scene 9 of La Cintia (E7v).

Act 3. Scene 10· This scene is based on the first part of

La Cintia III.9.

258   Secede to   Addressed to Crispinus.

Act 3. Scene 11. This scene forms a parallel to La Cintia III.8.

286-7 <u>nihil dulce est in vita, cui non admiscetur/Timoris aliqui</u>

<u>et periculi</u>

c.f. Apuleius, <u>Florida</u> 18 "nihil quicquam homini tam

prosperum divinitus datum, quin ei tamen admixtum sit

aliquid diffkultatis".

Act 4. Scene 1. This scene is based on <u>La Cintia</u> IV.1.

7 <u>loquentem semel pudere satius est, quam tacentem pavere</u>

<u>   indies</u>

c.f. "Satius est subire semel quam semper pavere" (Hans

Walther, <u>Proverbia sententiaeque Latinitatis medii aevi</u>,

6 vols, Göttingen, 1963-9, 27554c).

12 <u>Quae necessitas fert mala, ferendo corrigas</u>

c.f. Virgil, <u>Aeneid</u> V, 710 "superanda omnis fortuna

ferendo est".

19 <u>Socrates fiam. Sobrie, caute, callide.</u> Presumably

Tiberius intends to broach the subject of the marriage

of Lydia and Lepidus by the familiar Socratic method of

cross-questioning. c.f. Cooper, <u>Thesaurus</u> (Ooooooo vi v)

"Under sharpe and mery tauntes in the fourme of argument

called <u>Inductio</u> he ⌐Socrates⌐ caused men to perceyve

their ignorance".

Act 4. Scene 2.   This scene is based on La Cintia IV.2.

47   denarium   "The Romaine pennie" (Cooper, Thesaurus).

49   Por mis peccados, por mis peccados   (Spanish) "For my
          sins, for my sins".

54-5   Intolerabil pestilentia/Y mortall te consuma   (Spanish)
          "May a terrible and deadly plague put an end to you".

56   Vamos ... vamos   (Spanish) "Let's go ... let's go".
          See also IV.57.

Act 4. Scene 3.   This scene is loosely based on La Cintia IV.3.

Act 4. Scene 4.   This scene is loosely based on La Cintia IV.4.

119   an videns vigilans somnias?   c.f. Plautus, Captivi 848
          "Hic vigilans somniat".

125   Cave obsecro quid agas?   Presumably Lepidus has lost his
          temper and has struck out at Horatius.

132   An tu eam de genere leporum autumas, ut et praegnans sit,
          et praegnantes faciat?
          c.f.   John Lyly, Midas II.2.   "Hares we cannot be, because

they are male one yere, and the next female".

(The Complete Works of John Lyly, edited by R. Warwick Bond,
3 vols, Oxford, 1902).

38   Ubi vis, non moror   c.f. Terence, Eunuchus 460.

43   Quaenam sunt haec tempora?   c.f. Cicero, In C. Verrem
        II.4.25 "O tempora, o mores!"

50   Facito quod virum decet; aut corrigas, aut feras.
        c.f. IV.12 above.

Act 4.   Scene 5.   This scene closely follows La Cintia IV.5. with
         some omissions.

52   hoccine credibile est, aut memorabile!   c.f. Leander III.4.
        and Terence, Andria 625.

64   Sive foemina illa mortalis fuit, sive dea   c.f. Ovid
        Metamorphoses IV.321-2 "seu tu deus es .../Sive es mortalis".

65-6   Amo/Neque quid amo, scio   c.f. Hugo Grotius, Poemata Omnia
        (Leyden , 1645), Silvae III, Epithalamium Philippi Guilielmi
        "Nec, quid amet, novit, sed amat" (E10v).

168 <u>Certum est, remistam inultam non amittere</u> c.f. Plautus,

<u>Amphitruo</u> 847 "istam re: inquisitam certumst non amittere".

Act 4. Scene 6. This scene is closely based on <u>La Cintia</u> IV.6.

174 <u>Quin reprime impetum hunc</u> c.f. Senea, <u>Medea</u> 381 where

the Nurse says to Medea, "resiste et iras comprime ac

retine impetum".

182 <u>Non est miseria mori, cui misera est vita; optare mortem,</u>

<u>et vivere illa est miseria</u>

c.f. <u>Biblia Sacra</u>, Eccesiastici 30.17. "Melior est mors,

quam vita amara".

203 <u>Servare nolentem, mater, crudelis est misericordia</u>

c.f. Seneca, <u>Hercules Octaeus</u> 929-30 "Quicumque misero

forte dissuadet mori,/crudelis ille est".

204 <u>Caetera prius experiri sapientem addecet, mortem adire</u>

<u>ultimo</u>

c.f. Terence, <u>Eunuchus</u> 789 "Omnia prius experiri quam armis

sapientem decet".

Act 4. Scene 7. This scene is closely based on <u>La Cintia</u> IV.7.

228 <u>Aliud ex alio malum</u> c.f. Terence, <u>Eunuchus</u> 987.

250-1   <u>O anima! Ut quid non fugis etiam e turbato hoc et misero/</u>

<u>Corporis ergastulo</u>

c.f. Prudentius, <u>Peristephanon</u> V.358-9

    quae corporali ergastulo
    mentem resolvit liberam

(<u>Prudence</u>, edited by M. Lavarenne, 4 vols, Paris 1943-   ).

Seneca too speaks of the body as a prison of the mind,

c.f. <u>De beneficiis</u> III.20.1 "mens quidem sui iuris.

quae adeo libera et vaga est, ut ne ab hoc quidem carcere,

cui inclusa est, teneri queat ... ".

260   <u>O homines!</u> c.f. Shakespeare, <u>Othello</u> IV.3.60 "O, these

men, these men!"

Act 4. Scene 8. This scene is closely based on <u>La Cintia</u> IV.8,

although Hawkesworth introduces Crispinus earlier in the

scene and increases his part.

293   <u>aequiparabilem</u> Found only in Plautus among classical

writers.

Act 4. Scene 9. This scene is based on <u>La Cintia</u> IV.9. with some

changes toward the end.

378   <u>Id quod rei solent, tacet et metuit</u>

c.f. Michael Drayton, <u>The Owle</u> 1.174 "A/guiltie Conscience feeles continuall feare".

(The Works of Michael Drayton, edited by J. William Hebel, 5 vols, Oxford, 1931-41.)

383-4   Immo ventrem potius,

Tantae ingratitudinis semen ipsum ut extinguas insuper

i.e. the child in her womb. c.f. Seneca, Oedipus 1038-9

Jocasta seeks to punish her womb for the troubles it has

caused: "hunc dextra, hunc pete/uterum capacem, qui virum

et natos tulit".

Act 4.   Scene 10.   This scene is an almost literal translation of

La Cintia IV.10.

401   Sumne hic, an apud inferos   c.f. Leander IV.7. "Ubi ego sum?

hic, an apud inferos?" and Plautus, Mercator 602 "ubi, ubi

ego sum? hicine an apud mortuos".

423   Proteum   A minor sea god who knew all things and had the

power to take all manner of shapes in order to escape being

questioned, as "Lucretius" seemingly changed sex. c.f. Ovid

Metamorphoses VIII,730-1.

> Sunt, quibus in plures ius est transire figuras,
> Ut tibi, complexi terram maris incola, Proteu.

ct 5. Scene 1   This scene is closely based on __La Cintia__ V.1.,
although there are some omissions.

1   __Propere, propere, bene est, sat bene, sat est__
c.f. St. Jerome, __Epistulae__ LXVI.9 "sat cito, si sat bene".
(__Lettres__, edited by J. Labourt, 8 vols, Paris, 1949-1963.)

7   __Quid primum querar__   c.f. Seneca, __Hercules Octaeus__ 180
"quae prima querar?".

3   __Faustule__   The context shows that, in the lines following,
Synesius is addressing the nurse rather than Faustulus,
who knew nothing of Ersilia's secret until Lucretia told
him (I.4). Perhaps Synesius simply calls to the servant
for his stick, which Faustulus has brought from the house,
and then turns back to the nurse.

9   __ab incepto desisteret__   c.f. Virgil, __Aeneid__ I.37 "incepto
desistere".

ct 5. Scene 2.   This scene is based on __La Cintia__ V.2.

6   __Nuntium apporto tibi, cuius minime te fieri participem velles__
c.f. Terence, __Heauton Timorumenos__ 427-8 "Nuntium adporto
tibi,/Quoius maxume te fieri participem cupis".

55-72   c.f. Plautus, Rudens (954-966) where Trachalio tricks Gripus into declaring his own sentence, as Synesius does here with Cassander.

Act 5. Scene 3.   This scene is closely based on La Cintia V.3.

108   Ita nunc pudeo   c.f. Plautus, Casina 877. The use of pudeo as a personal verb is extremely rare in classical Latin, but is found in the works of Plautus and Terence. See also Labyrinthus IV.108.

124-5   ut Lepidae vice .../Nescio quod supposuerit scortum exoletum mihi   c.f. V, 49-50 where Cassander uses almost the same words.

154   tuasque suspiciens virtutes   c.f. V.87 Cassander is echoing Synesius' words.

158   O Cupido, quantus es!   c.f. Plautus, Mercator 854.

168   Cor miserum hoc continuis suspiriis guttatim contabescet c.f. Plautus, Mercator 204-5 "Edepol cor miserum meum,/Quod guttatim contabescit".

172   Siste, quaeso, hunc impetum   c.f. IV.174 the nurse and Cassander comfort the young people with almost the same word.

Act 5.   Scene 4.   This scene is based on <u>La Cintia</u> V.4. and 5.

Hawkesworth brings forward the beginning of Cintia's labour

pains from the end of V.5. and omits the entrance of Dulone

and his reconciliation with Cintia.

182   <u>hanccine ego te ad rem natam miseram memorabo</u>   c.f. Plautu.

           <u>Rudens</u> 188 "Hancine ego ad rem natam miseram memorabo?"

188-9   c.f. Seneca, <u>Medea</u> 387-9 where the nurse describes Medea's

           emotional behaviour:

                   flammata facies spiritum ex alto citat,
                   proclamat, oculos uberi fletu rigat,
                   renidet: omnis specimen affectus capit.

189-90   <u>cui multae certe insunt/Curae exanimales</u>   c.f. Plautus,

           <u>Rudens</u> 221 "ita mihi multae in pectore sunt curae

           exanimales".

232-3   <u>Nulla mihi res posthac potest intervenire tanta, quae</u>

                                                         <u>mihi ullam</u>

           <u>Aegritudinem adferat.</u>

           c.f. Terence, <u>Heauton Timorumenos</u> 679-80

                   Nulla mihi res posthac potest iam intervenire tanta,
                   Quae mi aegritudinem adferat.

238   <u>Vivamne, an apud inferos sim</u>   c.f. IV,401 above.

242   <u>Annon tu me satis noveras</u>   c.f. I.431, Horatius echoes

           Faustulus' words to Lucretia.

252   <u>Vivamus dehinc, atque amemus</u>   c.f. Catullus, <u>Carmina</u> 5.1 "Vivamus, mea Lesbia, atque amemus".

255   <u>Calor insuetus per venas discurrit meas, atque omnes</u> <u>mihi artus occupat</u>

Hot flushes are not among the usual symptoms of labour, but in this case serve merely to draw attention to the imminent birth of Lucretia's son. For the phrase <u>artus occupat</u> c.f. Virgil, <u>Aeneid</u> VII.446; XI,424.

Act 5.   Scene 5.   For this scene Hawkesworth completely recasts <u>La ^Cintia</u> V.6, and draws heavily on Roman comedy for Tiberius' attitude to the young and his good-natured acceptance of his son's adventures.

266-7   <u>Volo amari a meis, volo mei patris/Me esse similem</u> c.f. Plautus, <u>Asinaria</u> 67-8 "volo amari a meis,/Volo me patris mei similem".

269   <u>boni frugi</u>   The usual expression is <u>frugi bonae</u> (c.f. Plautus, <u>Trinummus</u> 321), <u>frugi</u> being a dative form used as an undeclinable adjective. Hawkesworth may be using the two adjectives separately here, <u>boni</u> agreeing with <u>qui</u>.

271-2   Quin et adhuc, Tiberi, amoris aliquantum habes, humorisque
                                                                tuo

Etiam   aliquid in corpore; neque dum exaruisti.

c.f. Plautus, Miles Gloriosus 640-1:

> Et ego amoris aliquantum habeo umorisque etiam in corpore
> Nequedum exarui ex amoenis rebus et voluptariis.

275   quasi mulso vinum austerum, temperabo   The wine of the

sixteenth century and earlier was often of such bad

quality that spices and sweeteners were added to make it

palatable.

281   Et vitae quod est reliquum, voluptate, vino, et lubentia

consumere   c.f. Plautus, Mercator 547-8:

> Breve iam relicuom vitae spatiumst: quin ego
> Voluptate, vino, amore id delectavero

283   Si quid a nobis peccatum sit, profer   c.f. Terence,

Hecyra 253 "siquid est peccatum a nobis, profer".

284   quid sic acetum loqueris, et intueris sinapi   He speaks

sharply and looks hotly.   c.f. Thomas Tomkis, Lingua

(1607) II.3. "There's a Musterd maker lookes as keene as

Viniger will have another".   See also Plautus, Truculentus

315-6 "Si ecastor hic homo sinapi victitet, non censeam/

Tam esse tristem posse".

286   Hey! Quid agis?   Presumably Cassander is making threatening

gestures towards Tiberius.

294-6   ... Nam ut nunc mos est maxime,

Quid novum fecit? Quid mirum adolescens homo si amet,

Si amoribus potiatur suis?

c.f. Plautus, Pseudolus 433-5:

> ... ut nunc mos est, maxume,
> Quid mirum fecit? quid novom, adolescens homo
> Si amat, si amicam liberat?

299-300   fecere tale antehac/Alii spectati viri   c.f. Plautus

Mercator 318 "Fecere tale ante aliei spectatei virei".

305   Plus potest, qui plus valet   c.f. Plautus, Truculentus 812.
Hawkesworth draws considerably on the scene in Truculentus
in which Callicles discovers that Diniarchus has raped his
daughter, and arrangements are made for their marriage
(ll. 775-853).

306-7   Nulla ... foemina/Vim invita patitur

c.f. Ovid, Ars Amatoria I.673-4

> Vim licet appelles, gratast vis ista puellis:
> Quod iuvat, invitae saepe dedisse volunt.

307-8   tu istuc insipienter factum/Sapienter feras   c.f. Plautus,

Truculentus 826-7 "per tua obsecro/Te genua, ut istuc

insipienter factum sapienter feras".

321   Nam haud mansit dum ego darem, ipse sumpsit sibi.

c.f. Plautus, Truculentus 843 "Nam haud mansisti, dum

ego darem illam: tute sumpsisti tibi".

351   **Martium, Valerium, Areotinum, Quintianum, Aemilium, et**

    Alphonsum aulicum

Only two names on this list may refer to historical person-

ages. "Areotinum" may be Pietro Aretino (1492-1557), who

wrote five comedies among other works. "Quintianum" may

be Giovanni Francesco Conti (1484-1557), known as

Quintianus Stoa, a Latin poet who also wrote on prosody.

Neither man can be considered among "primos omnes

Florentiae"; Aretino lived in Venice for most of his life

and Quintianus spent much time in France. "Alphonsum

aulicum" is, of course, Flaminia's suitor in Leander.

    The names on this list are probably entirely fictional.

Compare a similar list of guests invited to a dinner in

Samuel Brooke's Adelphe V.8 (Trinity College, Cambridge

MS R.3.9):

> Flaminius. Aurelius. Martepalvenerius. adolescens
>
>   optimus. Flaminius. Quintilianus. Albertus.
>
> Aemilius,/Rondinellus aulicus, et quidam alii.

352-3   **Quique heri etiam in filiae suae nos nuptias vocavit,**

                                Gerastum imprimis,

    Et Leandrum generum suum.

This refers to Leander, Hawkesworth's earlier play, which

was revived with additions for the Bachelor's Commencement

1602/3. See discussion on dating pp. 43-4.

354-6   This passage is interesting as a critical assessment of
the role and character of the hero of <u>Leander</u>, as
Hawkesworth not only wrote the part but also acted it.
The words "aeque ac meipsum amo" are ironic as everyone
in the audience who had seen the play the night before
would know that Hawkesworth, now playing Tiberius, was
speaking of himself.

365-7   <u>Edamus iam, bibamus/Atque animo obsequamur .../</u>
<u>Hilaritudine nos ... onerabimus hodie</u>
c.f. Plautus, <u>Miles Gloriosus</u> 677 "Es, bibe, animo
obsequere mecum atque onera te hilaritudine".

Act 5. Scene 6.   This scene is closely based on <u>La Cintia</u> V.7.

385   <u>Quantis me hodie cumulasti bonis</u>   c.f. V.159, Cassander
echoes Horatius' words.

Act 5. Scene 7.   This scene is closely based on <u>La Cintia</u> V.8.

389   <u>spem inter et metum</u>   c.f. Virgil, <u>Aeneid</u> 218 "spemque
metumque inter".

392   <u>metu ego hoc miserum eximam</u>   c.f. Terence, <u>Andria</u> 338-9
"sed ubi inveniam Pamphilum,/Ut metum inquo nunc est adimam".

Act 5. Scene 8. This scene is original.

416   vamos, Petre vamos   (Spanish) "let's go, Peter let's go".

         etc.   This is presumably a cue for the actor to

         improvise.

429-45   This episode is based on Lazarillo de Tormes pp. 55-7.

         Hawkesworth changes the story slightly and makes the

         servant abscond rather than the master.

436-8   The description of Don Piedro's house is from Lazarillo

         de Tormes pp. 38-9.

438   quod ille thorum appellavit suum   Don Piedro says thorum

         for torum. The th sound seems to have been considered a

         feature of the Spanish accent, c.f. Ben Jonson, The

         Alchemist IV.3. where Subtle pretends to speak Spanish:

         "Entratha the chambratha".

440-1   Quin et animalia quaedam memorare bene laeta, et perpinguia

         Quae somno tantum vescebantur

         Don Piedro was probably thinking of the bear. Pliny reports

         that the males come out of hibernation remarkably fat,

         although during this period no signs of food are to be

         found in the stomach of the animal and only a very slight

quantity of liquid: "primis diebus bis septenis tam gravi
somno premuntur ut ne vulneribus quidem excitari queant.
tunc mirum in modum veterno pinguescunt" (<u>Naturalis Historia</u>
VIII.36).

448 <u>hodierno in convivio</u> Numerous Latin comedies end with a
banquet, either on stage or behind the scenes, e.g. Plautus
<u>Bacchides</u>, <u>Curculio</u>, <u>Pseudolus</u>. <u>Labyrinthus</u> combines the
classical and romantic, ending with a banquet and two
marriages. Northrop Frye suggests that these celebrations
signalize the appearance of a "new society" as the hero
and heroine triumph over the characters who had the upper
hand at the beginning of the play and obstructed their
desires (<u>Anatomy of Criticism: Four Essays</u> (Princeton, 1957)
pp. 163-4).

460 <u>exedit mihi paene ventris medullam fames</u> c.f. Plautus,
<u>Stichus</u> 341 "medullam ventris percepit fames".

462 <u>Honestas fraudes</u> A comedy called <u>Fraus Honesta</u>, written
by E. Stubb of Trinity College, was performed at Cambridge
in 1618/9 and 1629, and was printed in 1632.

APPENDIX A

Lineation

The problems posed by the lineation of the various extant copies of Labyrinthus have already been discussed in the section on the metrical features of the play. A comparison of the lineation of all texts in a sample passage (III, 136-220) was made to show the differences between them.

The results show that only two manuscripts completely match any other in their system of lineation. Closer resemblances are found between members of the same genetic groupings than between the other manuscripts but, as in the case of substantive variants, there is little evidence of any direct derivation. For example, a comparison of J with the other texts reveals a very close relationship with D, with only one difference in lineation (ll. 216-7), and many resemblances to L, with only four cases of differing line division, at l. 151 caused by omission in L, ll. 153-5, ll. 197-8, ll. 209-10 caused by omission in L. J is also quite close to P where, except for three discrepancies in line division (ll. 145-7, ll. 188-9, ll. 216-7), the differences are accounted for by P printing many of J's lines as two. However it must be noted that J is closer to CYT in lineation than it is to N, with which, according to variant readings, it forms a group.

The grouping CYT is very close, as C and T correspond exactly in this sample passage and together have only two differences in lineation from Y, which omits part of lines 153-4 and reverses the order of lines 148-9. The group CYT has twenty-six lines divided as P out of the eighty-four lines of the sample section. The lineation of N is almost entirely different from that of any other of the manuscripts. It has only three lines in common with LJ, four with D, seven with P, and eleven with CYT.

Thus we find the split between CYT and PDNLJ, which occurred also in the sample collations of variants, and yet variation within PDNLJ is even greater than between the two major groupings. It is in the light of such variation that I have resorted to adopting the lineation of P as it stands, for, although it has several discrepancies P shares many lines with the majority of the manuscripts, as well as being the base text for my edition of Labyrinthus.

APPENDIX B

Revisional changes in D in the hand of D[1]

The reading of D[1] is before the bracket, that of D follows it.

ACT I

123   ⌐line omitted.

133   ipsasque ⌐ ipsas

134   aliquis misericors ⌐ aliquis

154   adolescentulos ⌐ adolescentos

169   Tiberi crepuerunt fores: ⌐ Tiberi:

175   ubi vero ⌐ ubi

179   vero. manus huic et ⌐ vero

185-7   Cick, ah viveret? Deum fidium, ut ego hoc nunc
            gestio, Huiusmodi aliquem interficere.
        Hor. Sumne ego infoelix.   ⌐
                        Viveret? lepidum hoc esset.

197-8   Hor. Dii illud perdant, ita est astute callidus.
            Quam confidenter autem sese intulit iam inde
            a principio. ⌐
                        Hor. Quam confidenter.

213-4   impudens! Quam ego te ob istam confidentiam
        Non possum quin deosculer! Vah delicias facis:
            neutiquam nevis. — hem tibi.   ⌐
                        impudens! hem tibi.

219   me toties ⌐ me

241   est hic ⌐ est

250   Quam tremo forte. ⌐ Quam tremo.

321-2   ⌐lines omitted.

342 Horatius medium per parietem _/_ Horatius

359 praestiterem _/_ praestarem

362 sibi cum illo _/_ cum illo

366 permanasseret _/_ permanaret

372 penes, nos _/_ penes

396 Dii omnes _/_ Dii

412 mutua propinantes _/_ propinantes

426 est _/_ esse

432-3 _/_ lines omitted

448 cape haec _/_ cape

452 illi nec _/_ illi

457 et illius _/_ illius

459 virginis _/_ sanguinis

464 ut sit _/_ sit

515 elegans es _/_ elegans

520 ut abstineas _/_ abstineas

549 _/_ line omitted.

571 non tu _/_ non

629-30 _/_ lines omitted.

646 Pu. Bene _/_ Bene

   Tib. iuxta _/_ iuxta

672 Pu. Cancro _/_ omitted.

675 ocyus. Puer _/_ ocyus.

685 e Neapoli _/_ Neapoli

695 Est potus in febre _/_ omitted.

708 filia quem ⟋ quem filia

727 de filia. Tiberi? ⟋ filia.

804 unquam crudelitas ⟋ unquam

808 coelestium scelestissime ⟋ scelestissime

892 haud te ⟋ haud

ACT II

3 visi sunt ⟋ sunt

15 prospiciendum tibi intelligo ⟋ prospiciendum est tibi

60 in timore spem quaerens, In dolo fidem, in flammis
      refrigerium. ⟋ omitted

114 ultimo die ⟋ ultimo

120 oboriretur ⟋ obiretur

158 ut se uxorem . . desponderet ⟋ ut eam desponderet

186 Eamus ad coenam. ⟋ omitted.

213 fuego ⟋ fa, ego

232 cielos ⟋ cibos

237 ego igitur ⟋ igitur

254 es nactus ⟋ nactus

270-5 Gril. Sine me modo.
Ego istuc recte fecero. Don. Vamos. Gril. I prae Here,
Quando tu duos passus confeceris, hinc ego insequar
Unus, duo, tres. O here rursum incipe. Don. Vamos
     vamos. Gril. Vamos vamos.   ⟋
                          vamos Grille vamos. Gril. Vamos vamos.

309   animo te ⫐ animo

311   composui hodie ⫐ composui

365   propriis suis ⫐ propriis

390   sic ⫐ hic

434   aliquot puellis ⫐ aliquot

450   compareret ⫐ comparet

457   et ·convoca ⫐ et ..... (illeg.)

551   quaenam ⫐ quanta

575   cordi ⫐ vidi

ACT III

 59   minime minime ⫐ minime

101   mihi ⫐ tibi

116   oculis atque auribus ⫐ oculis

117   Miror me ⫐Miror

120   Quarum ⫐ Quorum

141   hic exclusus exhilarus ⫐ hic exhilarus

258   Descende obsecro ad ostium.   Secede tum.⫐ Secede Lepida.

287   Lys. Hem ⫐ Hem

304   mihi hercle ⫐ hercle

314   eiah: ⫐ etiam

320   sum domi ⫐ sum

ACT IV

20	Signior Tiberi!] Tiberi!
207	sinas] serius
327	exosculabere] osculabere

ACT V

1	sat bene. sat est sic] sat bene. sic
194	]line omitted.
209	priusquam] praeterquam
327	illam uxorem] uxorem
365	statim] iamdudum
377	]line omitted.
414	O benedicto Iddio] omitted.
450	nuptiis nobiscum] nuptiis

STAGE DIRECTIONS

Dramatis Personae

Tiberius senex Domus Dec. superior.] Tiberius senex
Cassander senex Domus Bac. in medio.] Cassander senex
Synesius senex Domus Dec. inferior.] Synesius senex
Hispanus semper e Foro] Hispanus

ACT I

1	Don Piedro must passe over the stage. Exit viso Horatio. ⟋ Don Piedro must passe over the stage.
116	Horatius abigit cum fuste. Exit Grillus per forum Decani. ⟋ Exit Grillus per forum Decani.
121	Tiberius e domo propria. Ingreditur cantans ad cytharam Buon di, Buon di, Madonna Modina etc. ⟋ Tiberius e domo propria.
176	Cantus. Buon di, buon di etc. ⟋ omitted.
177	Crispinum vidit a tergo ad fenestras. ⟋ omitted.
189	desilit Crispinus ⟋ He spies Crispinus in the window.
214	Pecunias offert Crispino. ⟋ omitted.
220	She spies Horatio and nods to him to be gone. ⟋ omitted.
432	Ostendit ventrem. ⟋ omitted.
502	Lucretia steps back againe. ⟋ omitted.
585	Dat plures nummos. ⟋ omitted.
587	aurem Lysettae insuserat. ⟋ omitted.
623	vidit Lepidus patrem egredientem ⟋ omitted.
659	Cassander e domo propria consulens horologium. ⟋ Cassander e domo propria.
671	ostendit ei Cassandrum ⟋ omitted.
672	Cantat et ingredientem revocat Cassander. ⟋ omitted.
719	The boy gives him a boule of wine. propinat Cassandro, ille vero recusat. ⟋ The boy gives him a boule of wine.

732 Exit puer] omitted.

764 inerat hic Lepida osculans Lydiam.] omitted.

859 He kisses her.] omitted.

890 dat pecunias] omitted.

ACT II

86 Exit Lucretius maestus ac plangens ad forum Decani.] Exit Lucretius ad forum Decani.

221 Citharaedus canit ad citharam Stava la gentil dama etc.] omitted.

381 Lepida singes within] omitted.

399 Lysetta e fenestra Cassandri starching a bande.] Lysetta e fenestra Cassandri

455 Horatius incedit domum. Lysetta, Lidia in fenestra.] Lysetta, Lidia in fenestra.

ACT III

218 Lydia on the stage.] omitted.

APPENDIX C

Results of trial textual analyses

A. Collation of missing lines in the texts of Labyrinthus.

  i Single MSS containing unique variants

      P omits II,221; II,304.

      D omits I,123; I,186; I,187; I,432-3; I,549;
             II,270-4; V,194; V,377.
             All omissions in D have been corrected
             in the course of revision except I,187.

      Y omits I,91; I,219; I,408-9; I,693-4; III,100-1;
             IV,301-2; V,285.

      N omits I,235-6 (later corrected); I,238-9; II,100-1;
             II,334; II,544-5; III,311; V,434; V,460.

      L omits I,464-5; I,509-10; I,582; I,666-7; I,720-1;
             I,792; II,14; II,36; II,41; II,309; II,330;
             II,333; III,177; III,203; III,210-1; III,294-5;
             IV,8; IV,50; IV,55; IV,83-4; IV,106-7; IV,301;
             IV,369-71; V,49; V,211; V,302; V,317-9; V,416.

      J omits III,274-5.

      T omits IV,281-2; V,131; V,159.
             All omissions in T have been later corrected.

  ii Groups of two MSS.

      CY omit V,59.

      NJ omit III,3-4.

      DL omit III,25c. D is corrected in the course of revision.

iii Groups of three MSS.

    CYT omit I,889-91; II,537; IV,80.

    PYN omit II,304.

iv Groups of four MSS.

    DNLJ omit I,1; I,186; I,198; I,213-4.
           In all cases D has been corrected in the
           course of revision.

    NLJT omit IV,11.   T is later corrected.

v MSS and groups of MSS which include lines omitted elsewhere.

    L has extra material at II,419; II,453; II,476.

    PD has extra material at I,518; I,321-2 (after
        revision of D).

    NJ has extra material at II,502.

    PDL has extra material at I,486-7; III,5-6; IV,9-10.

    NLJ has extra material at V,415.

vi Omissions explicable by homoeoteleuton and homoeoarchy.

    P omits II,221 (Incipe).

    D omits I,629-30 (O generosam!); III,45-6 (passa).

    Y omits II,10-12 (amat colit intime); IV,87-8 (Lepida).

    N omits II,495 (venias).

    L omits I,654-5 (Pu. Ah); II,221 (Incipe); III,43-6
        (Unica); IV,368-72 (nuptiis ... nuptias).

    J omits I,806 (meum).

    T omits IV,310-15 (Tune); IV,350-1(pellexeras ...
        compuleras); V,63-4 (Syn.).
        T has been later corrected in all cases.

CY omit I,182 (Viveret).

YN omit II,303-7 (Reginas ha ha he ... Reginam ha ha he).

YL omit III,153-4 (vamos).

LT omit I,252-4 (Faust. Foemina). T later corrected.

CDY omit V,377 (Cass. Quid). ν is corrected in the
        course of revision.

CYT omit II,19-20(iterum); II,297-8 (inquam).

B Collation of Acts I and III.

These collations are based on non-grammatical variants
wherever possible. Letters in brackets represent manuscripts
which have been changed to or from the reading of the grouping.

  i Groupings of two MSS.

    PC   I,421.

    PD   I. 74; 77; 99; 135; 136; 160; 169(D); 179;
                179(D); 185(D); 188(D); 198(D); 241; 249;
                269; 272; 308; 321-2(D); 335; 342(D); 352;
                353(D); 363; 366(D); 372(D); 388; 391;
                396(D); 399; 412(D); 455; 460; 459(D);
                487; 512; 515-16(D); 518; 536; 566; 575;
                627; 628; 643; 646(D); 658; 659; 675(D);
                678; 686; 695(D); 696(D); 704; 713;
                728(D); 736; 738; 742; 752; 783; 797;
                798; 804(D); 840; 869(D); 888.

          III. 10; 13; 16; 20; 27; 34(D); 38; 47; 51;
                59(D); 82; 83; 90(D); 95; 123; 126; 128;
                143; 148; 166; 176(D); 185; 203; 217;
                223; 225; 254(D); 258(D); 276; 311;
                314(D); 316; 333.

    PY   I,177; III,73.

YT   I.   159;372; 412(T); 658; 852(T).

NL   I.   71; 330; 376(N); 417(L); 452; 504; 702; 750; 785.

      III,169.

NJ   I.   77; 149(N); 206; 279; 311; 311; 525; 678; 725; 798.

     III.   3; 4; 10; 88; 95; 110; 119; 121; 175; 241; 315; 320; 336; 343.

LJ   I.   163; 212; 283; 317; 650; 784(J); 790(J); 790.

    III.   27; 47; 291.

LT   I.   239(T); 252-4(T); 498(T); 719(T); 738(T); 765.

JT   I,153.

ii   Groupings of three MSS.

CYT   I.   11; 38;46;58; 63; 77; 89; 98; 104; 120; 123; 124; 127(T); 131(T); 146; 149; 152; 153; 155; 158; 165; 166; 168(T); 171; 173; 180; 193; 196; 198; 213; 214; 214; 231; 249; 251; 254(T); 260; 262; 263; 280; 281; 281; 290; 303; 309; 317; 319; 330; 336; 336(T); 338; 340; 344; 351; 358; 369; 371; 372; 379; 389; 394; 403; 403; 405; 406; 410; 411; 431; 436(T); 437(T); 444; 445; 445; 447; 452; 455; 461; 466; 469; 485; 494; 501; 516; 527; 529; 534(C); 541; 546; 550; 574; 580; 588; 590; 593(T); 596; 599; 603; 607; 627; 637; 638; 642; 652; 654; 656; 656; 659; 663; 672(T); 675; 679; 679; 681; 684; 695; 695; 696; 697; 700(T); 706; 707; 708; 713; 716; 729(T); 736; 737(T); 739; 741; 743; 746; 747; 752; 755-7; 759; 760; 761; 763; 765; 773; 776; 783; 785; 790; 791; 793; 801; 802; 804; 823; 825; 830; 840; 840; 845; 851;

NJT I. 267(T); 857(T).

   III. 41; 254(NT); 258(T).

DLJ I,367(D).

   III,89(D).

There are also 12 cases of unique groupings of three MSS:

DYT I,284; CLT I,669; YLJ I,162; PLJ I,224; LJT I,225;
YJN I,371; PYL I,398; CNJ I,537; CLT I,669; PYN III,178;
PJT III,112; PDT I,437(T).

iii Groupings of four MSS.

  PDLJ I. 32(D); 165; 179; 180; 190; 207; 283; 289;
       330; 371; 395; 401; 406; 411; 438; 445;
       447; 454; 461; 485; 501; 515; 580; 697; 708;
       710; 744; 765; 791; 792; 839.

     III. 12; 15(J); 38; 40; 60; 85; 100(D); 147;
       218; 254; 303.

  CYNT I. 32; 179; 283; 401; 438; 461; 658; 792.

     III. 15; 60; 85; 100; 147; 218; 254; 303.

  DNLJ I. 1(D); 125(D); 186(D); 198(D); 213-4(D);
       263(D); 344; 491(N); 515(D); 571(D); 675(D);
       695(D); 708(D); 887.

     III. 176(D); 195; 293; 327.

  PCYT I. 407; 491(T).

  PDNJ I. 95; 102; 105; 150; 494; 534; 605; 661; 669;
       738; 743; 811; 869; 872; 895; 895.

     III. 11; 31; 66; 116(D); 178.

  CYLT I. 102; 105; 150; 403; 581(L); 605; 674; 745;
       811; 872; 895.

     III,95.

CYJT   I.   158; 356; 575; 719.

      III.   109; 143.

PDNL   I.   356; 670; 719.

PCDT   I.   66; 185(D); 283; 371; 715.

CNJT   I.   91; 245; 536; 742; 769.

NLJT   I.   54; 74.

      III,196(T).

PNLJ   I,284.

      III,38.

There are also 9 cases of unique groupings of four MSS:

PCDY I,54; CNLJ I,648; PDYT I,648; PDYN I,89; CLJT I,89;
PDYL I,245; PDJT I,463; DNLT III,287(D); CDYT I,436(D).

iv   Groupings of five MSS.

PDNLJ   I.   11; 38; 46; 58; 89; 115; 120; 124; 126; 146;
               149; 152(L); 166; 168; 171; 173; 196; 213;
               253; 260; 262; 263; 280; 280; 281; 290; 298;
               303; 309; 318; 319; 320; 336; 338; 340; 358;
               367; 365; 369; 369; 372; 394; 397; 403; 403;
               405; 408; 410; 430; 436(J); 444; 445; 445; 455;
               461; 466; 469; 516; 527; 529; 541; 546; 550;
               574; 581(L); 584; 588; 590; 592; 596; 599;
               603; 607; 627; 630; 637; 652; 654; 656; 656;
               658; 658; 659; 679; 679; 692; 696; 705; 706;
               707; 716; 722; 739; 741; 746; 747; 752; 755-7; 760;
               761; 763; 765; 773; 776; 783(D); 795; 801; 802;
               804; 823; 825; 830; 845; 848; 851; 858; 859;
               864; 865; 875; 877; 878; 879; 888; 889-91.

III.   12; 16; 18; 19; 19; 22; 26; 28; 35; 38; 38; 40; 41; 42; 51; 52; 55; 56; 58; 59; 63; 64; 66; 66; 73; 74; 84; 88; 88; 91; 102; 105; 122; 129; 131; 137; 137; 147; 148; 150; 158; 160; 176; 178; 180; 181; 181; 184; 200; 201; 214; 216; 222; 223.

PCDYT   I. 1(D); 20; 186(D); 197(D); 262(D); 280(T); 554; 571(D); 627; 708(D); 713(D); 760; 776; 857.

III. 73; 175; 196(T); 291; 299; 307.

PDNJT I. 23; 30; 404; 689; 779; 851(T).

CYNJT I. 486-7; 741.

III. 5-6; 203; 274.

CYLJT I,515-16.

III. 13; 20; 37; 65.

CNLJT I. 308; 391.

III. 186; 251.

PDLJT I. 20; 711.

III,289.

CYNLT I. 221; 258.

III,258.

PCDJT I. 520; 651.

There are also 7 cases of unique groupings of five MSS:

CDLJT III,178; PDNLT I,178; CDYNT I,224; CDYJT I,714; PCNLT I,225; PDYLT I,537; CDNJT I,398(T).

APPENDIX D

Scribal errors in Labyrinthus

An authorial reading is probably determined most often by
the identification of the variant most likely to have given rise
to the others in the tradition. By studying the types of error
scribes make while copying, one is able to trace the process of
corruption and identify such a variant with some certainty and,
where possible, to reconstruct the original. This study of
specific types of scribal error leads one to the theory of
difficilior lectio potior:

> Difficilior et obscurior lectio anteponenda est ei,
> in qua omnia tam plana sunt et extricata, ut librarius
> quisque facile intelligere ea potuerit.[1]

It is the tendency of scribes to replace an uncommon expression
by a common one. I have used the knowledge of scribal tendencies
in Labyrinthus to make editorial decisions about the most
authoritative readings and I, therefore, give here a description
of the types of scribal errors found in the manuscripts of
the play.

As there is no wholly derivative manuscript in the tradition
of Labyrinthus one must turn to errors made within the texts and
corrected by the scribe to find examples where the direction of

---

[1] Novum Testamentum Graece, edited by J. J. Griesbach (London,
1809), I, lxiv.

error is clear. Also when a variant is supported by one
manuscript only it is easier to assume one error than several
independent errors. In such a case then the single reading
may be used as a definite corruption for the purposes of
this study.

Because of the circumstances of the tradition of the
play, for example the number of relatively independent
manuscripts, we have to deal mostly with simple corruptions
which have arisen in one copying rather than with complex
corruptions where later scribes have further corrupted the
initial error. The scribal errors in the manuscripts of
Labyrinthus can be divided into two types, mechanical errors
and those caused by scribal editing. Mechanical errors arise
from inattention through fatigue or boredom, from external
distractions, internal distractions of memory and from ignorance.
Errors due to scribal editing are sometimes unconscious but
involve a positive effort on the part of the scribe to change
his copy.

A. MECHANICAL ERRORS

1. The largest class of identifiable errors are those due
   to misreading.

   a) confusion of letters

      Many scribal mistakes consist of a change of only
      one letter in a word. However because many Latin

words differ by one letter from other Latin words,
even if different case forms are not included, it is
difficult to distinguish between a case where a scribe
has misread a single letter and where he has mistaken
one word for another closely resembling it.

i   vowels

marito] merito D II, 310; male] mele J V, 5;
aperiam] cperiam D IV, 6; affectas] affectus
L I, 68; contracta] contructa C V, 312; solutione]
solatione N V, 433; evenissent T^c] evanissent
T V, 244; deficiunt] dificiunt P IV, 88; specula]
spicula Y IV, 179; Lydia T^c] Lydea T III, 198;
color] calor N V, 254; morum] mirum L III, 168;
tuto L^b] toto L V, 251; incoenatum] incanatum L
I, 74; deluctari] delectari Y I, 106.

ii consonants

oliva] obiba L III, 42; flagravit] flagrabit L
V, 155; Ahi] Abi Y II, 58; charissime] clarissime
Y IV, 26; obtectam] oblectam L IV, 391; rimatores]
rivatores L II, 536; vino] vivo N V, 281; Lydia]
Lydra L II, 471; quisquam] quispiam C II, 326;
pacto] facto J V, 75; hic L^c] his L Prol., 3;
leviter] leniter D I, 143; vi N^c] ni vi N V, 206;
angit] augit N V, 115.

iii   groups of letters

    esclamo L^b _7_ esdamo L II, 193; Luscinia _7_ Lusania

    L II, 382; observent _7_ obssvent N I, 61; concelebras _7_

    conceterras L II, 217; videns T^a _7_ videris T IV, 119;

    corraseris _7_ convaseris Y II, 249; verum L^c _7_ utrum L

    II, 93.

During the period when the manuscripts of <u>Labyrinthus</u> were
being copied (i.e. early seventeenth century) a gradual change
was taking place in the fashion of handwriting, italic gradually
replacing the old English secretary hand. As a result there is
often confusion between the letters characteristic to each hand
as well as the usual misreading of similar letters.

ᴦ/r   Ardelia _7_ Arcdelia L I, 71

ᴦ/c   curatio _7_ iuratio L I, 101; suspicacem L^b _7_ suspicarem
    L I, 211; praeriperet _7_ praeciperet C II, 389;
    decipiat _7_ deripiat J III, 204; sic _7_ sit Y IV, 273.

σ/e   advorte _7_ adverte L II, 162; sedato _7_ sodato N III, 291.

ʂ/h   Ah quam _7_ aliquam L IV, 149; prehendat _7_ perpendat L
    I, 61; operi operi _7_ dheri o heri Y II, 314; hic _7_ sic L
    III, 83.

ſ/s   miseram _7_ inferam L IV, 42; siet _7_ fiet N V, 44;
    infamia _7_ insania Y V, 118.

ʒ/x   eximias N^b _7_ opimias N V, 246; ditto V, 181.

Pride of place among misreadings of letters however goes to the confusion of m, n, i, u, v.

> sumne _/ summus Y I, 58; gemmis _/ geminis Y I, 132; unice _/ vince Y I, 525; annos _/ avos L III, 132; inquam _/ unquam N III, 238; iniuriam _/ iniuiriam T IV, 49; inultum _/ multo N IV, 60; innui _/ inivi Y, munum N V, 315; nimium _/ omnium L I, 90.

There is remarkably little confusion about abbreviations in view of their widespread use. The majority of errors lie in the confusion of scribes when expanding the contractions for the prefixes p/per, p/pro, p$^\varepsilon$ /prae and in the use of the macron for m and n.

> persederint _/ procederint Y I, 126; perperam _/ properam P III, 225; promoveam _/ praemoveam D II, 394; praeclusum_/ perclusum N, proclusum L V, 156; adiuvantem _/ adiuvante N V, 33; consilium (ꝏ) _/ consiliud Y III, 12; scilicet (scil.) _/ scit Y IV, 157.

b) mistakes made by forming a wrong visual impression

When one is reading rapidly, even a well-printed book, it is not uncommon to substitute one or two similar words since the letters of the word are not read individually but as a group.

regnum _7_ reginam Y I, 100; et sum an _7_ resumat Y I, 146; culminis _7_ cumulus L II, 11; pridem _7_ pridie P II, 165; harum _7_ earum Y II, 252; unica _7_ amica Y II, 453; cognitissima J^c _7_ notissima cognitissima J II, 112; senectutem T^c _7_ servitutem T IV, 87; altrices T^c _7_ alterius altrices T IV, 214; coeleste N^c _7_ scaeleste N V, 250; cum illo _7_ Camillo Y V, 361.

Errors in word division may be due merely to the spacing of the letters in the copy or they may be due to the scribe taking in the word or phrase in small sections rather than as a whole. It may also of course be a form of unconscious emendation on the part of the scribe.

de via _7_ devia Y I, 161; inquam _7_ in quam N II, 144; te geris _7_ tegeris L III, 170; in vita T^c _7_ invita T III, 286; amaverim _7_ ama veram Y III, 260; autumas T^a _7_ Hoc tua mas T IV, 132; de sponsalibus _7_ desponsalibus T IV, 222; dic clare _7_ declare N V, 117; in posterum _7_ imposterum P V, 230.

Where the scribe has been unable to read his copy he has sometimes tried to reproduce the shape of the word. There is little significance in this tendency as it usually produces nonsense.

harum me rerum _7_ hay me xam Y I, 175; reniego _7_ cein ego Y II, 232.

2. Errors due to distraction of memory and verbal association.
Such errors are due to miswriting rather than misreading. The
copy is taken in correctly but some disturbance takes place
which results in the scribe writing down the word or phrase
wrongly.

a) synonyms

The tendency of the scribe to use synonyms may be
partly due to a wrong visual impression of the word he
is to copy, but it may also be the result of some
distraction while the scribe is holding his copy in his
mind, so that the sense is retained although the original
form is not. Most corruptions of this kind cannot be
detected except by the presence of a rival reading
elsewhere in the manuscript tradition.

ergo ⟧ igitur P I, 60; quam ⟧ ac Y I, 123; cur ⟧ quod Y
I, 151; Heus tu ⟧ Hem tibi Y I, 215; Ancillare huic ⟧
Comitare hanc Y I, 862; hercle J^c ⟧ autem hercle J II, 19;
atque ⟧ et Y II, 75; glaucomam T^c ⟧ nebulam T II, 180;
coenam ⟧ prandium L II, 305; probum C^c ⟧ dignum probum C
II, 232; habet C^c ⟧ amet habet C III, 283; senex es ⟧
annos habes L III, 333; intelligo D^{c}N^c ⟧ scio intelligo
DN IV, 166; sorore tua ⟧ Lydia L IV, 330; censeo C^b ⟧
sentio C V., 56.

b) word order

This type of error can frequently be explained by a
visual or memorial slip on the part of the scribe. There
is usually little change to the sense of the passage and,
because there is no recognizable metre in ᴸabyrinthus, such
errors do not produce obvious metrical anomalies.
Transposition has been recognized as one of the most
common scribal errors and the principle of simplex ordo
has been evolved to deal with it.[2] A complex word order
is often resolved by the scribe into a simple order by
rearranging the words, sometimes with further changes,
e.g. alterations to terminations, to simplify constructions.

   i inversion of two or more words

materies in mundo deridiculi _7 in mundo materies deridiculi Y
I, 760; amicos inter _7 inter amicos N II, 61; mihi
praetereunti _7 mihi praetereunti mihi Y II, 80; amare
vellete ^{cc}_7 velle amare te C III, 193; modo ex illius _7
ex illius modo N III, 316; tu concubitu usus es meo _7 usus es
tu concubitu meo Y, concubitu tu usus es meo N IV, 116;
splendeant aedes _7 aedes splendeant N V, 366; adhuc ut
potero c^b _7 ut potero adhuc C V, 192.

---

[2] Walter Headlam, "The Transposition of Words in MSS", Classical
Review, 16 (1902), 243-4.

"The error which the copyist commits in such a case does
not consist in writing the words in any order at haphazard,
but in arranging them according to the order which they would
have in prose; according to their grammatical construction."

See also George Thomson, "Simplex Ordo", Classical Quarterly,
15 (1965), 161-75.

ii change in position of one word in a sentence

Per lachrymas eius, et mortes, intimumque _7 intimumque
per lachrimas eius et mortes L I, 487.

iii change in order of lines

I, 128-9 T^c _7 order of lines reversed in T; III, 148-9 _7
order of lines reversed in Y.

c) transposition of letters

 This is often the result of unconscious suggestion
as well as fatigue or carelessness, for the resulting words
are usually legitimate.

sine _7 nisi L I, 102; fatigo _7 flagito N I, 141; partui L^c _7
patrui partui L; eo solum _7 eum solo Y II, 39; certe _7
recte J II, 433; regerat _7 ageret N III, 184; aegre _7
agere L IV, 65; obversatur _7 observatur J V, 239; feceras _7
faceres J V, 335.

d) verbal association

 If a familiar phrase is met in the course of copying,
there is a tendency to take in only the first word or so
and assume that the rest is known.

tum primo _7 tum primum Y I, 295; dispice impera _7 despice
respice N II, 32; fili mi ridicule C^b _7 fili mi dulcissime
C (cf. I, 249-50) II, 342; diildent N^c _7 diildent quae velis N

IV, 21; se afflictet adeo C^c _/ se afflictet misere adeo C
IV, 209; taces etiam _/ quid taces Y IV, 275.

e)   perseveration and anticipation

These two classes of mistake arise from the influence
upon any given word of a word coming shortly before or
shortly after.

verba fecit: lepide lusit _/ verba facit: lepide facit Y
I, 212; facio ... fiam _/ fiam ... fiam J II, 50; foemina
foeminam _/ feminam feminam N V, 291; filia tua istum _/
filia tua ista N IV, 43; falsiloquam, et infidum _/
falsiloquum, et infidum L IV, 262.

f)   failures of auditory memory

Such errors may be made in the course of dictation or
simply by the scribe repeating his copy to himself as he
wrote.

renidet _/ renitet Y I, 122; holla _/ o la L II, 190; de
cavaliero _/ delavagliero L II, 247; supprimam _/ supremam L
II, 397; concede _/ con sede Y (c was pronounced soft in
17th cent.) III, 18.

3. Omission

  a) haplography

This is the unintentional writing of a letter, word,
or series of letters or words once, when it should be
written twice.

i letters and syllables

It is often difficult to say if the loss of one of
a pair of double letters within a word is due to haplography
or is merely a peculiarity of spelling on the part of the
scribe.

absterrere $D^b J^b$ _/ absterere DJ I, 8; innupta _/ inupta L
II, 160; humillimus _/ humilimus C II, 322; paululum _/
paulum L I, 98; ditto N I, 99; fefellero _/ fellero N
III, 213; supposititia _/ suppositia L III, 276; mentitum _/
mentium L IV, 147.

ii words

est et L^b _/ est L I, 139; credere. <u>Crisp</u>. Quid ni
credas T^b _/ credere. <u>Crisp</u>. Quid ni. T : II, 135;
profecto profecto _/ profecto Y III, 310; eamus,
eamus _/ eamus N III, 329; Vale, vale, vale _/ vale,
vale, ~~vale~~ N V, 357.

Haplography can sometimes be the result of emendation on
the part of the scribe who, imagining the repetition to be
due to an error of dittography in his copy, omits one of
the letters etc. There are errors in the texts of
<u>Labyrinthus</u> where this process has been carried one step
further and both words omitted.

mi mi _/ om. N I, 213; alloqueris, Don? nam ... video. /
<u>Don</u>. O _/ alloqueris nam ... video / O N II, 227-8.

b)   homoeoteleuton

This is the occurrence of similar endings in two
neighbouring words, clauses, or lines of writing as a
source of error in copying. Having copied as far as the
first of the two letters etc., the scribe looks back at his
copy but his eye accidentally falls on the second letter etc.
and he continues copying from that point, so that all
intermediate material is omitted. This phenomenon is more
often seen in lines and phrases than in words and syllables.

I, 109-10 C (Vale) corrected by C^b; II, 132 L (unum/unquam)
corrected by L^b; II, 221 P (incipe); II, 495 N (venias);
III, 289-94 C (carnifex) corrected by C^b; IV, 87-8 Y
(Lepida! Lepida!); V, 63-4 T (Syn.) corrected by T^a;
V, 108 P (inferam / fugiam).

c)   omission of syllables

There seems to be little consistent reason for this
type of error for it cannot be blamed purely on one thing,
for example visual aberrations, haplography etc. The most
important factor may be syncope.

penitus L^b ⨆ pentus L I, 228; elegantes T^b ⨆ egantes T
II, 341; dominum ⨆ domum Y I, 171; accurassem D^b ⨆
curassem D I, 182; gravidam T^c ⨆ gravdamⲦII, 104.

d) inability of scribe to interpret copy

When a scribe came upon an illegible word or something
he did not understand, he often left it out altogether, in
some cases leaving a space which presumably he meant to
fill later after further thought. If he never returned
to correct his omission the error would be passed on in
any copy made from such a manuscript, without a sign that
a word or phrase had been omitted.

inaerem   _/ om. L (space left) I, 75;   me _/ om. L
(space left) I, 232; redamares _/ red C (space left)
III, 187; nunc mos _/ om. L (six dashes show position
of words) V, 294.

4. Additions

a) dittography

This is the inadvertent repetition of a word,
syllable, or letter.

i letters

As in the case of the opposite tendency, haplography,
it is difficult to distinguish between an unconscious
error and a peculiarity of spelling.

tibialia J^b _/ tibillia J II, 204; sumus _/ summus C II, 294;
varia J^b _/ varria J II, 319; aditum _/ additum T V, 156.

ii syllables

ad mores D^c _7_ ad amores D I, 154; at Delia _7_ at Ardelia J
I, 234; aufugere T^c _7_ aufugugere T III, 275; rabies _7_ rabibies
L IV, 418; hilariter _7_ hila/lariter L V, 280.

iii words

Found especially at the end of lines.

tristis _7_ tristis tristis N I, 702; totam _7_ totam totam Y
II, 7; eam _7_ eam/eam L II, 105; sponsam _7_ sponsam sponsam Y
III, 195; eius T^c _7_ eius / eius T IV, 5.

There is much evidence in the texts of Labyrinthus to
show that in the majority of cases the scribes copied correctly
and tried to rectify their own errors. They wrote the correct
word after the mistake, inserted words omitted, and, when
defeated by a word, left a space for a later addition or copied
the shape of the words literally. It is therefore unlikely
that all the variants in the manuscripts of 'Labyrinthus are
the result of scribal carelessness and inattention. It is
often impossible to make a clear distinction between mechanical
and unconscious errors and conscious emendations but some
errors cannot be ascribed to the physical features of the text
and must originate with the scribe.

B. SCRIBAL EDITING

1. Omissions

Accidental omissions, especially of whole lines, are often identifiable because the causes of the omission remain in other complete texts. For others there seems to be no specific reason. Such omissions are usually of unimportant words like prepositions, conjunctions, pronouns etc. The errors may have occured because the scribe took in too much copy at one time and forgot the least important elements of the phrase or sentence as he wrote, or they may have been made purposely by the scribe in the belief that the material was unnecessary.

meas / om. N I, 155; tu / om. N II, 474; ditto III, 165; ego / om. Y II, 549; ipse / om. Y II, 549; illum / om. L V, 59; tua / om. N V, 25; O / om. N II, 508; hercle T^a / om. T IV, 46; porro / om. L IV, 181; nimis T^a / om. T V, 85; si / om. L I, 99; se / om. N II, 540; iam / om. L III 29; ad / om. L III,8; ab / om. Y III, 230.

2. Additions

On the other hand similar elements have been interpolated into the text by the scribes, and again the action may just be an unconscious addition to bring the copy into line with the scribes idiomatic habits.

eloquere / hoc eloquere Y II, 144; nunc / tu nunc N II, 454;
mancipium / mancipium es Y II, 151; quae haec / quae est
haec P IV, 237; obsecro ... dic / obsecro atque ... dic N
IV, 24; oblivionē / in oblivione Y V, 146; pɔh / o poh T V,
266; tale / tale autem N V, 299.

There are some more extensive cases of interpolation where
there can be no doubt about the scribes intentions. In L lines
have been added in an attempt to improve the text. For the
most part such emendations can be identified easily as they
are of an obviously superficial nature.

II 419, 453, 476 / after these lines the scribe of L makes
the eavesdropper repeat the words he has just heard following
the precedent found in the earlier part of the scene (II.6).

3. Changes in grammar

   i cases

Cases are often altered to make a word agree with an
adjacent one when the scribe has been misled by the juxta-
position of the two words into supposing that they were
related.

habet male T^b / habet malum T I, 233; quales ego / qualis
ego L II, 61; cum perfidiae / cum perfidiis N II, 151;
illud / illa N II, 419; istuc est solatio / istuc est
solatium Y III, 241; pectus perfido / pectus perfidum Y
IV, 171; vitae male metuo / vitam male metuo L V, 5.

ii   verb forms

autumare / autumañt N I, 151; cogitare / cogitasse L II, 157;
paterere / patereris N III, 230; Cedo / Cede Y V, 453.

iii   constructions changed to fit the scribes interpretation

latere / laturum N II, 514; sibi / tutibi L II, 560; quid illud
ut sit gratiae / Quid illa ut sit gratia Y II, 424; memorior /
ne moriar Y IV, 91; versatum / versari L IV, 154.

Unfortunately the majority of such cases could be explained
alternatively as being due to other scribal tendencies, e.g.
anticipation, perseveration, misreading, etc.

The texts of Labyrinthus contain all the most typical scribal
errors found in manuscripts but in general, as far as can be
determined, they tend to be mechanical errors rather than
conscious changes.   Mechanical mistakes in copying are in the
main easy to detect. The substitution of synonyms or the
rearranging of phrases by someone who fully understands his
material are harder to detect but less damaging to the text.
The copyists of the extant manuscripts were probably university
men with a good knowledge of Latin and possibly capable of
emending the text so skilfully as to render the finished product
indistinguishable from the original.   It can be seen that the
majority of examples have been taken from only three manuscripts
N, L, and Y, a fact which is perhaps an indication of the high
level of skill and care used in the copying of Labyrinthus.

LIST OF WORKS CITED

Manuscripts and Unpublished Works

Brooke, Samuel   Adelphe, Trinity College, Cambridge, MS R.3.9.

Hawkesworth, Walter   Labyrinthus, University Library, Cambridge,
MS Ee.v.16.

———   Bodleian Library, Oxford, Douce MS
515.

———   Yale University Library, New Haven,
Conn., MS.

———   Warwick County Record Office,
Newdigate MS CR136/B761.

———   Lambeth Palace Library, MS 838.

———   St John's College, Cambridge, MS J.8.

———   Trinity College, Cambridge, MS R.3.9.

———   Leander, University Library, Cambridge, MS Ee.v.16.

———   Bodleian Library, Oxford, Rawlinson MS
D 341.

———   Trinity College, Cambridge, MS R.3.9.

———   Letter to Sir Robert Cotton, British Museum,
Cotton MS Julius C III 3509.

Meade, Joseph   Letters to Sir Martin Stuteville, British Museum,
Harleian MS 389.

Stratman, Carl Joseph   "Dramatic Performances at Oxford and Cambridge,
1603-1642" (unpublished Ph.D. dissertation, University of Illinois,
1947).

Zelotypus, Trinity College, Cambridge, MS R.3.9.

Books and Articles

Aeschylus   Oresteia, edited by George Thomson, 2 vols (Camoridge, 1938).

Alciatus, Andreas   Emblemata ... denuo ab ipso auctore recognita, ac, quae desiderabantur, imaginibus locupleta (Leyden, 1551).

Arber, E.   A Transcript of the Registers of the Company of Stationers of London, 1554-1640 A.D., edited by E. Arber, 5 vols (London, 1875-94).

Athenae Cantabrigienses, compiled by Charles Henry Cooper and T. Cooper, 3 vols (Cambridge, 1858-1913).

Bacon, Francis   The Works, collected and edited by J. Spedding, R.L. Ellis and D.D. Heath, 7 vols (London, 1859-64).

Baker, David Erskine   Biographica Dramatica; or, A Companion to the Playhouse ... Originally compiled by D.E. Baker. Continued by Isaac Reed and Stephen Jones, 4 vols (London, 1812).

Baldwin, Thomas Whitfield   William Shakspere's Small Latine and Lesse Greeke, 2 vols (Urbana, Ill., 1944).

Beaumont, Francis and Fletcher, John   The Works, edited by A.G. Glover and A.R. Waller, 10 vols (Cambridge, 1905-12).

Bentley, Gerald Eades   The Jacobean and Caroline Stage, 7 vols (Oxford, 1941; reprinted 1949-68).

Boas, Frederick Samuel   Introduction to Stuart Drama (Oxford, 1946).

_____   University Drama in the Tudor Age (Oxford, 1914)

_____   "University Plays, 1500-1642", in Cambridge Bibliography of English Literature, Volume I, 600-1600, edited by F.W. Bateson (Cambridge,1940), pp. 654-663.

Bocchi, Francesco   Le bellezze della citta di Fiorenza (Florence, 1591; facsimile reprint, Farnborough, 1971).

Bradford, John   The Copye of a Letter ... to ... the Erles of
     Arundel, Darbie, Shrewsburye, and Penbroke, Declaring the
     Nature of the Spaniardes, and Discovering the Most Detestable
     Treasons, which Thei Have Pretended ....agaynste ... Englande
     (Rouen?, 1555?).

Brooke, Samuel   Melanthe: A Latin Pastoral Play of the Early
     Seventeenth Century, edited by J.S.G. Bolton, Yale Studies in
     English, 79 (New Haven, Conn., 1928).

Campion, Thomas   Works, edited by Percival Vivian (Oxford, 1909).

Chamberlain, John   The Letters of John Chamberlain, edited by N.E.
     McClure, American Philosophical Society Memoirs, 12, 2 vols
     (Philadelphia, Pa., 1939).

Chambers, Sir Edmund Kerchever   The Elizabethan Stage, 4 vols (Oxford
     1923).

Churchill, George B. and Keller, Wolfgang   "Die lateiniscnen
     Universitäts-Dramen Englands in der Zeit der Königin Elisabeth"
     Shakespeare Jahrbuch, 34 (1898), 221-323.

Clubb, Louise George   Giambattista Della Porta: Dramatist (Princeton,
     N.J., 1965).

Cole, William   Manuscript of Athenae Cantabrigienses, quoted in Notes
     and Queries, 2nd series, 11 (1855), p. 147.

Cook, David   "Dramatic Records in the Declared Accounts of the
     Treasurer of the Chamber 1558-1642", edited by David Cook
     with assistance from F.P. Wilson, Malone Society Collections,
     6 (1961).

Cooper, Charles Henry   Annals of Cambridge, 3 vols (Cambridge, 1842-
     1845).

Cooper, Thomas   Thesaurus linguae Romanae et Britannicae (London,
     1578).

Courtney, W.P.   s.v. John Moore, DNB.

D'Avenant, Sir William   Dramatic Works, edited by J. Maidment and
   W.H. Logan, 5 vols (London, 1872-4; reprinted New York, 1964).

Dee, John   "Compendious Rehearsal of John Dee his Dutifull
   Declaration" in Johannis confratris et monachi Glastoniensis
   chronica sive historia de rebus Glastoniensibus, edited by
   T. Hearne, 2 vols (Oxford, 1726).

Dekker, Thomas   The Dramatic Works, edited by Fredson Bowers, 4 vols
   (Cambridge, 1953-61).

Della Porta, Giambattista   Le commedie, edited by Vincenzo
   Spampanato, 2 vols (Bari, 1910-11).

_____   La Cintia, commedia (Venice, 1601).

_____   I due fratelli rivali, commedia (Venice,
   1601).

Despauter, John   Ninivitae artis versificatoriae compendium
   (Edinburgh, 1631).

Drayton, Michael   Works, edited by J.W. Hebel, 5 vols (Oxford, 1931-
   1941).

Duckworth, George Eckel   The Nature of Roman Comedy: A Study in
   Popular Entertainment (Princeton, N.J., 1952).

Dyer, Thomas Firminger Thiselton   Folk-Lore of Shakespeare (New York,
   1966).

Eckhardt, Eduard   Die Dialekt- und Ausländertypen des älteren
   englischen Dramas, 2 parts (1. Die Dialekttypen. 2. Die
   Ausländertypen.) Materialen zur Kunde des älteren englischen
   Dramas, 27, 32, (Louvain, 1910-11).

Elyot, Sir Thomas   The Castel of Helth (London, 1539).

Enciclopedia dello spettacolo, 9 vols (Rome, 1955-62).

Erasmus, Desiderius   Adagia quaecumque ad hanc diem exierunt, Paulli
   Manutii studio atque industria (Florence, 1575).

————   Apophthegmatum ex optimis utriusque linguae
scriptoribus libri iix Paulli Manutii studio, atque industria
(Venice, 1577).

————   Apophthegmes, translated by Nicholas Udall
(London, 1542).

————   Opus epistolarum Des. Erasmi Roterodami, edited
by P.S. Allen,12 vols (Oxford, 1906-58).

————   An Epystell unto ... Christofer Byssnop of
Basyle Concernyng the Forbedynge of Eatynge of Flesshe (London,
1530?).

Eruditorum aliquot virorum de comoedia et comicis versibus
commentationes (Basle, 1568).

Eyre, G.E.B. and Rivington, C.R.   A Transcript of the Registers of
of the Company of Stationers of London, from 1640 to 1708 A.D.,
edited by G.E.B. Eyre and C.R. Rivington, 3 vols (London, 1913-
14; reprinted New York, 1950).

Fleay, Frederick Gard   A Biographical Chronicle of the English Drama,
1559-1642, 2 vols (London, 1891).

Florio, John   Queen Anna's New Worlde of Words; or, Dictionarie of
the Italian and English Tongues (London, 1611).

Fraunce, Abraham   Victoria, a Latin Comedy, edited by G.C. Moore
Smith, Materialen zur Kunde des älteren englischen Dramas, 14
(Louvain, 1906).

Frye, Northrop   Anatomy of Criticism: Four Essays (Princeton, N.J.,
1957).

Fulwell, Ulpian   An Enterlude Intituled Like Wil to Like, Quod the
Devel to the Colier (London, 1568).

Gerard, John   The Herball; or, Generall Historie of Plantes (London,
1597)

Gilb   Sir Humphrey   Queene Elizabethes Achademy, edited by F.J.
    Furnivall, Early English Text Society, extra series 8 (London,
    1869).

Goodwin, Gordon   s.v. Walter Hawkesworth, DNB.

Gosson, Stephen   Playes Confuted in Five Actions (London, 1582).

Greg, Sir Walter Wilson   Bibliography of the English Printed Drama
    to the Restoration, 4 vols (London, 1939-59).

_____   The Calculus of Variants: An Essay on
    Textual Criticism (Oxford, 1927).

Grotius, Hugo   Poemata omnia, fourth edition (Leyden, 1645).

Gwinne, Matthew   Vertumnus; sive, Annus recurrens (London, 1607).

Hacket, John   A Century of Sermons, published by Thomas Plume
    (London, 1675).

Hakluyt, Richard   The Original Writings and Correspondence of the
    Two Richard Hakluyts, with an introduction and notes by E.G.R.
    Taylor, Hakluyt Society Publications, series 2, 76-77, 2 vols
    (London, 1935).

Halliwell, James Orchard   A Dictionary of Old English Plays, Existing
    either in Print or in Manuscript from Earliest Times to the
    Close of the Sixteenth Century (London, 1860).

Harbage, Alfred Bennett   Annals of English Drama, 975-1700, revised
    by S. Schoenbaum (London, 1964).

Harmonius, Joannes Marsus   Comoedia Stephanium, edited by Walther
    Ludwig, Humanistische Bibliothek, Abhandlungen und Texte,
    2nd series, 7 (Munich, 1971).

Harvey, Gabriel   Letter Book of Gabriel Harvey ... A.D. 1573-1580,
    edited by E.J.L. Scott, Camden Society Publications, new series
    33 (London, 1884; reprinted 1965).

Hawkesworth, Walter   Labyrinthus, comoedia (London, 1636).

Hazlitt, William Carew   A Manual for the Collector and Amateur of Old English Plays (London, 1892; reprinted New York, 1967).

Headlam, Walter   "The Transposition of Words in MSS", Classical Review, 16 (1902), 243-56.

Herrick, Marvin T.   Italian Comedy in the Renaissance (Urbana, Ill., 1960).

Heylyn, Peter   ΜΙΚΡΟΚΟΣΜΟΣ: A Little Description of the Great World (Oxford, 1627).

Heywood, James and Wright, Thomas   Cambridge University Transactions during the Puritan Controversies of the 16th and 17th Centuries, 2 vols (London, 1854).

Hodgson & Co.   A Catalogue of XVIth and XVIIth Century Books from Shipdham Church Library ... which will be sold by Auction by Messrs. Hodgson and Co. ... Thursday, March 29th, 1951 and Following Day, Sale 6 (London, 1951).

Holinshed, Raphael   The First and Second and Third Volumes of Chronicles (London, 1587).

Honigmann, E.A.J.   The Stability of Shakespeare's Text (London, 1965).

Hunter, Joseph   Familiae minorum gentium, edited by J.W. Clay, Publications of the Harleian Society, 37-40, 4 vols (London, 1894-6).

Hutton, W.H.   s.v. Thomas Tenison, DNB.

James, Montague Rhodes   A Descriptive Catalogue of the Manuscripts in the Library of St John's College, Cambridge (Cambridge, 1913).

———   The Manuscripts in the Library at Lambeth Palace, Cambridge Antiquarian Society, octavo series, 33 (Cambridge, 1900).

St Jerome   Lettres, edited by J. Labourt, Collection Budé, 8 vols (Paris, 1949-63).

Jonson, Ben   Works, edited by C.H. Herford and Percy Simpson, 11 vols (Oxford, 1925-52).

Juvenalis, D. Junius   Saturae, edited by A.E. Housman (Cambridge, 1931).

Kane, George   Piers Plowman: The A Version. Will's Visions of Piers
    Plowman and Do-well: An Edition in the Form of Trinity College
    MS R.3.14, Corrected from Other Manuscripts, with Variant
    Readings (London, 1960).

Langius, Josephus   Florilegii magni; seu, Polyantheae floribus
    novissimis sparsae, libri XXIII (Leyden, 1681).

Latham, Simon   Latham's Falconry (London, 1615).

"Latin Plays Acted Before the University of Cambridge", Retrospective
    Review, 12 (1825), 1-41.

Law, Ernest   "Shakespeare at Whitehall", London Topographical Record,
    7 (1912), 31-48.

The Pleasaunt Historie of Lazarillo de Tormes, Drawen out of Spanish by
    David Rouland of Anglesey, 1586, edited by J.E.V. Crofts, Percy
    Reprints, 7 (Oxford, 1924).

La vida de Lazarillo de Tormes y de sus fortunas y adversidades, edited
    by R.O. Jones (Manchester, 1963; reprinted 1965).

Lea, Kathleen Marguerite   Italian Popular Comedy; A Study of the
    Commedia Dell'Arte 1560-1620, with Special Reference to the
    English Stage, 2 vols (Oxford, 1934).

Lily, William and Colet, John   Shorte Introduction of Grammar (London,
    1567).

Lothian, John M.   "Sforza d'Oddi's 'Erofilomachia' the Source of
    Hawkesworth's 'Leander'", MLR, 25 (1930), 338-41.

Lyly, John   The Complete Works, edited by R.W. Bond, 3 vols (Oxford,
    1902).

Maas, Paul   Textual Criticism, translated from the German by Barbara
    Flower (Oxford, 1958).

McAfee, Helen   Pepys on the Restoration Stage (New Haven, Conn., 1916;
    reprinted New York, 1968).

Madan, Falconer   Summary Catalogue of Western Manuscripts in the
Bodleian Library at Oxford, edited by F. Madan, R.W. Hunt, and
others, 7 vols (Oxford, 1895-1953).

Manly, J.M. and Rickert, E.   The Text of the Canterbury Tales, 8 vols
(Chicago, Ill., 1940).

Masson, David   The Life of John Milton Narrated in Connexion with the
Political, Ecclesiastical and Literary History of His Time,
6 vols (London, 1859-80).

Mayor, John Eyton Bickersteth   Early Statutes of St John's College,
Cambridge (Cambridge, 1859).

Middleton, Thomas   The Works, edited by A.H. Bullen, 8 vols (London,
1885-6).

Milano, F.   "Le commedie di Giovanbattista della Porta", Studi di
Letteratura Italiana, 2 (1900), 311-411.

Milton, John   An Apology against a Pamphlet Call'd A Modest Confutation
(London, 1642).

Minsheu, John   A Dictionary in Spanish and English: First Published
into the English Tongue by Ric. Percivale Gent. Now Enlarged
and Amplified by John Minsheu (London, 1623).

_____   A Spanish Grammar, First Collected and Published by
Richard Percivale Gent. Now Augmented and Increased, with the
Declining of All the Irregular and Hard Verbs in that Tongue ...
Done by John Minsheu (London, 1623).

Moxon, Joseph   Mechanick Exercises on the Whole Art of Printing,
1683-4, edited by H. Davies and H. Carter (London, 1958).

Murray, James Ross   The Influence of Italian upon English Literature
during the Sixteenth and Seventeenth Centuries (Cambridge, 1886).

Newdigate-Newdegate, Lady A.E.   Gossip from a Muniment Room; Being
Passages in the Lives of Anne and Mary Fytton, 1574-1618,
transcribed and edited by Lady Newdigate-Newdegate (London, 1897).

Nicol, John Ramsay Allardyce   A History of English Drama, 1660-1900, 6 vols (Cambridge, 1952-9).

Nichols, John   The Progresses, Processions, and Magnificent Festivities of King James the First, His Royal Consort, Family, and Court, 4 vols (London, 1828).

Novum testamentum graece, edited by Johann Jacob Griesbach, 2 vols (London, 1809).

Orr, David   Italian Renaissance Drama in England before 1625 (Chapel Hill, N. Carolina, 1970).

Palsgrave, John   The Comedy of Acolastus Translated from the Latin of Fullonius by John Palsgrave, edited by P.L. Carver, Early English Text Society, original series, 202 (London, 1937).

Pepys, Samuel   Diary, edited by R. Latham and W. Matthews (London, 1970-).

Prudentius, Aurelius Clemens   Prudence, edited by M. Lavarenne, Collection Budé, (Paris, 1943-).

Publilius Syrus   Sententiae, edited by R.A.H. Bickford-Smith (London, 1895).

Querolus, comédie latine anonyme, edited by L. Havet (Paris, 1880).

Rebora, Piero   L'Italia nel dramma inglese (1558-1642) (Milan, 1925).

Renart, Jean   Le Lai de l'ombre, edited by J. Bedier (Paris, 1913).

Reynolds, L.D. and Wilson, N.G.   Scribes and Scholars: A Guide to the Transmission of Greek and Latin Literature (Oxford, 1968).

Ruggle, George   Ignoramus, comoedia, edited by J.S. Hawkins (London, 1787).

Sanesi, Ireneo   La commedia, 2 vols (Milan, 1911-1935).

Scott, Mary Augusta   "Elizabethan Translations from the Italian", PMLA, 10 (1895), 249-93.

_____   "Elizabethan Translations from the Italian", PMLA, 14 (1899), 465-571.

Sidney, Sir Philip   An Apology for Poetry; or, The Defence of Poesy, edited by G. Shepherd (Edinburgh, 1965).

Simon, Joan   Education and Society in Tudor England (Cambridge, 1966).

Smith, George Charles Moore   "Academic Drama at Cambridge: Extracts from College Records", edited by G.C. Moore Smith, Malone Society Collections, 2, Pt. 2 (1923), 150-230.

———   College Plays Performed in the University of Cambridge (Cambridge, 1923).

———   Fucus Histriomastix, a Comedy Probably Written by R. Ward and Acted at Queen's College, Cambridge in Lent, 1623, first printed with an introduction and notes by G.C. Moore Smith (Cambridge, 1909).

———   Hymenaeus, a Comedy Acted at St John's College, Cambridge, edited by G.C. Moore Smith (Cambridge, 1908).

———   Pedantius, a Latin Comedy Formerly Acted in Trinity College, edited by G.C. Moore Smith, Materialen zur Kunde des älteren englischen Dramas, 8 (Louvain, 1905).

———   "Plays Performed in Cambridge Colleges before 1585", in Fasciculus Joanni Willis Clark Dicatus (Cambridge, 1909), 265-73.

Stäuble, Antonio   La commedia umanistica del Quattrocento (Florence, 1968).

The Stage Cyclopedia: A Bibliography of Plays, compiled by Reginald Clarence (London, 1909).

Stobaeus, Johannes   Florilegium, edited by A. Meineke, 4 vols (Leipzig, 1855-7).

Stub, Edmund   Fraus honesta, comoedia (London, 1632).

Terentius, Publius Afer   Comoediae, una cum scholiis ex Donati, Asperi et Cornuti commentariis decerptis (Basle, 1538).

———   P. Terentius Afer, cum commentariis Aelii Donati ... accesserunt A. Goveani ... annotationes (Venice, 1560).

_____   Comoediae, edited by Richard Bentley (Cambridge, 1720).

Thomson, George   "Marxism and Textual Criticism", Wissenschaftliche Zeitschrift der Humboldt-Universität zu Berlin, Gesellschafts- und Sprachwissenschaftliche Reihe, 12 (1963), 45-52.

_____   "Simplex Ordo", Classical Quarterly, new series 15 (1965), 151-75.

Thorpe, James   Principles of Textual Criticism (San Marino, Cal., 1972).

Threnodia in obitum D. Edouardi Lewkenor equitis (London, 1606).

Todd, H.J.   A Catalogue of the Archiepiscopal Manuscripts in the Library at Lambeth Palace (London, 1812).

Tomkis, Thomas   Lingua; or, The Combat of the Tongue (London, 1607).

Turberville, George   The Booke of Faulconrie or Hauking (London, 1575).

Venn, John and Venn, John Archibald   Alumni Cantabrigienses, Part I, From the Earliest Times to 1751, 4 vols (Cambridge, 1922-7).

Walther, Hans   Proverbia sententiaeque latinitatis medii aevi, 6 vols (Göttingen, 1963-9).

Warton, Thomas   History of English Poetry, edited by W.C. Hazlitt, 4 vols (London, 1871).

Willis, Robert   The Architectural History of the University of Cambridge and of the Colleges of Cambridge and Eton, edited by J.W. Clark, 4 vols (Cambridge, 1886).

Winwood, Sir Ralph   Memorials of Affairs of State in the Reigns of Q. Elizabeth and K. James I. Collected (Chiefly) from the Original Papers of the Right Honourable Sir Ralph Winwood Kt., edited by Edmund Sawyer, 3 vols (London, 1725).

Yates, Frances Amelia   John Florio: The Life of an Italian in Shakespeare's England (Cambridge, 1934).

Young, Karl   "William Gager's Defence of the Academic Stage", edited
        by Karl Young, *Transactions of the Wisconsin Academy of Sciences,
        Arts and Letters*, 18 (1915), 593-630.

Addenda

Bennett, J.A.W.   Review of *Piers Plowman: The A Version*, edited by
        G. Kane (London, 1960), *Review of English Studies*, new series
        14 (1963), 68-71.

Bessinger, J.B.   Review of *Piers Plowman: The A Version*, edited by
        G. Kane (London, 1960), *Journal of English and Germanic Philology*,
        60 (1960), 571-6.

Guazzo, Stephen   *The Civile Conversation of M. Stephen Guazzo,
        Divided into Foure Bookes, The First Three Translated ... by G.
        Pettie ... The Fourth ... Translated by Barth. Young* (London,
        1586).

Heywood, Thomas   *The Dramatic Works*, first collected with illustrative
        notes and a memoir of the author by R.H. Shepherd, 6 vols (London,
        1874).

Lawlor, J   Review of *Piers Plowman: The A Version*, edited by G. Kane
        (London, 1960), *MLR*, 56 (1961), 243-5.

Smith, George Charles Moore   *Laelia, a Comedy Acted at Queen's College,
        Cambridge, Probably on March 1st 1595*, printed with an
        introduction and notes by G.C. Moore Smith (Cambridge, 1910).

                        "Notes on Some English University Plays",
        MLR, 3 (1907-8), 141-156.

Manuscripts

Hawkesworth, Walter   Leander, British Museum, MS Sloane 1762.

Stub, Edmund   Fraus Honesta, Bodleian Library, Oxford, Douce MS 234.